American Contract Bridge League

Introduction to Bridge

Defense

"Heart Series"

by Audrey Grant

ISBN–0-943855–06–3

The American Contract Bridge League

presents

 The ACBL Heart Series

"Defense"

This is the third book in the four–book series that forms the basis of the ACBL teaching program. The other books:

♣ *The ACBL Club Series* — "Bidding: An Introduction"

♦ *The ACBL Diamond Series* — "The Play of the Hand"

♠ *The ACBL Spade Series* — "Introduction to Duplicate Bridge"

American Contract Bridge League

American Contract Bridge League (ACBL) is dedicated to the playing, teaching and advancement of contract bridge.

The current membership of 180,000 includes a wide range — from the thousands who are just learning the joys of bridge to the most proficient players in North America.

ACBL offers a variety of services. These include:

• Tournament play. Thousands of tournaments — North American Bridge Championships (three a year), as well as tournaments at the regional, sectional, local and club levels — are sanctioned annually.

• A monthly magazine. *The BULLETIN* offers articles on tournaments, card play, the Laws, personalities, special ACBL activities, etc.

• A ranking plan. Each time a member does well in any ACBL event, whether it be at the club level or at a North American Bridge Championship, that member receives a masterpoint award. Players achieve rankings and prestige as a result of their cumulative masterpoint holdings.

• A teaching program. This book is one in a series of volumes being used in the ACBL Teaching Program.

• A novice program. ACBL offers special games and programs for players new to bridge and duplicate.

• A charity program. Each year the ACBL Charity Foundation selects a "Charity of the Year," which becomes the main beneficiary of ACBL charity games and general donations by the membership. All ACBL clubs participate to raise money for the charity.

• An education program. The ACBL Educational Foundation is dedicated to bringing the enjoyment of bridge to people of all ages through bridge education. Grants are provided for special bridge projects.

• A college program. ACBL cooperates with the nation's colleges in making bridge instruction and play available to college students.

• A youth program (for players age 19 and under). ACBL offers a funded teaching program, youth membership, special events and a quarterly youth newsletter.

• Products. ACBL offers a wide variety of bridge supplies, books, clothing and other bridge-related items through its Customer Service Department.

• Membership in the World Bridge Federation. Each year ACBL sends premiere players to compete in the world championships. In alternate years, ACBL's Junior Team is entered in the World Competition.

• Membership benefits. Credit card programs, member discounts on product purchases, special hotel rates at tournaments, airline discounts for NABCs and supplemental insurances are offered.

ACBL has long been the center of North American bridge activity. In 1987 ACBL celebrated its 50th anniversary. We invite you to enjoy our second half-century with us.

TABLE OF CONTENTS

LESSON 1 — OPENING LEADS AGAINST NOTRUMP CONTRACTS

Introduction to Defense 2
The Opening Lead 2
Choosing the Suit 3
Choosing the Card 7
Bidding Review 22
Play of the Hand Review 24
Summary 25
The Finer Points 26
WORKSHOP MATERIAL
Group Activities 28

LESSON 2 — OPENING LEADS AGAINST SUIT CONTRACTS

Choosing the Suit 38
Choosing the Card 51
Bidding Review 55
Play of the Hand Review 57
Summary 58
The Finer Points 59
WORKSHOP MATERIAL
Group Activities 60

LESSON 3 — THIRD-HAND PLAY

Third Hand High 72
Third Hand Not So High 75
Unblocking 85
Bidding Review 87
Play of the Hand Review 88
Summary 90
WORKSHOP MATERIAL
Group Activities 91

LESSON 4 — SECOND-HAND PLAY

Second Hand Low 104
Second Hand Not So Low 110
Covering Honors 115
Bidding Review 124
Play of the Hand Review 127
Summary 131
WORKSHOP MATERIAL
Group Activities 132

LESSON 5 — DEFENSIVE SIGNALS

Attitude Signals 147
Count Signals 156
Suit Preference Signals 163
Bidding Review 165
Play of the Hand Review 167
Summary 168
WORKSHOP MATERIAL
Group Activities 169

LESSON 6 — DEVELOPING DEFENSIVE TRICKS

Taking Sure Tricks 180
Promoting Tricks 183
Establishing Long Suits 186
Finessing 190
Trumping 194
Bidding Review 196
Play of the Hand Review 199
Summary 201
WORKSHOP MATERIAL
Group Activities 202

LESSON 7 — INTERFERING WITH DECLARER

Defending Against Suit Establishment 216
Defending Against Declarer's Small Cards 223
Defending Against Finesses 227
Defending Against Declarer's Trumps 231
Bidding Review 234
Play of the Hand Review 236
Summary 238
WORKSHOP MATERIAL
Group Activities 239

LESSON 8 — MAKING A PLAN

The Defenders' Plan 252
Before the Opening Lead 257
After the Opening Lead 262
Bidding Review 271
Play of the Hand Review 273
Summary 275
WORKSHOP MATERIAL
Group Activities 276

APPENDIX

Glossary of Terms 288
Answers to Exercises 291

LESSON 1
Opening Leads Against
Notrump Contracts

Introduction to Defense
The Opening Lead
Choosing the Suit
Choosing the Card
Bidding Review
Play of the Hand Review
Summary
The Finer Points

Workshop Material
Group Activities

INTRODUCTION TO DEFENSE

Playing bridge is a combination of skill, luck, and your ability to communicate with your partner. Nowhere is partnership communication more important than on defense. When you are declarer, you can look at all 26 cards held by your side before making any decision about how to play the hand. When you are a defender, you and your partner need to work as a team to try to defeat the contract even though you cannot see the cards in each other's hand. That's quite a challenge.

During the auction, you work with your partner to exchange information through your bids in order to reach a suitable contract. As defenders, you must give each other as much information about your hand as possible in order to achieve your goal of defeating the contract. This is done by the means of the cards you choose to play on each trick. With each card played, the defenders get a clearer picture of each other's hand and can use this information to try to defeat the contract. The defenders are not only trying to take their tricks but are also trying to do what they can to prevent declarer from taking his tricks.

After defending a hand, you and your partner may wonder, "Could we have defeated that contract?" In the *Heart Series*, we will look at techniques for defeating contracts that declarer would make if we did not defend carefully. We start by looking at the guidelines for handling specific situations on defense: opening leads, third-hand play, second-hand play and signals. We move on to look at how the defenders establish winners and take their sure tricks. Then we see how the defenders can interfere with declarer's plans to make the contract. Finally, we take a look at how the defenders formulate their plan and put it into action.

In this lesson let's start at the beginning, with the opening lead.

THE OPENING LEAD

Declarer's objective is to make the contract. The defenders' objective is to defeat the contract. With the opening lead, the defenders get the opportunity to choose the suit that seems to have the best potential for their side. Many of the greatest players in the game have said that opening leads alone can make the difference between winning and losing a world championship. In this lesson we will look at how you can choose an effective lead when defending against a notrump contract. First, you have to consider which suit you should lead, then you have to decide which card in the suit you should lead.

♥ CHOOSING THE SUIT ♥

There are many bridge sayings designed to guide you on defense. One of the best known is "Lead the fourth highest from your longest and strongest suit against notrump contracts." It is necessary to understand what this guideline means and when it applies so you can use it in the right place at the right time.

In a notrump contract, rarely do either the defenders or declarer start with enough winners to reach their objective. The defenders need to develop tricks in the same manner that declarer does. The most common method is by developing tricks from long suits. By repeatedly leading the suit until all the high cards are gone, you can manufacture winners from small cards. The advantage of playing in notrump is that once your winners in a long suit have been established, there is no trump suit to stop you from taking them. It becomes a race to see which side can set up its *spot* (small) cards in time to make or break the contract.

Since the defenders have the opening lead, they have a head start in the race to establish winners. The opening leader should start the suit that offers the greatest potential for developing the winners needed to defeat the contract. This suit will usually be the longest combined suit in the defenders' hands. For example, compare the following notrump holdings:

1)	YOU A K 4		2)	YOU J 10 9 7 4 2
	PARTNER Q 8 3			PARTNER Q 8 3

In the first case, you have the top three cards in the suit and can take three tricks. This does not develop any further tricks for your side, and it will establish at least one long-card winner for declarer. In the second holding, you have less high card strength, but because of the length of the suit you may be able to establish four tricks by driving out declarer's ace and king. The length of the suit rather than the location of the high cards tends to determine the best suit to attack.

When making the opening lead, you have to choose the suit without seeing partner's hand. Usually the bidding helps you to make the best decision. At other times, the decision has to come from examining only the cards held in your hand.

Partner's Suit

If partner has opened the bidding or overcalled in a suit, *lead partner's suit* unless you clearly have a better alternative. Partner normally opens the bidding or overcalls in his longest suit. Even if you have only one or two small cards, partner's suit may well be your longest combined suit. If partner opened the bidding or overcalled, he will usually have the majority of strength for your side and is most likely to have an *entry* to his suit once it is established. Even if your suit is longer, you may have no way to get in and take your winners once they are established. It is also a good idea to lead partner's suit in the interest of the ongoing harmony of the partnership.

For example, consider the following hand. You are on lead against 3 NT after partner has opened the bidding 1♠.

♠ Q 7
♥ 9 6 2
♦ J 9 6 4 3 2
♣ 10 4

Lead a spade, partner's suit, rather than a diamond, your long suit. For his opening bid, partner should have length in spades, as well as some high cards in other suits with which to get the lead once his small spades are established as winners. If you were to lead a diamond, you would probably not have an entry to the suit even if you could establish it.

Your Suit

If there is no help from partner during the auction, you will have to choose the suit to lead by looking at your own hand, taking into account any information you have from the opponents' bidding. The guideline here is straightforward: with no information about the opponents' suits, choose your longest suit. This may not work out to be the best lead 100% of the time, but with nothing else to go on it certainly gives your side the most potential to establish winners.

For example, suppose you are on lead against 3 NT with the following hand and have no information from the auction:

♠ 9 5
♥ J 10 9 6 5 2
♦ A K 5
♣ 7 3

Lead a heart, your long suit, even though the diamonds contain more high cards. The heart suit provides the opportunity to establish tricks for your side while the diamonds are already winners. You want to keep the ♦A and ♦K as entries to get to the heart suit.

If you have two suits of equal length, choose the **stronger**, which will usually require less help from partner to establish. For example, suppose you are on lead against 1 NT with the following hand:

♠ K J 8 6 3
♥ 7 4
♦ J 9 6 4 2
♣ Q

Lead a spade rather than a diamond. If partner has the ♠A or ♠Q, you may be able to establish winners in the suit quickly. On the other hand, if partner has the ♦A or ♦Q diamonds will take longer to establish.

The Unbid Suit

The opponents may have bid one or more suits before arriving at their final contract. It is usually best to **avoid leading the opponents' suit** when you have a reasonable alternative. If the opponents bid a suit, they will normally have some length and strength in it. For example, suppose the auction proceeds as follows:

NORTH (DUMMY)	EAST (PARTNER)	SOUTH (DECLARER)	WEST (YOU)
1 ♦	Pass	1 ♥	Pass
1 ♠	Pass	1 NT	Pass
3 NT	Pass	Pass	Pass

Here are three possible hands that you might hold:

1)	2)	3)
♠ Q 3	♠ J 9 7 2	♠ K Q J 10 8
♥ K J 8 3	♥ Q 7 4 3	♥ J 8
♦ Q 6 3	♦ Q 5	♦ J 7 2
♣ J 10 7 2	♣ 10 9 7	♣ A 8 4

In the first hand, your heart suit is stronger than your club suit. The opponent on your right, however, has bid hearts — this tends to make a heart lead unattractive. It is not likely that your partner has much length or strength in the heart suit. You may even be helping declarer to establish tricks in the suit. Instead, lead a club, the unbid suit. Since the opponents have never bid clubs, it is reasonable to expect that partner will have some help in that suit.

In the second hand, your only long suits are spades and hearts, both of which have been bid by the opponents. Again, leading the unbid suit, clubs, is the most attractive alternative, even though you have only a three-card suit. Since the opponents did not bid the suit, there is a reasonable possibility that partner has some length and strength in this suit.

You do not always avoid leading the opponents' suit. In the third example, your spade suit is strong enough to lead even though it was bid by the opponents. You expect to drive out their ace and establish four winners, keeping the ♣A as an entry to your hand.

Considering the Contract

The level of the contract is another factor that affects your choice of lead. Consider the following hand:

♠ 8 6
♥ J 10 9 7 3
♦ A K
♣ 7 6 4 2

If you are leading against a contract of 1 NT or 3 NT with no help from the bidding, lead hearts, your longest suit, keeping the ♦A and ♦K as entries to your hand to help you establish and take your winners. If the contract is 6 NT, however, you would take your ♦A and ♦K right away since you need only two tricks to defeat the contract. If you lead a heart, the opponents may be able to take 12 tricks right away, giving you no second chance. Always keep your eye on the contract you are defending. If you see enough tricks to defeat it, take them.

♥ CHOOSING THE CARD ♥

Once you have decided on the suit, the next decision is which card to lead. This is an important consideration for two reasons. First of all, since the defenders cannot see each other's hand, every card they play sends a message, including the opening lead. Secondly, the card you choose can make it easier to take the tricks to which your side is entitled. Your choice of card depends on whether you are leading partner's suit or your own long suit. Let's take a look at each in turn.

Leading Partner's Suit.

When you are leading partner's suit rather than your own, you will often be leading from a short suit. With a singleton, you have no choice of cards to lead, but with two or more cards use the following guideline:

- Lead the top card from a doubleton (e.g., **7** 2, **Q** 5)
- Lead the top of touching honors (e.g., **Q** J 3, **10** 9 5)
- Otherwise, lead low (e.g., K 8 **3**, Q 9 4 **2**, 9 7 **6***)

---

*From three small cards some partnerships prefer to lead the top card (e.g., **9** 7 6) or the middle card (e.g., 9 **7** 6).

Let's see why these guidelines usually work well. Consider the following suit layout where you are on lead with a doubleton in partner's suit:

DUMMY
6 4 2

YOU
K 8

PARTNER
A Q 9 7 3

DECLARER
J 10 5

If you lead the 8, rather than the king, partner would win the first trick and could then lead back to your king — but you would have no cards left to lead. Partner's winners would be stranded unless he has an entry in another suit. The principle involved is *lead the high card from the short side first*. The situation is identical when you are trying to establish the suit by driving out declarer's high cards.

Suppose this is the layout:

DUMMY
9 8 3

YOU
Q 5

PARTNER
K J 7 4 2

DECLARER
A 10 6

If you lead the 5 and partner plays the king, declarer can win with the ace and the suit is *blocked*. If your side regains the lead, you have all the winners in the suit, but after winning a trick with your queen, you have no small card left to get to partner's winners. Partner will need an entry in a side suit.

Alternatively, declarer may *hold up*, allowing partner to win the first trick with the king. When partner leads the suit again, declarer can hold up again, letting you win the trick with the queen. The suit is still not established and you have no small card left to lead. Partner will need two entries to both establish the suit and get in to take his winners. By leading the queen, high card from the short side, you avoid these problems.

Leading the top of touching high cards can be useful in **trapping** declarer's high cards. Consider the following layout:

DUMMY
K 8 3

YOU
J 10 2

PARTNER
A Q 7 6 5

DECLARER
9 4

If you lead the 2 and declarer plays a small card from dummy, partner can win the first trick with the queen. Whether partner now takes the ace or leads a small card, he cannot lead the suit without letting declarer win a trick with dummy's king. He would have to wait until you got the lead again if he wanted to trap dummy's king. If you lead the jack initially, top of your touching honors, declarer's king is trapped immediately. If declarer plays a small card from dummy, partner can play a small card and let your jack win the trick so that you can lead the suit again. If declarer covers the jack with the king, your side takes all five tricks. If declarer held the king rather than dummy, it would still do no harm to lead the jack:

DUMMY
9 4

YOU
J 10 2

PARTNER
A Q 7 6 5

DECLARER
K 8 3

Declarer is entitled to one trick with the king whether or not you lead the jack. Once your jack has driven out declarer's king, your side's winners are ready to take.

When you have three or more cards without touching honors, the objective is also to trap one of declarer's high cards whenever possible. Consider this layout:

DUMMY
5 3

YOU
K 8 4

PARTNER
A J 10 7 2

DECLARER
Q 9 6

If you lead the king and then a small card to partner's ace, declarer ends up winning a trick with the queen. If instead you lead a small card to partner's ace, partner can lead back the jack, trapping declarer's queen. If declarer covers the jack with the queen, you can win the trick with the king and still have a small card left to lead over to partner's established tricks.

Here are some examples of leading partner's suit. The contract is 3 NT and partner has bid diamonds during the auction:

♠ 8 7 5
♥ 10 8 3
♦ J 3
♣ K 8 6 5 2

Although your longest suit is clubs, lead partner's suit since the club suit is not clearly a better choice. With a doubleton lead the top card, the ♦ **J**.

♠ Q 10 8 4
♥ 9 2
♦ Q J 6
♣ J 10 8 3

Again, lead partner's suit rather than one of your own. With touching honors, lead the top card, the ♦ **Q**.

♠ J 7 3
♥ 9 4 2
♦ Q 7 3
♣ Q 7 4 2

Once more you would lead partner's diamond suit rather than your meager club suit. With a three-card suit and no touching honors, lead a low card, the ♦ **3**.

Here is an example of the effectiveness of leading partner's suit in a complete hand. The contract is 3 NT and partner overcalled 1 ♥ during the auction.

Contract: 3 NT
Lead: ♥ 8

DUMMY
♠ A K 4
♥ 9 4
♦ A K J
♣ Q J 10 9 3

YOU
♠ Q 10 9 3 2
♥ 8 2
♦ 10 9 6 4
♣ 7 2

PARTNER
♠ J 7
♥ K J 10 7 6 5
♦ 8 7
♣ A K 5

DECLARER
♠ 8 6 5
♥ A Q 3
♦ Q 5 3 2
♣ 8 6 4

Although you have a long suit of your own, lead the suit partner overcalled. With a doubleton, lead the top card, the ♥8. Declarer can win partner's ♥K with the ♥A and still have the ♥Q left as a second trick in the suit. However, declarer needs nine tricks. Together with the two heart tricks, declarer has two spade tricks and four diamond tricks for a total of eight. Declarer will have to lead clubs to establish a ninth trick. When declarer leads a club, partner can win the ♣K and lead the ♥J (or ♥10) to drive out declarer's ♥Q. When declarer leads another club, partner can win the ♣A and take his four established heart winners to defeat the contract by two tricks.

Notice what would happen if you led your long suit, spades. You may be able to drive out declarer's ♠A and ♠K, but you will have no high card left as an entry to take your winners. In the meantime, declarer will drive out partner's high clubs and end up taking 10 tricks, making the contract with an overtrick!

Leading Your Long Suit

When you are leading your own suit, you will have four or more cards in the suit. In this case, you can use the following guideline:

- Lead the top of the touching honors from a three-card sequence, a broken sequence or an interior sequence (e.g., **K** Q J 3 2, **Q** J 9 6 4, K **J** 10 8)
- Otherwise, lead low (e.g., Q 10 8 **3**, K J 4 **2**, A K 7 **5**)

There is a subtle difference between leading your suit and leading partner's suit when you have a suit headed by touching honors. When leading partner's suit, you lead the top of two touching honors. When leading your suit, lead the top of three touching honors but lead a low card when you have two touching honors. Let's look at why this usually works best. First let's see why it is normally best to lead the top card from three or more touching honors. Consider the following suit layout:

	DUMMY	
	7 6 2	
YOU		PARTNER
K Q J 8 3		9 4
	DECLARER	
	A 10 5	

If you were to lead a small card from this holding, declarer would win the first trick with the 10 and still have a second trick left, the ace. Declarer would get an undeserved trick, and your suit still would not be established. By leading the king, the top of your three-card sequence, declarer gets only one trick, the ace, and the remainder of your cards are established as winners. The idea of leading high from such a strong sequence is to prevent declarer from winning a trick with a small card when partner has no help for you in the suit. If partner does have some help, so much the better.

Why the top card, rather than the queen or jack? While leading the top card from a sequence makes no difference to you, it provides information to partner about the other cards you hold. If you lead the queen from your long suit, for example, partner knows you have the next lower card, the jack, but not the next higher card, the king.

Leading from a suit headed by a three-card sequence can often lead to the rapid establishment of tricks for your side. Consider this layout:

	DUMMY	
	Q 4 3	
YOU		PARTNER
J 10 9 2		K 6 5
	DECLARER	
	A 8 7	

If you lead the jack and it is covered by dummy's queen, partner's king and declarer's ace, your 10 and 9 have been promoted into winners. Not only that but your 2 will be the last card in the suit and can also take a trick. Three tricks from a suit headed by the jack.

Here is a complete hand that illustrates the value of leading a suit headed by a three-card sequence:

Contract: 3 NT
Lead: ♥ Q

DUMMY
♠ A 10 3
♥ A 5
♦ 10 9 7 6 2
♣ Q 9 6

YOU
♠ J 6 2
♥ Q J 10 7 2
♦ A K 4
♣ 8 4

PARTNER
♠ Q 8 7 5
♥ 6 4 3
♦ 3
♣ 10 7 5 3 2

DECLARER
♠ K 9 4
♥ K 9 8
♦ Q J 8 5
♣ A K J

Against a contract of 3 NT, you (West) choose to lead your longest suit, hearts. With a three-card sequence, lead the top card, the ♥ Q. Declarer needs nine tricks and has two sure tricks in spades, two in hearts and three in clubs — for a total of seven. Two more tricks must be established, and they can come only from the diamond suit.

After winning a heart trick, declarer leads a high diamond to promote winners in the suit. When you win the diamond trick, lead another high heart to drive out declarer's remaining winner. Declarer wins the trick and leads another diamond. You win the race, however, taking your three heart winners and two diamond winners to defeat the contract.

If you originally lead a high diamond or any suit other than a heart, you would lose the race. Declarer would be able to establish his diamond winners before you could establish enough winners to defeat the contract. If you lead a low heart rather than a high heart, declarer will end up winning three heart tricks, and again you would not defeat the contract.

A *broken sequence* is one in which you have the top two cards but are missing a card before the next highest card (e.g., K Q 10, Q J 9, J 10 8). Suits headed by a broken sequence are treated in a similar fashion to suits headed by a three-card sequence: lead the top of the touching honors (e.g., *K* Q 10 7 4, *Q* J 9 4 3). The idea is not to let declarer win a trick with a small card.

For example, consider this layout:

```
            DUMMY
             8 4
   YOU                PARTNER
  Q J 9 6 2            7 5 3
           DECLARER
            A K 10
```

If you lead a small card, declarer will win the first trick with the 10 since partner has no high cards in the suit to help out. Declarer ends up with three tricks in the suit. If you lead the top of your touching honors, the queen, declarer can win the trick with the king and the remaining cards will look like this:

```
            DUMMY
              8
   YOU                PARTNER
  J 9 6 2              7 5
           DECLARER
            A 10
```

Declarer has not yet won a trick with the 10. If partner gets the lead, he can return the suit and, whether declarer plays the 10 or the ace, he ends up with only two tricks in the suit.

Notice that if you, rather than partner, lead the suit the second time, declarer will still get a trick with the 10. This is often the case when you lead from a broken sequence and partner has no help in the suit. Partner may have to lead the suit next if you want to trap the card missing from the broken sequence. On the other hand, if partner does have some help in the suit, it usually will not matter which defender leads the suit next.

An *interior sequence* is one in which the top card of the suit is not part of the sequence (e.g., K J 10, Q 10 9, A 10 9). Suits headed by an interior sequence are also treated in a similar fashion to suits headed by a three-card sequence: lead the top of the touching honors (e.g., K *J* 10 8 4, Q *10* 9 4 3, A *J* 10 9). Again, the idea of leading one of your high cards is to avoid letting declarer win an undeserved trick with a small card. By not leading the highest card in the suit, however, you retain the possibility of trapping one of declarer's high cards when partner has some help in the suit.

For example, look at this layout:

```
              DUMMY
               Q64
YOU                      PARTNER
AJ109          ■■■        K72
              DECLARER
               853
```

When you lead the jack, top of the touching cards in your interior sequence, dummy's queen is trapped. If declarer covers the jack with the queen, partner wins the trick with the king and the rest of the tricks are yours. If declarer plays a small card from dummy, partner lets your jack win the trick and you can lead the suit again and take all the tricks.

It would make no difference if declarer held the queen rather than dummy. You would still be able to trap it:

```
              DUMMY
               864
YOU                      PARTNER
AJ109          ■■■        K72
              DECLARER
               Q53
```

When you lead the jack and a small card is played from dummy, partner can win the trick with the king and lead a small card back to trap declarer's queen. Whether or not declarer plays the queen, your side takes all four tricks. This shows the value of not leading the highest card when you have an interior sequence. If you start by leading the ace and then a card over to partner's king, declarer will get a trick with the queen.

How does partner know to play the king when you lead the jack and there are only small cards in the dummy? Since you always lead the top of your touching honors, partner knows you do not have the queen when you lead the jack. If he plays a small card, declarer will win the trick with the queen. By playing the king, he will be able to trap declarer's queen if you are leading from an interior sequence. Of course, you may be leading the top of a three-card sequence:

```
              DUMMY
               864
YOU                      PARTNER
J1093          ■■■        K72
              DECLARER
               AQ5
```

If this is the case, it still does partner no harm to play the king on your jack. Declarer is always entitled to two tricks in the suit no matter what your side does.

When your suit is not headed by a three-card sequence or a broken or interior sequence, the guideline is to lead a small card. The idea behind this is that, since you do not have a strong holding of high cards in the suit, you are probably going to need some help from partner. You want to preserve your high cards to help trap any high cards in declarer's hand and as entries to your suit once it is established. Here is a typical example:

DUMMY
97

YOU   ■   PARTNER
K J 6 5 2   A 8 3

DECLARER
Q 10 4

When you lead a small card, partner wins the trick with the ace and leads the suit back, trapping declarer's high cards. Whether declarer plays the queen or 10, you win the trick and can take all five tricks in the suit.

If you start by leading one of your high cards, the king or the jack, declarer will get a trick in the suit. If partner held the queen rather than the ace, leading a small card would still be effective. Partner would play the queen to help drive out the ace and establish the suit. But what if declarer holds both the ace and queen?

DUMMY
97

YOU   ■   PARTNER
K J 6 5 2   10 8 3

DECLARER
A Q 4

When you lead a small card, the best partner can contribute is the 10 and declarer wins with the queen. All is not lost, however. When you regain the lead, you can drive out declarer's ace and establish three winners in the suit.

Notice that you *sacrificed* a trick by leading a card into declarer's ace and queen. If you did not lead the suit, declarer would get only one trick, the ace. If, for example, declarer led the suit from dummy and tried a finesse by playing the queen, you would win the trick with your king.

The objective of leading your long suit originally, however, is to try to establish enough winners to set the contract. In the above layout, you sacrifice one trick by leading the suit but are rewarded by eventually establishing three tricks in the suit. Since the contract is notrump, you can take all your winners once you get the opportunity. If you sit back and do not lead your long suit, declarer can go about establishing his long suits without having to worry about giving up the lead while doing it.

It may seem odd to be leading a small card when you have a suit such as A K 8 6 3. After all, declarer may well win a trick with the queen or jack. Let's see why it usually works out best. First, suppose this is the layout of the entire suit:

DUMMY
10 7 2

YOU
A K 8 6 3

PARTNER
Q 5

DECLARER
J 9 4

If you were to start by leading the ace and king, partner's queen would have to be played on the second trick and declarer would end up getting a trick with the jack. Even if you played only one high card and then led a small card to partner's queen, your remaining winners would be stranded. Unless you had an entry in another suit, your side would again end up with only two tricks. By leading a low card over to partner's queen, partner can win the trick and lead the 5 back to your winners and you end up taking all five tricks in the suit. Notice that the way you take or establish your winners in a suit is similar to the way declarer does. You are following the principle of *play the high card from the short side first.*

Suppose, instead, the complete layout looked like this:

DUMMY
10 7 2

YOU
A K 8 6 3

PARTNER
5 4

DECLARER
Q J 9

If you lead the ace, king and then a small card to establish your remaining cards as winners, declarer wins the third round of the suit with the queen. Your winners are stranded once again unless you have an entry in another suit. However, if you start by leading a small card, declarer wins the first trick with the 9 (or queen or jack), but partner still has a small card left in the suit. If *either* you **or partner** regains the lead, your side will be able to take four tricks in the suit. Leading a small card preserves the *link* to partner's hand. You are *taking your losses early* (ducking a trick to preserve an entry).

Let's look at an example of leading low from your long suit in a complete hand:

Contract: 3 NT
Lead: ♠6

DUMMY
♠ 975
♥ 642
♦ AK64
♣ K83

YOU
♠ AQ862
♥ 75
♦ 97
♣ J1074

N
W   E
S

PARTNER
♠ 43
♥ A983
♦ 10852
♣ Q52

DECLARER
♠ KJ10
♥ KQJ10
♦ QJ3
♣ A96

On lead against 3 NT, start by leading a small spade from your long suit (we will look at which small spade in a moment). It turns out that partner does not have much help in the suit and declarer wins the first trick with the ♠10. Declarer has four sure diamond tricks and two sure club tricks to go with the spade trick, but that is only a total of seven. To make the contract, declarer will have to establish tricks in the heart suit. When declarer leads a high heart to drive out the ♥A, partner wins the trick and still has a small spade to lead back. Declarer's remaining ♠K and ♠J are trapped. Whichever one declarer plays, you win with the next higher card and take the rest of the spade tricks. You give declarer a spade trick early but end up taking a heart trick and four spade tricks to defeat the contract.

If you did not lead a spade at all, declarer would make the contract by driving out partner's ♥A before your side has established enough tricks to defeat the contract. Also, if you started by leading one of your high spades, you would no longer be able to trap declarer's ♠K later on to defeat the contract. Now let's take a look at which small spade you choose when leading from your long suit.

Fourth Highest

When leading a small card from a long suit, most players traditionally lead their *fourth highest* ranking card in the suit. The fourth highest (*fourth best*) card is determined by counting down from the top. For example, you would lead the underlined card from each of the following holdings: Q 8 7 **5** 3 2, A Q 8 **6** 2, K 10 5 **4**.

So we finally come to the source of the saying, *"Lead the fourth highest from your longest and strongest suit against notrump contracts."* Against a notrump contract, you generally lead from your longest suit and, with a choice of suits, pick your strongest suit. When leading a small card, you choose your fourth highest. The saying puts it all together. Notice that it must be put in context, however. You do not necessarily lead from your longest suit if partner has bid a suit, and you do not necessarily lead your fourth highest if you have a suit headed by a three-card sequence.

It may not appear to make any difference which low card you lead, but remember with every card you play you are trying to give as much information as possible to partner. When you lead the fourth highest card, partner may be able to glean some extra information. For example, if you lead the 2 from K J 6 2, partner can figure out that you have only four cards in the suit since there are no lower cards you could hold if the 2 is your fourth card down from the top. If you lead a 5 and later follow suit with a lower card such as the 3, partner can figure out that you started with at least five cards in the suit (e.g., K 10 8 5 3). Another reason for leading fourth best has to do with the *Rule of Eleven* which is discussed in *The Finer Points*.

Putting everything together, let's see what you would lead from each of the following hands against a contract of 3 NT when you have no help from the bidding:

♠ A J 6 4 3   Start by picking your longest suit, spades. With no three-card sequence
♥ K 9 2   to lead from, lead the fourth highest card, the ♠ **4**.
♦ 7 5
♣ J 4 2

♠ 8 3   With a choice of suits, pick the stronger, hearts. With a three-card
♥ K Q J 4   sequence, lead the top card, the ♥ **K**.
♦ K J 8 2
♣ 9 4 3

♠ 9 2   Your longest suit is diamonds. With an interior sequence, lead the
♥ Q 7 5   top of your touching cards, the ♦ **10**.
♦ A 10 9 8 4
♣ J 6 2

♠ Q 7 4   With a broken sequence lead the top of your touching cards, the ♣ **Q**.
♥ J 9
♦ 10 8 2
♣ Q J 9 7 6

♠ K Q   Your longest suit is hearts, with nothing else to go on you would lead
♥ Q 10 6 4 2   one. With no sequence to lead from, lead the ♥**4**, your fourth highest.
♦ A 7 3
♣ 8 5 2

Here is a final example of leading against a notrump contract with a complete hand. First, the auction:

NORTH (DUMMY)	EAST (PARTNER)	SOUTH (DECLARER)	WEST (YOU)
		1 ♥	Pass
2 ♦	Pass	2 NT	Pass
3 NT	Pass	Pass	Pass

Next, your hand:

♠ A J 10 7
♥ A Q 6 2
♦ 5 2
♣ 9 7 3

Would you pick the ♠J? Here is the complete hand:

Contract: 3 NT
Lead: ♠J

DUMMY
♠ 8 5
♥ 5 3
♦ K Q J 10 8 4
♣ K Q 10

YOU
♠ A J 10 7
♥ A Q 6 2
♦ 5 2
♣ 9 7 3

PARTNER
♠ 6 4 3 2
♥ 9 7
♦ A 7 3
♣ 8 5 4 2

DECLARER
♠ K Q 9
♥ K J 10 8 4
♦ 9 6
♣ A J 6

With two equally long suits, you would normally lead the stronger — but always listen to the auction before making your decision. Declarer has bid hearts, so partner is unlikely to have much help in that suit. Instead choose the unbid suit, spades. With an interior sequence, lead the top of the touching cards, the ♠J. Look at what happens.

Declarer can win the first trick with the ♠Q (or ♠K) but must now lead diamonds to try to establish the tricks needed to make the contract. When partner wins the ♦A, he can return your suit, trapping declarer's remaining honor. You get three spade tricks and, together with partner's ♦A and your ♥A, that is enough to defeat the contract. If you led a heart or any suit other than spades, declarer would make the contract. Also, if you led the ♠A or the ♠7, declarer would also make the contract. By leading the ♠J, you do not have to worry about asking partner at the end of the hand, "Could we have defeated that contract?"

♥ *BIDDING REVIEW* ♥

As a refresher, here is a review of some of the bidding concepts covered in the *Club Series* and *Diamond Series* which may come in handy when bidding the practice hands.

Opening the Bidding

When you have the first opportunity to bid in an auction, value your hand using a combination of high-card points (HCPs) and distribution (length) points to determine whether or not you have enough strength to open the bidding. When you do have sufficient strength, start describing your hand to partner by opening the bidding at an appropriate level and in an appropriate denomination. Here are the guidelines for opening the bidding:

HAND VALUATION			
High-card Points (HCPs)		**Distribution Points**	
Ace	4 points	five-card suit	1 point
King	3 points	six-card suit	2 points
Queen	2 points	seven-card suit	3 points
Jack	1 point	eight-card suit	4 points

OPENING THE BIDDING AT THE ONE LEVEL

 /S - 17

- With fewer than 13 points, pass.
- With 16–18 points and a balanced hand, bid 1 NT.
- With 13–21 points:
  - With a five-card or longer suit:
    - Bid your longer suit
    - Bid the higher ranking of two five-card or six-card suits.
  - With no five-card or longer suit*:
    - Bid your longer minor suit.
    - Bid the higher ranking of two four-card minor suits or the lower ranking of two three-card minor suits.

---

*This applies only if you are playing a five-card major system. If you are playing a four-card major suit system
- With no five-card or longer suit:
  - Bid the lower ranking of two four-card suits
  - Bid the middle ranking of these four-card suits

OPENING THE BIDDING AT THE TWO LEVEL

- With an unbalanced hand of 22 or more points, open the bidding at the two level in your longest suit.
- With a balanced hand of 22–24 points, open the bidding 2 NT.
- With a balanced hand of 25–27 points, open the bidding 3 NT.

OPENING THE BIDDING AT THE THREE LEVEL

- An opening bid in a suit at the three level or higher (preempt) shows:
- A long suit — usually seven or more cards with three of the top five cards in the suit **and**
- A weak hand — less than the point count values for an opening bid.

Here are some examples of opening the bidding:

♠ K964
♥ A32
♦ Q8
♣ AJ84

With 14 HCPs, there is enough to open the bidding at the one level. With no five-card major suit, open the bidding in your longer minor suit, 1♣. (Playing a four-card-major system, you would also open 1♣, the lower ranking of two four-card suits.)

♠ AQ
♥ AKQ93
♦ 4
♣ AK1082

With 22 HCPs plus one point for each of the five-card suits, there is enough strength to open the bidding at the two level. With two five-card suits, use the same guideline as you would for opening at the one level and bid the higher ranking suit. Open the bidding 2♥.

♠ KQJ9762
♥ 8
♦ 942
♣ J3

There are not enough points to open the bidding at the one level, but with a good seven-card suit, you can open the bidding at the three level, 3♠. This is a preemptive opening bid, describing your hand and, at the same time, making it difficult for the opponents to enter the auction.

♥ *PLAY OF THE HAND REVIEW* ♥

Here is a review of some of the material from the *Diamond Series* that may be useful when you are playing some of the practice hands.

Declarer's Plan

When you are declarer, always take the time to make a PLAN before you start to play the hand:

1. **P**ause to consider your objective
2. **L**ook at your winners and losers
3. **A**nalyze your alternatives
4. **N**ow put it together

When playing in a notrump contract, consider your objective in terms of the number of winners you must take in order to make the contract. For example, in a contract of 3 NT you need nine winners. Look at the number of *sure tricks* you have — the tricks you can take without giving up the lead to the opponents. If you do not have enough sure tricks, examine each suit to see what alternatives you have for developing the extra tricks you need. Tricks can be developed in notrump contracts with the help of *promotion, long suits* and *finesses*. Finally, put your plan together by choosing the best alternative. Make sure to keep track of your *entries* between the two hands and watch out for the opponents if you are going to have to give up the lead.

♥ *SUMMARY* ♥

When you are on lead against a notrump contract, use the following guideline:

- If partner has bid a suit, lead it:

  - Lead the top card from a doubleton (e.g., **7** 2, **Q** 5)
  - Lead the top of touching honors (e.g., **Q** J 3, **10** 9 5)
  - With no sequence, lead low (e.g., K 8 **3**, Q 9 4 **2**, 9 7 **6**)

- Otherwise, lead your longest suit (unless bid by the opponents):

  - Lead the top of the touching honors from a three-card sequence, a broken sequence or an interior sequence
    (e.g., **K** Q J 3 2, **Q** J 9 6 4, K **J** 10 8)
  - With no sequence, lead fourth highest
    (e.g., Q 10 8 **3**, K J 6 **5** 4, A 9 7 **6** 4 3)

- With a choice of suits:

  - Lead the stronger
  - Lead the unbid suit

♥ *THE FINER POINTS* ♥

Disregarding the Guidelines

Your objective as a defender is to defeat the contract. The guidelines on opening lead are there only to help when you are unsure what to do. If you see a better alternative, do not blindly follow the guideline. For example, suppose you are on lead against 3 NT with the following hand:

♠ J 8 6 4 3
♥ Q J 10 9
♦ A K
♣ A 5

Your longest suit is spades, but leading a heart will give you the best chance to defeat the contract. By leading the ♥ Q, you will drive out declarer's ♥ K. When you regain the lead, you can lead another heart to drive out declarer's ♥ A. This will establish two sure heart tricks to go along with your club trick and two diamond tricks to defeat the contract. Leading a spade is much less likely to succeed since you will need considerable help from partner to establish the suit.

Rule of Eleven

If your partner leads his fourth highest card against a notrump contract, you can get some additional information about the cards in declarer's hand by using the *Rule of Eleven*. Subtracting the number of the card led by partner from 11 tells you how many higher cards there are in the other three hands. Since you will be able to see the number of higher cards in your hand and the dummy, you can determine the number of higher cards held by declarer. Let's see how this could be useful. Suppose partner leads the ♥ 7 against a notrump contract and you see the following cards:

DUMMY
♥ Q 8 6
PARTNER   YOU
♥ 7   ♥ K 10 3

Subtracting partner's card from 11 tells you that there are four (11 − 7 = 4) higher cards in the other three hands. You can see two of them in dummy, the ♥ Q and ♥ 8, and two in your hand, the ♥ K and the ♥ 10. That leaves no higher cards than the ♥ 7 in declarer's hand. Suppose declarer plays dummy's ♥ 8. You can confidently play the ♥ 10 to win the trick, rather than expending the ♥ K. The complete layout of the suit must be something like this:

DUMMY
♥ Q 8 6
PARTNER   YOU
♥ A J 9 7   ♥ K 10 3
DECLARER
♥ 5 4 2

If you played the ♥ K rather than the ♥ 10, declarer would eventually get a trick with dummy's ♥ Q. Using the Rule of Eleven helped you make the right decision.

♥ *GROUP ACTIVITIES* ♥

Exercise One — Choosing the Suit

You are on lead against a notrump contract with the following hand:

> ♠ 109762
> ♥ 86
> ♦ A943
> ♣ KQ

Which suit would you lead under each of these conditions:

1) The contract is 3 NT and your partner overcalled in hearts during the auction.
2) The contract is 1 NT with no bidding from your side.
3) The contract is 3 NT after one of the opponents opened the bidding 1♦.
4) The contract is 6 NT.

1) _____8 H_____ 2) _____10 S_____ 3) _____3 D_____ 4) _____A D_____

Exercise Two — Choosing the Card in Partner's Suit

In each of the following examples, you are leading partner's suit. Which is the best card to lead? Why?

1)

	DUMMY	
	962	
YOU	■	PARTNER
J3		KQ875
	DECLARER	
	A104	

2)

	DUMMY	
	K85	
YOU	■	PARTNER
QJ3		A10962
	DECLARER	
	74	

3)

DUMMY
9 6

YOU
Q 7 ⑤

PARTNER
A 10 8 4 2

DECLARER
K J 3

1) _____   2) _____   3) _____

Exercise Three — Leading the Top of a Sequence

In the following examples, you are leading your own suit against a notrump contract. Which is the best card to lead? How many tricks can your side develop from the suit? What must the defenders do to ensure that they take all the tricks they have coming?

1)

DUMMY
K 3

YOU
Ⓙ 10 9 6

PARTNER
A 7 5 2

DECLARER
Q 8 4

2)

DUMMY
A 7

YOU
Ⓠ J 9 6 3

PARTNER
8 4 2

DECLARER
K 10 5

3)

DUMMY
K 2

YOU
A Ⓙ 10 4 3

PARTNER
8 7 6

DECLARER
Q 9 5

4)

DUMMY
74

YOU
K Q J 8 3

DECLARER
10 9 5

PARTNER
A 6 2

1) _____ J _____   2) _____ Q _____   3) _____   4) _____

Exercise Four — Leading a Low Card

Once again you are leading your suit against a notrump contract. Which is the best card to lead? How many tricks can your side develop from the suit? What must the defenders do to ensure that they take all the tricks they have coming?

1)

DUMMY
6 5

YOU
K 9 8 7 2

DECLARER
A Q 10

PARTNER
J 4 3

2)

DUMMY
A 2

YOU
Q 7 6 3

DECLARER
J 10 9

PARTNER
K 8 5 4

3)

DUMMY
8 7 5

YOU
A Q 4 3 2

DECLARER
10 9 6

PARTNER
K J

1) _____   2) _____   3) _____

Exercise Five — Leading Against Notrump Contracts

The opening bid is 1 NT by the opponent on your right and everybody passes. Which card do you lead from each of the following hands?

1) ♠ A K
   ♥ Q 10 8 4 3
   ♦ J 9 5
   ♣ 7 4 2

2) ♠ J 9 6 3
   ♥ Q 4
   ♦ Q J 10 5
   ♣ K 8 3

3) ♠ A J 8 6 5 2
   ♥ K 8 3
   ♦ 8 4
   ♣ 9 2

1) _____   2) _____   3) _____

Exercise Six — Listening to the Bidding

You are on lead against a contract of 3 NT after the auction has progressed as follows:

NORTH (DUMMY)	EAST (PARTNER)	SOUTH (DECLARER)	WEST (YOU)
		1 ♥	Pass
1 ♠	Pass	2 ♣	Pass
3 ♠	Pass	3 NT	Pass
Pass	Pass		

Which card do you lead from each of the following hands?

1) ♠ 7 4
   ♥ K Q 8 3
   ♦ K J 6 2
   ♣ 9 8 5

2) ♠ Q 6 5 2
   ♥ Q 8 4
   ♦ J 10 9
   ♣ J 8 3

3) ♠ 6 3
   ♥ J 9 4 2
   ♦ Q 8 3
   ♣ K Q J 10

1) _____   2) _____   3) _____

Exercise Seven — Review of Opening the Bidding

What would your opening bid be with each of the following hands?

1) ♠ Q 10 8 5 2
   ♥ 9 4   *13 + 1*
   ♦ A K 8 3
   ♣ A 4

2) ♠ K 7 3   *16 + 1*
   ♥ A J
   ♦ K 10 9 6 4
   ♣ A J 10

3) ♠ 7 4
   ♥ A J 9 2   *13*
   ♦ K 10 4 3
   ♣ A J 8

1) _____/ S_____   2) _____/ N_____   3) _____/ D_____

4) ♠ Q J 9
   ♥ A K 7   *22*
   ♦ K Q 8 4
   ♣ A Q J

5) ♠ K Q J 10 8 3
   ♥ A K J   *22 + 2*
   ♦ K Q
   ♣ K 4

6) ♠ 8 6
   ♥ 10
   ♦ A Q 10 9 6 4 3
   ♣ J 4 2

NOT 2N

4) _____2C_____   5) _____2 C_____   6) _____3 D_____

Exercise Eight — Review of Declarer's Plan

Go through the four steps of declarer's PLAN to decide how to play the following hand in a contract of 3 NT after the opening lead of the ♣Q.

DUMMY
♠ J 9 2
♥ 10 6 4
♦ Q J 10 7 3
♣ A 8

LEAD
♣ Q

DECLARER
♠ A 8 4 3
♥ A K 9
♦ K 8
♣ K 7 3 2

Exercise Nine — Leading Partner's Suit

Turn up the cards on the first pre-dealt hand. Put each hand dummy style at the edge of the table in front of each player.

Dealer: North

The Bidding

What would North open the bidding? How can East describe his hand? South passes. How many points does West have? At what level does the partnership belong? Is there a Golden Fit? What does West respond? How does the auction proceed from there? What is the contract? Who is declarer?

The Defense

Which player makes the opening lead? What would the opening lead be? Why? How does North plan to defeat the contract?

The Play

Review the steps in declarer's PLAN. How does declarer plan to make the contract?

Exercise Ten — Leading From a Sequence

Turn up the cards on the second pre-dealt hand. Put each hand dummy style at the edge of the table in front of each player.

Dealer: East

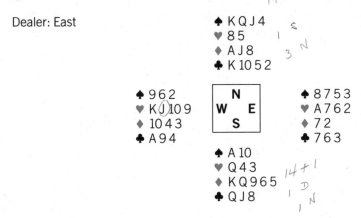

The Bidding

East and West pass throughout the auction. What would South open the bidding? What does North respond? How does South finish describing his balanced hand? At what level does the partnership belong? Is there a Golden Fit? What does North rebid? How does the auction proceed from there? What is the contract? Who is declarer?

The Defense

Which player makes the opening lead? What would the opening lead be? Why? From the opening lead, which card does East know that declarer has? How do the defenders plan to defeat the contract?

The Play

Review the steps in declarer's PLAN. How does declarer plan to make the contract?

Exercise Eleven — Fourth Highest

Turn up the cards on the third pre-dealt hand. Put each hand dummy style at the edge of the table in front of each player.

Dealer: South

```
                        ♠ 10 7 6 2
                        ♥ A K 9 6 2
                        ♦ 10 4
                        ♣ 6 3

       ♠ A K 8          N              ♠ Q 4
       ♥ Q J 5        W     E          ♥ 10 8 3
       ♦ A Q J 6        S              ♦ K 7 5 3
       ♣ K Q 4                         ♣ J 10 8 2

                        ♠ J 9 5 3
                        ♥ 7 4
                        ♦ 9 8 2
                        ♣ A 9 7 5
```

The Bidding

South passes. With a balanced hand and 22 HCPs, what is West's opening bid? North passes. Knowing that his partner has 22–24 points, what does East respond? How does the auction proceed from there? What is the contract? Who is declarer?

The Defense

Which player makes the opening lead? What would the opening lead be? Why? After the opening lead, which cards must North and South be careful to hold on to if declarer starts taking his tricks?

The Play

Review the steps in declarer's PLAN. How does declarer plan to make the contract?

Exercise Twelve — Listening to the Opponents

Turn up the cards on the fourth pre-dealt hand. Put each hand dummy style at the edge of the table in front of each player.

Dealer: West

```
Dealer: West          ♠ K Q J        1 ƒ + 1
                      ♥ 9 6
                      ♦ K J 9 4 3
                      ♣ A 7 6

   ♠ 9 8 7 6 5    ┌─────────┐    ♠ 4
   ♥ 7 4 2        │    N    │    ♥ A 8 5 3
   ♦ 6           │ W     E │    ♦ A 8 7 5
   ♣ K 9 4 3      │    S    │    ♣ Q 10 8 2
                  └─────────┘
                      ♠ A 10 3 2
                      ♥ K Q J 10
                      ♦ Q 10 2
                      ♣ J 5
```

The Bidding

West passes. What is North's opening bid? Why can East not overcall or make a takeout double? What does East do? Which suit does South bid at the one level? West passes. How does North describe his balanced hand? East passes. At what level and in what denomination does the contract belong? What does South bid? How does the auction proceed from there? What is the contract? Who is declarer?

The Defense

Which player makes the opening lead? After listening to the auction, which suit should he choose? Which card? What would happen if a different suit were chosen?

The Play

Review the steps in declarer's PLAN. How does declarer plan to make the contract?

LESSON 2
Opening Leads Against Suit Contracts

Choosing the Suit
Choosing the Card
Bidding Review
Play of the Hand Review
Summary
The Finer Points

Workshop Material
Group Activities

The presence of a trump suit influences both the way declarer plays the hand and the way the defenders try to defeat it. Starting with the opening lead, the defenders must take a different approach in choosing the suit to attack and in choosing the specific card to lead. In this lesson we will look at where the differences arise and will come up with guidelines for making the opening lead against a suit (trump) contract.

♥ CHOOSING THE SUIT ♥

"When in doubt lead trumps" is a popular saying to guide you when it is your lead. There are probably many situations where you are "in doubt" as to the best lead, but in only a few of these cases will leading trumps be the most effective defense. To help remove some of the doubt, let's start by looking at the major difference between suit contracts and notrump contracts.

When defending against a notrump contact, you look to your long suit as a potential source of tricks when you do not have enough sure tricks to defeat the contract. You are often willing to sacrifice a trick if it will help establish some winners in your long suit. When you eventually regain the lead, you can take your winners without interference from declarer.

All this changes when there is a trump suit. Even if you can establish your small cards as winners, it is unlikely you will be able to take many tricks with them. Why? Because declarer will be able to trump your winners once he runs out of the suit. For example, consider the layout of the following suit:

	DUMMY	
	9 6 3	
YOU		PARTNER
K J 7 5 2		10 8 4
	DECLARER	
	A Q	

Against a notrump contract, leading this suit will often be effective. Although declarer can win the first two tricks, you are compensated by eventually establishing three winners in the suit. If you can regain the lead, declarer can do nothing to stop you from taking your winners.

Against a suit contract, leading this suit from your side is unlikely to be a success. Declarer can win the first two tricks, and then his trump cards prevent you from taking any tricks in the suit. Declarer ends up with no *losers* in the suit. If you bide your time and wait for declarer or partner to lead the suit, you will be able to win a trick with the king.

The trump suit, therefore, shifts the defenders' focus away from their length toward their strength. Of course, the trump suit itself is a double-edged sword. Whereas declarer can use his trumps to *ruff* (trump) your winners, the trump suit also presents the defenders an opportunity to ruff some of declarer's winners.

Partner's Suit

If partner has bid a suit during the auction, that is a good place to look for tricks for your side. As when leading against notrump contracts, lead partner's suit unless you clearly have something better to do. It is often important to establish your side's tricks before declarer has an opportunity to discard some of his losers. For example, suppose your partner opens the bidding 1 ♥ and the opponents, undaunted, bid all the way up to 6 ♠ and it is your lead from the following hand:

♠ 8
♥ 7 4
♦ 9 6 3 2
♣ 10 9 8 7 4 3

Your hand is so weak that you may think it does not matter what you lead, but you are the player in the key position. Lead your partner's suit, hearts. Whatever tricks your side has coming are likely to come from the suit bid by partner. Even if partner cannot win the first trick, you may help your side establish winners. This could be the complete deal:

Contract: 6 ♠
Lead: ♥ 7

DUMMY
♠ A 10 5 4
♥ 9 8 3 2
♦ K Q J 7
♣ 6

YOU
♠ 8
♥ 7 4
♦ 9 6 3 2
♣ 10 9 8 7 4 3

N
W   E
S

PARTNER
♠ J 2
♥ K Q J 10 5
♦ A 8 4
♣ J 5 2

DECLARER
♠ K Q 9 7 6 3
♥ A 6
♦ 10 5
♣ A K Q

When you lead a heart, declarer can win the trick with the ♥A but eventually has to lead diamonds to drive out partner's ♦A. Partner can then take a heart trick to defeat the slam. If you lead anything other than partner's suit, declarer can make the slam. After drawing trumps, declarer loses a trick to partner's ♦A and, when partner leads a heart, wins the ♥A and discards the ♥6 on dummy's extra diamond winner.

Your Suits

When leading a suit of your own, the best choice is usually one in which you have a sequence of high cards. For example, suppose the opponents bid only spades during the auction and you are on lead against 4♠ with the following hand:

♠ 8
♥ Q 10 6 4 2
♦ K Q J
♣ K 8 6 3

Although both the heart and club suits are longer, leading from the strong sequence in diamonds is likely to work out best against a spade contract. By leading the ♦ K you should be able to drive out declarer's ♦ A and establish both the ♦ Q and ♦ J as winners. Because you have only three diamonds, declarer is less likely to have a singleton or doubleton, so you should be able to take both your winners. Notice that you do not need any help from partner to establish winners in the suit. If partner has the ♦ A, so much the better. If not, it should still work out well.

On the other hand, if you lead a heart, you will need some help from partner, either the ♥ A, ♥ K or ♥ J. If partner has none of these cards, leading a heart may well give up a trick for your side. The full layout of the heart suit might be something like this:

```
              DUMMY
              ♥ A 7 5
  YOU                    PARTNER
♥ Q 10 6 4 2             ♥ 9 8
             DECLARER
              ♥ K J 3
```

When you lead a small heart, declarer can play a small heart from dummy and win the first trick with the ♥ J. After drawing trumps, the ♥ A and ♥ K will also be winners. If you do not lead a heart, declarer has a loser in the suit. It is better to wait until partner can lead through declarer's high cards, or until declarer plays the suit himself. Leading a heart could cost a trick even if partner has some help and declarer's holding is not as strong. Consider this layout:

```
              DUMMY
              ♥ K 7 3
  YOU                    PARTNER
♥ Q 10 6 4 2             ♥ A 9 8
             DECLARER
              ♥ J 5
```

When you lead a small heart, declarer can play a small heart from dummy and partner will have to win the trick with the ♥ A to avoid letting declarer win the trick with the ♥ J. Now dummy's ♥ K is a trick. If you do not lead a heart, your side will get two heart tricks. If, for example, declarer were to lead the ♥ J, you could cover with the ♥ Q and partner would win dummy's ♥ K with the ♥ A. Now your side has the remaining high hearts.

Leading a club from the example hand could have equally unfortunate results if partner has no help in the suit. The complete layout of the suit might look like this:

DUMMY
♣ A 7
YOU PARTNER
♣ K 8 6 3 ♣ J 10 9 5 4
DECLARER
♣ Q 2

If you lead a small club, declarer can play a small club from dummy and win the trick with the ♣Q, ending up with no losers in the suit. If you do not lead a club, declarer has a loser in the suit.

It is often best against a trump contract to lead a suit containing a sequence even if it is not the longest suit in your hand. A suit with a strong two-card sequence has good potential for developing tricks for your side. For example, leading a suit such as K Q 4 will work very well if partner has either the ace or jack and will still develop one trick even if declarer has both those cards.

If you have bid a suit which partner has supported, it generally is safe to lead it even when it is not headed by touching high cards. For example, your suit is K J 8 6 3 and partner has raised it during the auction: it is likely that partner has either the ace or the queen. It is usually important to lead your suit as soon as possible, before declarer has an opportunity to discard any losers in the suit.

The Unbid Suits

On many hands, partner will not have bid and you will not have a strong sequence from which to lead. As when leading against notrump contracts, it is usually preferable to lead an unbid suit. The fact that the opponents have not bid the suit increases the probability that partner will have some strength there. For example, suppose the auction proceeds in this manner:

NORTH (DUMMY)	EAST (PARTNER)	SOUTH (DECLARER)	WEST (YOU)
		1♠	Pass
2♦	Pass	3♦	Pass
3♠	Pass	4♠	Pass
Pass	Pass		

You have to choose a lead from the following hand:

♠ 8 4
♥ K 7 6 3
♦ J 10 9
♣ K 8 7 5

You have a safe-looking sequence in diamonds, but that is one of the opponents' suits. It is better to choose one of the unbid suits. Which one? With no help from partner during the auction, it is difficult to say. Yet it is reasonable to hope that partner will have some strength in whichever suit you choose since the opponents have both bid spades and diamonds.

41

The complete hand might look like this:

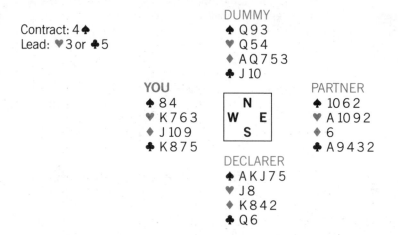

Contract: 4♠
Lead: ♥3 or ♣5

DUMMY
♠ Q93
♥ Q54
♦ AQ753
♣ J10

YOU
♠ 84
♥ K763
♦ J109
♣ K875

PARTNER
♠ 1062
♥ A1092
♦ 6
♣ A9432

DECLARER
♠ AKJ75
♥ J8
♦ K842
♣ Q6

It turns out that either lead is effective, letting you take the first four tricks: the ♥A and ♥K, and the ♣A and ♣K. If you lead one of the opponents' suits, declarer can draw trumps and discard one of his losers on dummy's extra diamond trick to make the contract. If the opponents have bid and supported two suits during the auction, lead one of the unbid suits quickly in order to take or establish your winners before they disappear.

Leading a Short Suit

Leading a short suit — a singleton or sometimes a doubleton — can be an effective way to get tricks in a trump contract. The idea is to put declarer's trump suit to work against him; you hope to be able to trump declarer's high cards when the suit is led again. For the lead of a short suit to work, one or both of the following conditions must be present:

- Partner must be able to win a trick in the suit and then lead the suit back so that you can trump it. This is a reasonable expectation if partner has bid the suit or if it is an unbid suit and the auction indicates that partner has some strength. If the opponents stop in a contract of 4♠ and you have only a couple of points, assume partner has some strength, but if you have a lot of points, assume partner has very little.

- If partner cannot win an early trick in the suit, partner will need to regain the lead before declarer draws all your trumps. This might be the case if partner has an early winner in the trump suit (the ace or, perhaps, the king), or if you have an early winner in the trump suit and can find an entry to partner's hand in another suit.

Without being able to look into partner's hand, the lead of a singleton carries some risk. You may be helping declarer to establish his suit, and your trumps may be drawn before you get an opportunity to use them. Nonetheless, the situation occasionally merits taking the chance. Suppose the auction proceeds as follows:

NORTH	EAST	SOUTH	WEST
(DUMMY)	(PARTNER)	(DECLARER)	(YOU)
		1♥	Pass
1♠	Pass	1NT	Pass
4♥	Pass	Pass	Pass

This is your hand:

♠ 8
♥ 652
♦ J97652
♣ 1083

You do not have much high card strength but partner is marked with some strength. Otherwise the opponents would probably be in a slam contract. Lead your singleton spade and see what develops.

The complete layout may be something like this:

Contract: 4♥
Lead: ♠8

DUMMY
♠ KQJ4
♥ Q983
♦ AK
♣ 654

YOU
♠ 8
♥ 652
♦ J97652
♣ 1083

PARTNER
♠ A 10753
♥ 10
♦ Q43
♣ A972

DECLARER
♠ 962
♥ AKJ74
♦ 108
♣ KQJ

When you lead the ♠8, partner wins the trick with the ♠A and leads back a spade for you to trump. Since the diamond suit does not look attractive, you now lead a club (we will see in a later lesson how partner may be able to help out in this situation). Partner wins the ♣A and leads another spade for you to trump. All of a sudden, your side has four tricks, despite the fact that the opponents started with 29 HCPs.

Of course, there is one more ingredient to making your lead of a singleton effective. Partner has to visualize the opportunity for you to trump declarer's winners and must cooperate by leading back the suit for you to ruff. Hopefully you will do the same when partner leads a singleton.

Leading a short suit is not a good idea when you are likely to get tricks with your trumps anyway. For example, if your holding in the trump suit is Q J 10 9, you will get two trump tricks even if declarer has both the ace and king. If you lead a singleton and partner returns the suit for you to trump, you have gained nothing. You were entitled to your trump tricks anyway. In the meantime, you may be helping declarer to establish winners. If you hold *natural trump tricks* (i.e., likely winners in the trump suit), it is better to try to establish winners in other suits.

Leading a Long Suit

Although it is not always advantageous to lead your long suit against a trump contract since declarer will be able to ruff it, this can be an effective defense when either you or partner has four or more trumps. Consider the following hand:

Contract: 4♠
Lead: ♣K

```
                    DUMMY
                    ♠ 8 7 4
                    ♥ Q 9 3
                    ♦ K 10 9 2
                    ♣ A 6 5
YOU                                 PARTNER
♠ 10 5 3 2     ┌─────────┐          ♠ 9
♥ A 8 5        │    N    │          ♥ 10 6 4 2
♦ 4            │  W   E  │          ♦ A 8 6 3
♣ K Q J 10 8   │    S    │          ♣ 9 7 4 2
               └─────────┘
                    DECLARER
                    ♠ A K Q J 6
                    ♥ K J 7
                    ♦ Q J 7 5
                    ♣ 3
```

If you start by leading the ♣K, declarer can win the ♣A and draw all your trumps. Since you have four of them, declarer is left with only one trump. When declarer leads a diamond to drive out your partner's ♦A, your partner can lead another club, forcing declarer to use up his last trump. Declarer can take the three diamond tricks while you discard your small hearts and a club, but when he leads a heart you win the ♥A and take your remaining two club tricks. Declarer, with no trump left, is powerless to stop you.

By continuing to lead the club suit at every opportunity, you force declarer to use up his trumps. This is called a *forcing defense*. The idea is to run declarer out of trumps so that you can take all your established winners when you regain the lead. If this happens, declarer will *lose control* of the hand.

Notice what would happen if you led your singleton diamond. Your partner can win the ♦A and lead one back for you to trump. You have two tricks and can see one more with the ♥A. If you now lead a club to promote a fourth winner, declarer wins it, draws your three remaining trumps and leads a heart to drive out the ♥A. With two trumps left and your partner's ♦A gone, declarer is firmly in control. Whatever you do, declarer has the rest of the tricks. When you have long trumps, leading your long suit to make declarer trump is often more effective than leading a singleton.

Leading a Trump

Leading the trump suit may be effective when declarer is planning to ruff some of the losers in his hand with dummy's trumps. If declarer has a limited supply of trumps, he often cannot afford to draw trumps and still have enough left in the dummy with which to trump all his losers. In such cases, declarer wants to delay drawing trumps until he has ruffed his losers. By leading trumps whenever you get the opportunity, you may be able to thwart declarer's plan.

How do you know when declarer is planning to trump losers in the dummy? You have to listen carefully to the auction and try to visualize the distribution of both declarer and dummy's hand. If it sounds as though dummy has shortness in one of declarer's long suits, it is likely that declarer will make use of dummy's shortness to ruff some of the losers in his long suit. To protect your side's winners in that suit, it may be the time to lead a trump. For example suppose the auction proceeds as follows:

NORTH	EAST	SOUTH	WEST
(DUMMY)	(PARTNER)	(DECLARER)	(**YOU**)
Pass	Pass	1♠	Pass
1 NT	Pass	2♥	Pass
2♠	Pass	Pass	Pass

You are on lead with:

♠ 8 4 3
♥ A K J 10
♦ K 10 7 5
♣ 9 3

What do you know about declarer's hand? Declarer has opened the bidding 1♠ and then bid hearts, so he probably has at least five spades and four hearts. What do you know about dummy's hand? Dummy did not raise declarer's spades right away but preferred to play with spades as trump rather than hearts. Therefore, dummy is quite likely short in hearts. Looking at the potential heart winners in your hand, it looks as though declarer will have some heart losers he will want to trump in dummy. It's time to lead a trump in order to spoil declarer's plan.

The complete hand might look like this:

Contract: 2♠
Lead: ♠3

DUMMY
♠ Q 7
♥ 5
♦ A 9 6 3 2
♣ 10 6 5 4 2

YOU
♠ 8 4 3
♥ A K J 10
♦ K 10 7 5
♣ 9 3

PARTNER
♠ 9 6 5
♥ 8 7 4 2
♦ Q J
♣ K Q J 8

DECLARER
♠ A K J 10 2
♥ Q 9 6 3
♦ 8 4
♣ A 7

With four heart losers, a diamond loser and a club loser, declarer needs to ruff a heart loser in dummy. Declarer plans to lose one heart trick and then trump a heart with one of dummy's trumps. By leading a trump, you spoil the plan. Declarer can win the trump lead and give up a heart trick but you win the heart and lead another spade to remove dummy's remaining trump. If your partner returns a heart when he gets the lead, declarer ends up losing all four heart tricks and is defeated. If your opening lead is anything except a trump, declarer would get the opportunity to ruff at least one of his losers in dummy and end up making the contract.

It is not always easy to tell from the auction whether a trump lead will be effective. Listening to the bidding, however, and trying to visualize the opponents' hands is always a useful exercise. When the dummy is actually put down, you get an opportunity to verify part of your prediction and, throughout the defense of the hand, the more you know about declarer's distribution, the easier it will be to defend. With practice, you will soon recognize some of the opportunities to lead trumps.

It is often a good idea to lead trumps when your side appears to have the majority of the high cards but the opponents end up playing the contract. They may have bid too much trying to prevent your side from getting the contract (*sacrificing*) and you may even have made a penalty double of the final contract. In such situations, the opponents are hoping to use their trumps to ruff your winners. By leading a trump, you cut down their ability to do so. For example, suppose the auction goes this way:

NORTH (DUMMY)	EAST (PARTNER)	SOUTH (DECLARER)	WEST (YOU)
Pass	1♣	1♦	1♥
2♦	4♥	5♦	Double
Pass	Pass	Pass	

A trump lead will protect your high cards if the complete hand is something like this:

DUMMY
♠ 6 4
♥ Q 10 2
♦ K J 5
♣ 9 7 6 4 2

Contract: 5 ♦ Doubled
Lead: ♦ 2

YOU
♠ Q 10 2
♥ K J 8 7 6
♦ 8 4 2
♣ J 5

N
W E
S

PARTNER
♠ A K 9 3
♥ A 9 5 3
♦ 7
♣ K Q 10 8

DECLARER
♠ J 8 7 5
♥ 4
♦ A Q 10 9 6 3
♣ A 3

South bid to the five level assuming that your side can make 4♥ and that the penalty for going down in 5♦ will be less than the value of your game. Since you know your side has most of the high cards, you double and lead a trump. South has four spade losers, a heart loser and a club loser. By leading a trump and continuing to lead trumps every time you gain the lead, you can prevent declarer from trumping his spade losers in dummy. Declarer is defeated four tricks. If you never lead trumps, declarer would go down only two tricks for a relatively inexpensive sacrifice.

One other time when you lead a trump is when you truly are "in doubt". It looks as if the lead of any other suit would be likely to give up a trick for your side. By making the passive lead of a trump you are biding your time, leaving it to declarer to play the other suits. For example, suppose the auction proceeds as follows:

NORTH	EAST	SOUTH	WEST
(DUMMY)	(PARTNER)	(DECLARER)	(YOU)
1♣	Pass	1♦	Pass
1♥	Pass	1♠	Pass
2♠	Pass	4♠	Pass
Pass	Pass		

With the opponents having bid all four suits, you have to find a lead from this hand:

♠ 9 4 2
♥ Q 10 9
♦ K 10 8 2
♣ K 7 5

You have finally come to the situation in which the saying "when in doubt, lead trumps" comes in handy. Lead a spade and let declarer play the other suits himself.

The complete hand might look like this:

DUMMY
♠ A Q 8 3
♥ K 8 4 2
♦ 7 4
♣ A 10 6

Contract: 4♠
Lead: ♠2

YOU
♠ 9 4 2
♥ Q 10 9
♦ K 10 8 2
♣ K 7 5

```
      N
   W     E
      S
```

PARTNER
♠ 10 5
♥ A 7 6 3
♦ 9 5
♣ J 9 8 4 2

DECLARER
♠ K J 7 6
♥ J 5
♦ A Q J 6 3
♣ Q 3

If you lead anything other than a trump on this hand, it costs your side a trick. By making the passive lead of a trump, you give declarer no help. Declarer will eventually lose two heart tricks, a diamond trick and a club trick — one too many.

Putting together the various options you have when leading against a suit contract, let's look at which suit you would lead from various hands after this auction:

NORTH	EAST	SOUTH	WEST
(DUMMY)	(PARTNER)	(DECLARER)	(**YOU**)
1 ♦	Pass	1 ♥	Pass
2 ♥	Pass	4 ♥	Pass
Pass	Pass		

♠ K 8 4 2
♥ 7 3
♦ Q 9 4
♣ Q J 10 6

With no bidding from partner, you will have to choose the suit. Leading the opponents' suits is unlikely to be profitable, so pick an unbid suit. With a strong sequence in clubs, that suit is preferable to spades. If partner has no help in spades, leading a spade might cost a trick. Lead a **club**.

♠ 6
♥ A 8 3
♦ 10 9 6 2
♣ J 8 6 4 2

To establish the club suit will require a lot of help from partner. Even if partner has some help, it is unlikely you can get more than one or two tricks before declarer can trump the suit. Instead, lead a **spade**, your singleton, hoping to get a ruff. Since you have the ♥A, declarer will not be able to draw all your trumps right away even if partner cannot win the first spade trick.

♠ 8
♥ J 10 7 3
♦ Q 6 2
♣ K Q J 9 8

Although you have a singleton, leading it is unlikely to work out best. You will likely get a trump trick anyway, even if the opponents have the ♥A, ♥K and ♥Q. Instead, lead a **club**, your long suit. Perhaps you can force declarer to trump too often and lose control of the hand.

♠ K Q 3
♥ 9 7
♦ J 8 5
♣ A 10 8 6 3

Your touching honors in spades are more attractive than the long club suit. If partner has either the ♠A or ♠J, a **spade** lead will work out well. Even if he does not, you will establish one spade winner and will then have the opportunity to lead a club if it seems necessary.

♠ K 10 5
♥ 8 7 4
♦ K J 8 7
♣ K J 3

Nothing looks particularly attractive here. You do not want to lead a diamond since the opponents bid that suit. You could guess whether partner has something in spades or clubs, but maybe this is the time to lead a **trump** since you are in doubt.

♥ CHOOSING THE CARD ♥

Once you have decided on the suit, picking the card is relatively straightforward since the guidelines are similar to those for leading against notrump contracts, with only a couple of exceptions.

Leading Partner's Suit

The card you choose when leading partner's suit is identical to that when leading against notrump with the proviso that you do not lead a small card if you hold the ace. Why is it better to lead the ace against a suit contract rather than a small card? Consider the following layout:

DUMMY
8
YOU   PARTNER
A 7 3 2   Q J 9 6 5
DECLARER
K 10 4

If you lead a small card *away from the ace,* declarer can win the first trick with the king. Defending against a notrump contract, this would not be a problem. When your side regained the lead, you could take all the established winners in the suit. When defending against a suit contract, however, your side may never get a trick in the suit since declarer can trump his remaining small cards in dummy. It is usually safer to lead an ace than to lead away from it.

In summary, when leading partner's suit:

- Lead the ace, if you have it (e.g., **A** 8 3, **A** J 10 4)
- Lead the top card from a doubleton (e.g., **7** 2, **Q** 5)
- Lead the top of touching honors (e.g., **Q** J 3, **10** 9 5)
- With no sequence, lead low (e.g., K 8 **3**, Q 9 4 **2**, 9 7 **6***)

---

*From three small cards, some partnerships prefer to lead the top card (e.g., **9** 7 6) or the **middle** card (e.g., 9 **7** 6).

Leading Your Suit

When you are leading your own suit, the guidelines are similar to leading against a notrump contract with a couple of exceptions. First, if your suit is headed by the ace, lead the ace rather than a small card. The reason for not leading away from an ace, if you are leading the suit, is the same as when leading partner's suit — you do not want declarer to win the first trick and then have no cards left in the suit when you later try to take your ace.

The other change from leading against notrump contracts is that you lead the top of touching honors even if you have only a two-card sequence. Consider this layout:

```
              DUMMY
                87
  YOU       ▮▮▮▮   PARTNER
  KQ654     ▮▮▮▮   932
            DECLARER
              A J 10
```

Against a notrump contract, leading a small card from your holding will not usually cost a trick even though partner has no help in the suit. Declarer will win the first trick with the 10, but you can later drive out the ace and establish three winners in the suit. Declarer is always entitled to two tricks in the suit once you lead it, whether you lead a small card or the king. Against a suit contract, however, leading a small card does not work out well. Declarer could win the first trick with the 10, take the ace and ruff the jack with one of dummy's trumps. You end up with no tricks in the suit. By leading the king, you make sure of getting at least one trick even if partner has no help in the suit.

Leading a high card from a holding headed by the ace and king can be very effective. You will still be on lead after the first trick, so you will be able to look at dummy before deciding whether or not to continue leading the suit. If you have a long suit headed by the ace and king, you may even be able to use declarer's trump suit against him.

Take a look at this hand:

Contract: 4♥
Lead: ♦ A

DUMMY
♠ A K J
♥ 10 8 7
♦ 10 9 5
♣ K Q J 10

YOU
♠ Q 10 7 4
♥ 5
♦ A K 8 6 3
♣ 7 6 3

PARTNER
♠ 8 3 2
♥ 6 4 3 2
♦ 7 2
♣ A 8 4 2

DECLARER
♠ 9 6 5
♥ A K Q J 9
♦ Q J 4
♣ 9 5

After leading the ♦ A and seeing dummy, no other suit looks particularly attractive. So you continue with the ♦ K and another diamond (we will see how partner can help in this situation in a later lesson). Partner can trump the third round of diamonds and take the ♣ A to defeat the contract. You can see the difference between leading from this holding in a suit contract and in notrump. If the opponents played this hand in 3 NT, you would have to lead a small diamond to defeat the contract. They would make it with any other lead.

When leading a low card from a suit of four cards or longer, lead the fourth highest, as when leading against a notrump contract (e.g., Q 8 7 **5** 3). The reasoning behind this is the same — you are trying to give information to partner about the number of cards you hold in the suit. This may help partner decide how many winners there are to take before declarer can trump. Against a suit contract, however, you also lead your lowest card from a three-card suit. Partner will not always be able to figure out exactly how many cards you have in the suit you started with.

In summary, when leading against a suit contract:

- Lead the ace, if you have it (e.g., **A** 9 7 3, **A** Q J 8 3)
- Lead the top of touching honors from a sequence (e.g., **K** Q 8 3 2, **Q** J 9 3, K **J** 10 8)
- With no sequence, lead low or fourth highest (e.g., J 8 **4**, Q 10 8 **3**, K J 7 **5** 2)

Let's put everything together and see which card you would lead from each of the following hands. The auction proceeds:

NORTH (DUMMY)	EAST (PARTNER)	SOUTH (DECLARER)	WEST (**YOU**)
1♣	Pass	1♠	Pass
3♠	Pass	4♠	Pass
Pass	Pass		

♠ J82
♥ KQ4
♦ J9632
♣ Q5

Rather than lead one of the opponents' suits, you would pick an unbid suit. The strong sequence in the heart suit offers better prospects than the diamond suit. Lead the top of touching honors, the ♥**K**.

♠ 64
♥ K932
♦ AK65
♣ 1084

This time, the diamonds look like the best bet. Lead the top of the touching honors, the ♦**A**. After seeing the dummy, you may still be able to change your mind and switch to another suit if that looks like a good idea.

♠ Q3
♥ Q964
♦ Q853
♣ J82

None of your choices is particularly attractive. Still it is probably best to pick one of the unbid suits. With no touching honors, lead a low card, either the ♥**4** or the ♦**3**.

♠ J2
♥ AJ98
♦ A1064
♣ Q64

Once again, you would like to avoid leading the opponents' suit if possible. If you have to pick one of the unbid suits, do not lead away from an ace. Choose either the ♥**A** or the ♦**A**, rather than a small card. After seeing the dummy, you will have a better idea of what to lead next.

♥ *BIDDING REVIEW* ♥

Responding to Opening Bids of One in a Suit

When partner starts describing his hand by opening the bidding at the one level in a suit, responder, as *captain*, does not yet have enough information to determine the final level and denomination of the contract. Instead, responder categorizes the strength of his hand and responds using the following guideline:

	RESPONSES TO OPENING BIDS OF ONE OF A SUIT
0–5	• Pass

6–10	*Responding to a major suit*
	    • Raise to the two level with three-card support.
	    • Bid a new suit at the one level.
	    • Bid 1 NT.
	Responding to a minor suit
	    • Bid a new suit at the one level.
	    • Raise to the two level with five-card support.
	    • Bid 1 NT.

11–12	*Responding to a major suit*
	    • Raise to the three level with three-card or longer support.
	    • Bid a new suit.
	Responding to a minor suit
	    • Bid a new suit.
	    • Raise to the three level with five-card or longer support.

13 or more	*Responding to a major suit*
	    • Jump to 2 NT with a balanced hand.
	    • Bid a new suit.
	Responding to a minor suit
	    • Bid a new suit.
	    • Jump to 2 NT with a balanced hand.

Responding to Opening Bids of Two in a Suit

A two-level opening bid is a forcing bid. Responder must bid again until game is reached. With a weak hand of 0–5 points, responder makes a *conventional (artificial)* response of 2 NT to keep the bidding going. Use the following guideline when responding to a *strong two-bid:*

RESPONSES TO OPENING BIDS OF TWO IN A SUIT	
0–5 points	• Bid 2 NT *(conventional)*.
6 or more points	• Raise to the three level with three-card or longer support. • Bid a new suit. • Bid 3 NT with a balanced hand.

Responding to Opening Bids of Three in a Suit

When partner starts the bidding at the three level or higher in a suit, he is making a *preemptive opening bid,* showing a seven-card or longer suit and less than the values for an opening bid at the one level. Since partner has a weak hand, likely of value only if played with his suit as trump, responder must proceed cautiously. Use the following guideline when responding:

RESPONSES TO OPENING BIDS OF THREE IN A SUIT	
0–15 points	• Pass.
16 or more points	• Raise partner to game. • Bid a new suit (forcing if below game level). • Bid 3 NT.

♥ *PLAY OF THE HAND REVIEW* ♥

Declarer's Plan

When you are declarer in a suit contract, you go through the same four planning steps as when playing in a notrump contract:

1. *Pause to consider your objective.*
2. *Look at your winners and losers.*
3. *Analyze your alternatives.*
4. *Now put it together.*

In a suit contract, consider your objective in terms of the number of *losers* you can afford and still make the contract. For example, in a contract of 2 ♥, you can afford five losers. Then look at the number of losers you have — the cards in your hand which may not win tricks even with the help of dummy's high cards. If you do not have more losers than you can afford, start by *drawing trumps.* You want to make sure that the opponents do not trump any of your winners.

If you have too many losers, look at each suit to see how the losers can be eliminated. In addition to the techniques available in a notrump contract — *promotion, long suits* and *finesses* — there are techniques for eliminating losers which are unique to suit contracts: *trumping losers* in the dummy and *discarding losers* on dummy's extra winners. Finally, put your plan together by choosing the best alternative and deciding whether you can draw trumps right away or have to delay drawing trumps until you have eliminated some losers.

♥ *SUMMARY* ♥

Use the following guidelines when choosing a suit to lead against a trump contract:

- Lead partner's suit
- Lead a strong sequence rather than low from an honor
- Lead an unbid suit
- Lead a short suit when partner is likely to be able to give you a ruff before trumps are drawn
- Lead a trump when declarer is likely to want to trump losers in dummy or when all other leads are unattractive
- Lead a long suit when you, or perhaps partner, have four or more trumps

When choosing the card to lead:

- Lead the top card from a doubleton (e.g., **7** 2, **Q** 5)
- Lead the top of touching honors (e.g., **K** Q 8 3 2, **Q** J 3)
- With no sequence, lead low (fourth highest) (e.g., K 8 **3**, Q 9 4 **2**, K J 7 **5** 2)
- Lead the ace, if you have it (e.g., **A** 8 3, **A** Q J 9 4)

♥ *THE FINER POINTS* ♥

Leading From Three Small Cards

When leading from a three-card suit with no honor card, some partnerships prefer leading the top card (e.g., **8** 6 2) rather than the lowest card. This is referred to as leading the *top of nothing.* Leading the highest of three small cards has the advantage that, when you lead a low card, partner can assume that you have at least one honor in the suit. This may be helpful when partner has to decide what to lead next. The disadvantage is that you also lead the top card when you have a doubleton (e.g., **8** 6) so, when you lead the top card, partner cannot tell whether you have two or three cards in the suit (or even a singleton).

Some partnerships prefer to get around the problem by leading the middle of three small cards (e.g., 8 **6** 2). By not leading a small card, they are not promising an honor in the suit and, when the suit is played again, they can play a higher card (i.e., the 8 from the remaining 8 2), so that partner will not think they have a doubleton. Because the idea is to lead the **M**iddle card, then play a higher card (**U**p) and finally the low card (**D**own), this is referred to as leading *MUD* (middle, up, down) from three small. While this has some advantages, partner will have to wait until the second or third round of the suit before being able to interpret your exact holding. By then, it may be too late to be of much use.

Rather than add a new guideline for leading from three small cards, it is easier to continue to lead low from three or more cards, whether or not you have an honor in the suit. Although partner may not know whether or not you have an honor, neither will declarer, so you will not be giving away any helpful information to the opponents.

Leading From the Ace and King

When leading from a suit headed by the ace and king, the guideline recommends leading the top of the touching honors, the ace. This is consistent with the lead from other touching honor combinations. Some partnerships, however, prefer to lead the *king from the ace and king* when leading against a suit contract. The reasoning behind this is that, since you do not want to lead away from an ace against a suit contract, you will sometimes lead an ace when you do not have the king. By always leading the king when you have both the ace and king, partner will know when you lead an ace that you **do not have the king** and can plan the defense accordingly. The disadvantage of this method is that, since you also lead the king when you have both the king and queen, partner will not know when you lead a king whether you also have the ace or the queen.

Again you want to be aware of variations such as this when playing with a new partner who might have come from a different school of thought. Until you have a regular partner with whom to discuss such variations, however, be consistent and always lead the ace when you have both the ace and king.

♥ *GROUP ACTIVITIES* ♥

Exercise One — Strength Versus Length

Compare what would happen if you led each of the following suits against a notrump contract and against a suit contract (assuming another suit is trump). Would you normally lead the suit against a notrump contract, a suit contract, or both?

1)
　　　　　　　　　　　DUMMY
　　　　　　　　　　　7 5 4
YOU　　　　　■　　　　　PARTNER
K 10 8 6 2　　　■　　　　　J 9 3
　　　　　　　　DECLARER
　　　　　　　　A Q

2)
　　　　　　　　　　　DUMMY
　　　　　　　　　　　7 4 3
YOU　　　　　■　　　　　PARTNER
K Q J　　　　　■　　　　　10 6 5
　　　　　　　　DECLARER
　　　　　　　　A 9 8 2

3)
　　　　　　　　　　　DUMMY
　　　　　　　　　　　9 8 5
YOU　　　　　■　　　　　PARTNER
A Q 7 4 2　　　■　　　　　10 6 3
　　　　　　　　DECLARER
　　　　　　　　K J

4)
　　　　　　　　　　　DUMMY
　　　　　　　　　　　K 9 5
YOU　　　　　■　　　　　PARTNER
Q J 10 8　　　■　　　　　6 4 2
　　　　　　　　DECLARER
　　　　　　　　A 7 3

Vs. Notrump: 1) _____ 2) _____ 3) _____ 4) _____

Vs. Suit: _____ _____ _____ _____

Exercise Two — Utilizing the Trump Suit

You are defending a contract of 4♠ with no other suits bid during the auction. What would be the advantage of leading a diamond rather than a club on each of the following hands?

1) ♠ 8 6 5   2) ♠ Q J 9 8   3) ♠ 8 6 5 2
   ♥ J 9 4   ♥ J 9 4 2   ♥ J 9 4
   ♦ 4   ♦ Q J 10 9   ♦ A K Q J 9
   ♣ Q 9 7 6 4 2   ♣ 5   ♣ 3

1) _____   2) _____   3) _____

Exercise Three — Leading Trumps

For each of the following auctions put down a possible suit distribution for both declarer's hand and the dummy (using X's to represent the cards). On which auctions might leading a trump prevent declarer from ruffing losers in the dummy?

1)	NORTH (DUMMY)	EAST (PARTNER)	SOUTH (DECLARER)	WEST (YOU)
	Pass	Pass	1♥	Pass
	1 NT	Pass	2♦	Pass
	Pass	Pass		

2)	NORTH (DUMMY)	EAST (PARTNER)	SOUTH (DECLARER)	WEST (YOU)
	1♦	Pass	1♠	Pass
	2♣	Pass	2♥	Pass
	3♥	Pass	4♥	Pass
	Pass	Pass		

3)	NORTH (DUMMY)	EAST (PARTNER)	SOUTH (DECLARER)	WEST (YOU)
			1♠	Pass
	2♣	Pass	3♣	Pass
	3♠	Pass	4♠	Pass
	Pass	Pass		

1) DUMMY
♠
♥
♦
♣

2) DUMMY
♠
♥
♦
♣

3) DUMMY
♠
♥
♦
♣

DECLARER
♠
♥
♦
♣

DECLARER
♠
♥
♦
♣

DECLARER
♠
♥
♦
♣

Lead
trump? _____   _____   _____

Exercise Four — Choosing the Suit

You are on lead against 4 ♥ with the following hand:

♠ Q92
♥ 863
♦ KQ82
♣ Q72

Which suit would you lead under each of these conditions:

1) Your partner overcalled in clubs during the auction.
2) The only suit bid during the auction was hearts.
3) The opponents bid all four suits during the auction.
4) The opponents bid hearts and diamonds during the auction.

1)_____ 2)_____ 3)_____ 4)_____

Exercise Five — Choosing the Card

In each of the following examples, which would be the best card to lead from the suit against a notrump contract? Which would be the best card against a suit contract?

1)
	DUMMY	
	7 5 3	
YOU	■	PARTNER
A K 8 4 2		10 6
	DECLARER	
	Q J 9	

2)
	DUMMY	
	8	
YOU	■	PARTNER
A J 10 9 3		7 5 4 2
	DECLARER	
	K Q 6	

3)
	DUMMY	
	6 4	
YOU	■	PARTNER
K Q 9 7 3		10 5
	DECLARER	
	A J 8 2	

1) _____ 2) _____ 3) _____

Exercise Six — Putting It Together

The auction proceeds:

NORTH	EAST	SOUTH	WEST
(DUMMY)	(PARTNER)	(DECLARER)	(YOU)
		1♣	Pass
1♥	Pass	1♠	Pass
2♠	Pass	4♠	Pass
Pass	Pass		

Which card would you lead from each of the following hands?

1) ♠ Q74
   ♥ J83
   ♦ QJ62
   ♣ J108

1) _____

2) ♠ J92
   ♥ J75
   ♦ AJ975
   ♣ Q4

2) _____

3) ♠ K8
   ♥ Q97
   ♦ Q10832
   ♣ Q54

3) _____

4) ♠ A93
   ♥ 108532
   ♦ 6
   ♣ J865

4) _____

5) ♠ 864
   ♥ J932
   ♦ K5
   ♣ Q874

5) _____

6) ♠ 753
   ♥ A105
   ♦ AQ10
   ♣ K1042

6) _____

Exercise Seven — Review of Responses to Opening Bids in a Suit

What would you respond with each of the following hands if partner opened 1 ♥? If partner opened 2 ♥? If partner opened 3 ♥?

1) ♠ Q7643
   ♥ 85
   ♦ 742
   ♣ J86

1) _____

2) ♠ KQ765
   ♥ Q8
   ♦ J92
   ♣ 1064

2) _____

3) ♠ AJ83
   ♥ Q862
   ♦ QJ9
   ♣ J6

3) _____

Exercise Eight — Review of Declarer's Plan

Go through the four steps of declarer's PLAN to decide how to play the following hand in a contract of 4♥ after the opening lead of the ♣K.

DUMMY
♠ Q
♥ J753
♦ AK52
♣ 7642

LEAD:
♣K

DECLARER
♠ A95
♥ Q10986
♦ Q3
♣ A83

Exercise Nine — Leading Partner's Suit

Turn up the cards on the first pre-dealt hand. Put each hand dummy style at the edge of the table in front of each player.

Dealer: North

```
                        ♠ Q 7 6 2
                        ♥ K J 5
                        ♦ Q J 10 8
                        ♣ A 6

   ♠ 9 3              N              ♠ 10
   ♥ 9 6 2        W       E          ♥ A Q 10 8 4
   ♦ 4 3 2            S              ♦ A K 7 5
   ♣ Q J 10 9 3                      ♣ 8 5 2

                        ♠ A K J 8 5 4
                        ♥ 7 3
                        ♦ 9 6
                        ♣ K 7 4
```

The Bidding

What would North open the bidding? How can East describe his hand? What does South bid? West passes. What rebid does North make to show support for partner's suit? East passes. How many points does South have? At what level does the partnership belong? Is there a *Golden Fit*? What does South rebid? How does the auction proceed from there? What is the contract? Who is declarer?

The Defense

Which player makes the opening lead? What would the opening lead be? Why? How does East plan to defeat the contract?

The Play

Review the steps in declarer's PLAN. How does declarer plan to make the contract?

Exercise Ten — Leading From a Sequence

Turn up the cards on the second pre-dealt hand. Put each hand dummy style at the edge of the table in front of each player.

Dealer: East

```
                    ♠ J 7 6
                    ♥ 9 7
                    ♦ 9 8 6 3
                    ♣ Q J 9 3
    ♠ 9 4 2          N          ♠ A Q
    ♥ K J 6 4    W       E      ♥ A Q 10 8 5
    ♦ A 10 7         S          ♦ 5 4 2
    ♣ 7 6 5                     ♣ A K 4
                    ♠ K 10 8 5 3
                    ♥ 3 2
                    ♦ K Q J
                    ♣ 10 8 2
```

The Bidding

North and South pass throughout the auction. What would East open the bidding? How does West show the trump support and the strength of the hand? What does East rebid? How does the auction proceed from there? What is the contract? Who is declarer?

The Defense

Which player makes the opening lead? What would the opening lead be? Why? What would happen if South led a spade against the contract?

The Play

Review the steps in declarer's PLAN. How does declarer plan to make the contract?

Exercise Eleven — Leading a Trump

Turn up the cards on the third pre-dealt hand. Put each hand dummy style at the edge of the table in front of each player.

Dealer: South

```
                    ♠ K 9 8 6 5
                    ♥ K J 10 6
                    ♦ K 8 3
                    ♣ A
    ♠ 7 4 2         ┌─────────┐      ♠ A Q J 10
    ♥ A 5           │   N     │      ♥ 7 4 2
    ♦ J 10 6 2      │ W   E   │      ♦ Q 7 4
    ♣ K Q 8 5       │   S     │      ♣ 10 9 7
                    └─────────┘
                    ♠ 3
                    ♥ Q 9 8 3
                    ♦ A 9 5
                    ♣ J 6 4 3 2
```

The Bidding

South and West pass. What is North's opening bid? East passes. Without support for partner's suit and no suit that can be bid at the one level, what does South respond? West passes. Can North conveniently show his second suit? East passes. Which suit does South prefer? What does South do? What is the contract? Who is declarer?

The Defense

Which player makes the opening lead? After listening to the auction, what would the opening lead be? Why? What does East plan to do when he regains the lead? How can West help?

The Play

Review the steps in declarer's PLAN. How does declarer plan to make the contract?

Exercise Twelve — Leading a Short Suit

Turn up the cards on the fourth pre-dealt hand. Put each hand dummy style at the edge of the table in front of each player.

Dealer: West

♠ 743
♥ 10 8 7 4
♦ 9
♣ 10 6 5 4 3

♠ K J 10 9 5   N   ♠ Q 8 6 2
♥ K J   W   E   ♥ A 9 5
♦ K Q 10 3   S   ♦ J 7 5
♣ A J   ♣ K Q 2

♠ A
♥ Q 6 3 2
♦ A 8 6 4 2
♣ 9 8 7

The Bidding

What is West's opening bid? North passes. What does East respond? South passes. What does West rebid? What is the contract? Who is declarer?

The Defense

Which player makes the opening lead? What hope is there to defeat the contract? What does North lead? How can South cooperate?

The Play

Review the steps in declarer's PLAN. How does declarer plan to make the contract? How many losers does declarer expect to have when the dummy goes down? What can go wrong?

LESSON 3
Third-Hand Play

Third Hand High
Third Hand Not So High
Unblocking
Bidding Review
Play of the Hand Review
Summary

Workshop Material
Group Activities

When your partner leads, you are in a position referred to as *third hand* because you are contributing the third card to the trick. As third hand, you have a special role to perform since it is your side's last opportunity to play to the trick. You are third hand to play on the first trick when partner makes the opening lead and dummy is put down on your right, as well as any other time partner has the lead. The card you choose to play depends not only on the cards you hold in the suit but the card partner led and the second card played to the trick. In this lesson, we will look at guidelines for choosing the card to play when you are third hand.

♥ THIRD HAND HIGH ♥

A common piece of advice handed down from the days of whist, a predecessor of the game of bridge, is *"third hand high."* This implies you should contribute your highest card to the trick when in third position. Let's see where this advice came from and how to apply it in the appropriate situation.

When Partner Leads a Low Card

Suppose partner's opening lead is the 2. After dummy is put down you can see the following cards in the suit:

	DUMMY	
	7 6 5	
PARTNER	■	YOU
2		A 4 3

When a small card is played from dummy, you are third hand to play. This is the last opportunity for your side to play to the trick. Play your ace, *third hand high*, in order to win the trick for your side. But will you always be able to play a high enough card to win the trick for your side?

Suppose we change your holding slightly:

	DUMMY	
	7 6 5	
PARTNER	■	YOU
2		K 4 3

You are again third to play for your side. The king will win the trick if partner has the ace, but suppose declarer has the ace and the complete layout looks like this:

	DUMMY	
	7 6 5	
PARTNER	■	YOU
Q J 8 2		K 4 3
	DECLARER	
	A 10 9	

When you play the king, third hand high, declarer can win the trick with the ace. All is not lost, however. By playing the king and driving out declarer's ace, you have helped promote partner's queen and jack into winners. If you played a small card instead of the king, declarer would win the trick with the 9 and still have the ace left. Your side would still not have established any winners in the suit. By playing third hand high, you are trying to win the trick for your side. Even if you cannot win the trick, you are hoping to promote eventual winners for your side.

How high should you play? Suppose this is the layout you see after partner's lead:

DUMMY
765
PARTNER
2
YOU
K J 3

Should you play the king or the jack? If partner has the queen and declarer the ace, it will not matter which high card you play — either one will force declarer to play the ace to win the trick.

Suppose, however, this is the layout:

DUMMY
765
PARTNER
A 10 8 2
YOU
K J 3
DECLARER
Q 9 4

If you play the jack, declarer will win the trick with the queen. This can be prevented by playing the king, the highest card you can afford, rather than the jack. The king wins the trick and you can lead back the jack to trap declarer's queen. Your side ends up taking all the tricks in the suit, no matter which card declarer plays. The guideline in such situations is to play as *high a card as you can afford* when trying to win the trick. It would do no harm to play the king even if declarer held both the ace and the queen.

For example:

DUMMY
765
PARTNER
10 8 4 2
YOU
K J 3
DECLARER
A Q 9

Playing the king will force declarer to play the ace. Later, your jack can be used to drive out the queen and partner's 10 is promoted to a winner. Playing as high as you can afford to try to win the trick also applies in the following situation:

DUMMY
K 9 3
PARTNER
2
YOU
Q 10 5

If a low card is played from dummy, play the queen, the highest card you can afford, in order to try to win the trick. If declarer has the ace, your queen will drive it out. If declarer does not have the ace, you will save a trick for your side by playing the queen, rather than the 10, if the layout is something like this:

DUMMY
K 9 3
PARTNER
A 8 6 2
YOU
Q 10 5
DECLARER
J 7 4

If you were to play the 10, declarer would win with the jack. Since your partner has the ace, declarer would later get a second trick in the suit with dummy's king. By playing the queen, you win the trick and can lead back to partner's ace. Declarer will only get one trick in the suit, with dummy's king. If dummy's king is played, there is no need to play third hand high since you cannot win the trick.

Here is an example of third hand high in action:

Contract: 1 NT
Lead: ♥ 6

DUMMY
♠ K J 2
♥ 7 4
♦ Q J 10 8 4
♣ Q 10 7

PARTNER
♠ 10 7 5
♥ K 10 8 6 2
♦ 5 3
♣ A 9 6

YOU
♠ 9 8 4 3
♥ Q 9 5
♦ A K 7
♣ J 4 2

DECLARER
♠ A Q 6
♥ A J 3
♦ 9 6 2
♣ K 8 5 3

Partner leads the ♥ 6, fourth best against declarer's 1 NT contract, and a small heart is played from dummy. Play third hand high, the ♥ Q. Declarer wins the trick with the ♥ A and, needing to establish some diamond tricks to make the contract, leads a diamond. On winning the ♦ K, you lead back a heart, trapping declarer's ♥ J, and your side takes four heart tricks. Together with your two diamond tricks and the ♣ A, that is enough to defeat the 1 NT contract. If you played the ♥ 9 or ♥ 5 on the first trick, declarer would win with the ♥ J and make the contract.

Using the Guideline

Here are a couple of examples of using the guideline *third hand high:*

DUMMY
8 6 3

PARTNER
5

YOU
J 9 4

Partner leads the 5 and the 3 is played from dummy. Play the **jack**, third hand high. You want to make the best effort to win the trick for your side. Even though the jack is unlikely to win the trick, it may help promote some winners for partner.

DUMMY
A 7 5

PARTNER
3

YOU
Q 10 2

When partner leads the 3 and the 5 is played from dummy, play the **queen**, the highest card you can afford, not the 10. If declarer had played the ace from dummy, there would be no need for you to play third hand high.

♥ *THIRD HAND NOT SO HIGH* ♥

While you want to play as high a card as you can **afford** when trying to win the trick by playing third hand high, you need play only as high a card as is **necessary**.

Touching Cards

Consider the following situation where partner leads the 4 and dummy plays the 3:

DUMMY
853
PARTNER
4
YOU
Q J 2

You want to play third hand high to try to win the trick for your side. Your queen and jack in this situation are *equals*. In such cases, play only *as high a card as necessary,* the jack, rather than the queen. It may seem odd to play the lower of touching honors in third hand since you play the higher of touching honors when leading to a trick. By playing the lowest card necessary to try to win the trick, however, you may give valuable information to your partner. For example, suppose you are defending a notrump contract and this is the complete layout of the suit:

DUMMY
853
PARTNER
K 10 6 4
YOU
Q J 2
DECLARER
A 9 7

When the 4 is led and you play the jack, declarer has to play the ace to win the trick. Partner can now figure out that you have the queen. If declarer held the queen, he would win the first trick with it, keeping the ace as a second trick. If partner regains the lead, he can safely lead the suit again, knowing your side has all the remaining high cards in the suit.

What difference would it make if you played the queen rather than the jack? Partner might think the complete layout of the suit was like this:

DUMMY
853
PARTNER
K 10 6 4
YOU
Q 7 2
DECLARER
A J 9

When he leads the 4, since you have no choice of equal cards. You have to play the queen to force out declarer's ace. If partner regains the lead, it would be a mistake to lead the suit again from his side since declarer would get a trick with the jack. Partner will want to wait until you can lead the suit, trapping declarer's jack. .By playing the lower of touching cards in third hand, you can help partner distinguish between the different situations. For example, if you play third hand "high" with the 10, partner knows you do not have the next lower card, the 9, but may have the next higher card, the jack, and perhaps the queen as well. Let's see this in a complete hand:

Contract: 3 NT
Lead: ♠4

DUMMY
♠ 6 3
♥ 9 4 2
♦ Q J 7 2
♣ A Q J 8

PARTNER
♠ K 9 7 4 2
♥ Q 7 5 3
♦ A
♣ 9 7 3

YOU
♠ Q J 10
♥ K 10 8 6
♦ 9 5 4
♣ 10 4 2

DECLARER
♠ A 8 5
♥ A J
♦ K 10 8 6 3
♣ K 6 5

When partner leads the ♠4 against 3 NT and a low card is played from dummy, you play the ♠10, third hand high — but only as high as necessary. When declarer wins this trick with the ♠A, partner knows you have the ♠J and ♠Q since declarer would have won the trick with one of those cards rather than winning with the ♠A. When declarer leads a small diamond toward dummy, planning to establish some diamond winners, partner wins the ♦A and can lead a small spade over to your ♠J since he knows you have that card. You lead back the ♠Q, and partner can overtake it with the ♠K and take his remaining spade winners to defeat the contract. What if you played the ♠Q on the first trick rather than the ♠10? Now partner might think the complete hand looked something like this:

Contract: 3 NT
Lead: ♠4

DUMMY
♠ 6 3
♥ 9 4 2
♦ Q J 7 2
♣ A Q J 8

PARTNER
♠ K 9 7 4 2
♥ Q 7 5 3
♦ A
♣ 9 7 3

YOU
♠ Q 10 5
♥ J 10 8 6
♦ K 9 4
♣ 10 4 2

DECLARER
♠ A J 8
♥ A K
♦ 10 8 6 5 3
♣ K 6 5

When partner leads the ♠4, you are forced to play the ♠Q, the highest card you can afford, to stop declarer from winning the first trick with the ♠J. When a diamond is led and partner wins the ♦A, he does not want to lead another spade and let declarer win the trick with the ♠J. Instead, he wants to bide his time until you get the lead and can lead back the ♠10, trapping declarer's ♠J. By playing the ♠10 on the first hand and the ♠Q on the second hand, you help partner decide what to do in each case.

Finessing Against Dummy

Another situation in which you play only as high a card as necessary is the following:

If partner leads the 3 and the queen is played from dummy, you would try to win the trick for your side by playing the king. If the 5 is played from dummy rather than the queen, however, there is no need to play the king. Playing the jack is all that is necessary. If partner has the ace, the jack will win the trick. If declarer has the ace, the jack will force him to play it if he wants to win the trick, and dummy's queen is still trapped by your king. For example, the complete layout might be:

If you were to play the king, declarer would win with the ace and still have the queen left as a second trick. By playing the jack, only as high a card as necessary, you restrict declarer to one trick in the suit. You can see how your king and jack effectively trap dummy's queen. This is similar to the way declarer takes a finesse. The difference here is that you can see the cards on your right but you cannot see partner's remaining cards. Being able to visualize what partner might hold comes in useful if we change the situation slightly:

Again partner leads a low card and a low card is played from dummy. You want to play third hand high, but only as high as necessary. How high is it necessary to play? That depends on which of the other players hold the ace and jack. If partner holds them both, then playing the 10 will be sufficient and will also let you keep dummy's queen trapped with your king. Partner might have the jack and declarer the ace. This would be a likely situation if you were defending against a suit contract since, as you saw in the last lesson, partner would not lead away from the ace. The complete layout might be something like this:

```
            DUMMY
            Q 7 3
PARTNER     ███      YOU
J 9 6 5     ███      K 10 4
          DECLARER
            A 8 2
```

Again, playing the 10 works better than playing the king. If you play the king, declarer wins with the ace and gets a second trick with dummy's queen. If you play the 10, declarer can win with the ace but dummy's queen remains trapped by your king. Declarer only gets one trick in the suit. Partner might have the ace and declarer the jack. This might be the case when you are defending against a notrump contract. Suppose this is the layout:

```
            DUMMY
            Q 7 3
PARTNER     ███      YOU
A 9 6 5     ███      K 10 4
          DECLARER
            J 8 2
```

If you play the 10 on the first trick, declarer wins with the jack, but has any harm been done? Declarer is entitled to one trick in the suit anyway. You will still be able to take your three winners when you regain the lead. If you had won the first trick with the king, declarer would eventually get a trick with dummy's queen. Nothing is lost by playing the 10. Finally, suppose declarer has both the ace and jack:

```
            DUMMY
            Q 7 3
PARTNER     ███      YOU
9 8 6 5     ███      K 10 4
          DECLARER
            A J 2
```

If you play the king, declarer will get three tricks in the suit, the ace, the jack and the queen. If you play the 10, declarer can win the first trick with the jack and still have the ace left as a second trick, but dummy's queen remains trapped by your king and declarer only gets two tricks in the suit.

In conclusion, playing the 10 works out best in most situations, even though declarer may win the first trick with the jack. The objective in all cases is to try to keep dummy's queen trapped by your king. This is the general idea when trying to decide how high a card it is necessary to play as third hand. You want to keep the opponents' high cards *trapped* whenever possible. Here is an example in a complete hand:

Contract: 3 NT
Lead: ♥2

DUMMY
♠ K 10 5
♥ K 8 4
♦ K 5
♣ Q J 10 6 2

PARTNER
♠ J 8 4
♥ J 7 6 2
♦ 10 4 2
♣ A K 8

YOU
♠ Q 7 6 2
♥ A 10 9
♦ 9 8 6 3
♣ 7 5

DECLARER
♠ A 9 3
♥ Q 5 3
♦ A Q J 7
♣ 9 4 3

Partner leads the ♥2 and the ♥4 is played from dummy. Since you want to keep dummy's ♥K trapped with your ♥A, play the ♥9, the lower of your touching cards. The ♥9 will win the trick if partner has both the ♥Q and ♥J, but on the actual hand declarer is able to win the trick with the ♥Q. With only two spade tricks, the heart trick and four diamond tricks, declarer needs to try to promote two extra tricks in clubs. Your partner wins the club trick and leads another heart. Dummy's ♥K is trapped. If declarer plays a small card, you can win the trick with the ♥10 and take the ♥A. Partner's other club winner and his remaining heart will be enough to defeat the contract.

An analogous situation for trying to keep declarer's high cards trapped is the following. Suppose partner leads your suit against a notrump contract and this is the complete layout:

DUMMY
Q 7 4
PARTNER
8 6
YOU
A J 10 5 3
DECLARER
K 9 2

Partner leads the 8 and a small card is played from dummy. If you play the ace, dummy's queen is no longer trapped and declarer ends with two tricks in the suit. Instead, play the 10, the lower of your touching high cards, and let declarer win the first trick with the king. When partner regains the lead, he can lead the suit again. This time dummy's queen is trapped by your remaining ace and jack. Whichever card declarer plays, he cannot prevent you from taking the rest of the tricks in the suit.

Here are more third-hand situations:

	DUMMY	
	8 5 2	
PARTNER		**YOU**
6		K Q 3

With touching high cards, play only as high as necessary, the **queen**. If declarer wins the trick with the ace, partner will know that you do not have the jack but may have the king.

	DUMMY	
	J 6 2	
PARTNER		**YOU**
5		Q 10 4

If a small card is played from dummy, play the **10**, keeping dummy's jack trapped with your queen.

	DUMMY	
	Q 6 2	
PARTNER		**YOU**
3		A J 5

When a small card is played from dummy, play the **jack**. This will win the trick if partner has the king. If declarer has the king, dummy's queen will remain trapped by your ace.

When Partner Leads a High Card

When partner leads a high card, rather than a low card, you may not have to play third hand high in order to win the trick. Whether you need to play third hand high can depend on which high cards are held by declarer and whether they are in declarer's hand or in the dummy. You want to trap the missing high cards whenever possible. Starting with a straightforward example, consider this situation, where partner leads the queen:

Partner's lead of the queen looks to be from the top of a sequence headed by the queen and jack. If the king is played from dummy, you would win the trick with the ace and, unless you had something clearly better to do, lead the suit back to partner's winners. If a low card is played from dummy, however, there is no need for you to play the ace. Partner's queen will win the trick since you can see the king in dummy. If you were to automatically play third hand high and win the trick with the ace, you would establish dummy's king as a winner. Instead you want to trap the king. The complete layout might be something like this:

When you let partner's queen win the trick, partner can continue by leading the jack, and the king is again trapped. Declarer cannot get a trick with it no matter which card he plays.

The situation is different if you cannot see the high card you would like to trap and suspect that it is in declarer's hand:

When partner leads the jack, you know declarer holds the queen. If you do not play the king, declarer will be able to win the trick with the queen and this may end up costing your side a trick if partner is leading from the top of an interior sequence and the complete layout is something like this:

DUMMY
762
PARTNER ■ YOU
A J 10 9 K 8 3
DECLARER
Q 5 4

By winning the first trick with the king, you can lead the suit back and trap declarer's queen. Your side takes all four tricks in the suit. If it turned out that partner was leading the top of a sequence and declarer held the ace as well as the queen, nothing is lost by playing your king. Declarer is always entitled to two tricks.

You and your partner have to work together carefully to capture declarer's high cards when your side is missing two high cards. Consider this layout where partner has led the jack against a notrump contract and declarer plays a small card from the dummy:

DUMMY
K 6 2
PARTNER   YOU
J   A 8 4 3

Partner's lead of the jack tells you that declarer has the queen. If you play a small card, declarer will be able to win the trick with the queen. You would have to play the ace to win the first trick for your side. Winning the first trick, however, may not be in the best long term interest for your side. Suppose the complete layout looks like this:

DUMMY
K 7 2
PARTNER   YOU
J 10 9 5   A 8 6 3
DECLARER
Q 4

If you play the ace on partner's jack, declarer will play the 4 from his hand. Declarer will now get two tricks from the suit, one with the queen and one with the king. Your side has not trapped either of declarer's high cards. Since declarer is entitled to at least one trick in the suit, suppose you do not play third hand high but instead let declarer win the first trick with the queen. The remaining cards now look like this:

DUMMY
K 7
PARTNER   YOU
10 9 5   A 8 6
DECLARER
4

If partner later regains the lead, he can lead the 10 and dummy's king is now trapped. Whether or not declarer plays it, your side takes three tricks in the suit and declarer ends up getting only one trick. Let's see this type of situation in a complete hand:

Contract: 4 ♥
Lead: ♠ 10

DUMMY
♠ Q 6 2
♥ Q J 7 3
♦ A K 8 4
♣ 8 7

PARTNER
♠ 10 9 8 3
♥ A 8
♦ 10 5 2
♣ A 5 4 2

YOU
♠ A J 7
♥ 5 4
♦ Q J 9 6
♣ 10 9 6 3

DECLARER
♠ K 5 4
♥ K 10 9 6 2
♦ 7 3
♣ K Q J

Your partner leads the ♠10 against declarer's 4♥ contract, and declarer plays a small spade from dummy. Is this the time to play third hand high and win the trick with the ♠A? If declarer has the ♠K and you play the ♠A on the first trick, you will not trap either of declarer's high cards and declarer will get two tricks in the suit. Instead, play the ♠7, letting declarer win the first trick with the ♠K but keeping dummy's ♠Q trapped. When partner later regains the lead, he can lead another spade. Whichever card declarer plays from dummy, you can play a higher card to prevent declarer from getting a second trick. On the actual hand, you get two spade tricks to go along with partner's ♥A and ♣A to defeat the contract. If you play the ♠A on the first trick, your side gets only one spade trick and declarer makes the contract.

What if partner were leading from an interior sequence and held the ♠K instead of declarer? The complete layout of the suit might have been this:

Again you should not play your ace on partner's 10. If partner has the king, his 10 will win the trick when you play the 7, and dummy's queen will remain trapped. If you were to play the ace on the first trick and lead back to partner's king, declarer would end up getting a trick with dummy's queen. In general, you do not want to play third hand high if it means giving up on trapping a high card held by the second hand to play to the trick. Against a suit contract, you may be afraid that the complete layout is something like this:

When partner leads the 10 and you play the 7, declarer wins the trick with the singleton king. Even though dummy's queen remains trapped, your side never gets a trick in the suit because declarer can trump the next time it is led. Nonetheless, it may not have cost your side a trick. Even if you were to guess to play the ace on the first trick while declarer had to follow suit with the king, dummy's queen would be established as a trick and declarer might be able to use it for discarding a loser from his hand. You should still try to keep dummy's queen trapped unless you can clearly see that taking your ace on the first trick will result in defeating the contract.

Here are more examples of third-hand play when partner leads a high card:

DUMMY
Q 7 4
PARTNER YOU
J ■ A K 8

When partner leads the jack and a low card is played from dummy, there is no need for you to play third hand high. Play the **8**. Partner's jack will win the trick and dummy's queen will remain trapped.

DUMMY
K 4
PARTNER YOU
J ■ A 7

Even though you know from partner's lead of the jack that declarer holds the queen, play the **7** and not the ace when a small card is played from dummy. Keep your ace to capture dummy's king to prevent declarer from getting two tricks in the suit.

DUMMY
6 5 4
PARTNER YOU
J ■ A 7

This time, there is nothing in dummy for your ace to capture. Partner's lead of the jack tells you that declarer has the queen, so you should win the first trick with the **ace** and return the 7. You may be able to trap declarer's queen if partner has led from an interior sequence and has a holding such as K J 10 8 3.

UNBLOCKING

Sometimes you have to play a high card from third hand even though it is not needed to win the trick. This is called unblocking and is used to avoid stranding partner's winners. Consider the following layout of a suit where your partner leads the king against a notrump contract:

Since your partner has led the king, it is not necessary for you to play the ace in order to win the trick. If you play the 3, however, the suit becomes *blocked*. Your only remaining card is the ace. When partner leads the suit again, you can win with the ace but now partner's remaining winners in the suit are stranded. Unless partner has an entry in another suit, your side ends up with only two tricks. Instead, you must *overtake* partner's king with your ace so that you can lead back your small card and partner can take his winners. By unblocking the suit, your side can take the first five tricks. This is really a variation of making sure you play the *high card from the short side first*. Here is another example:

If partner leads the queen and a small card is played from dummy, you must overtake with the king to unblock the suit. Now you can lead the 8 back and partner can drive out dummy's ace. If you let the queen win the first trick, you would win the second trick with the king if declarer held up dummy's ace again. However, you would have no small cards left to help establish the suit by driving out dummy's ace. You would need two entries to partner's hand to both establish the suit and take the winners once they are established. You must play the king even if declarer does not hold up but plays dummy's ace on the first trick. Otherwise, you will be able to win a trick with the king when your side regains the lead but once again partner's winners will be stranded.

85

Here is an example of unblocking in a complete hand:

Contract: 3 NT
Lead: ♠Q

DUMMY
♠ 9 4 2
♥ 6 4 3
♦ A 9 6
♣ A Q J 4

YOU
♠ J 7
♥ Q J 10 9 7
♦ 8 4 3
♣ 9 5 3

PARTNER
♠ Q 10 6 5
♥ A K 5
♦ 10 7 5
♣ 10 7 6

DECLARER
♠ A K 8 3
♥ 8 2
♦ K Q J 2
♣ K 8 2

Partner leads the ♥ Q against 3 NT. With both the ♥ A and ♥ K, you could let partner's ♥ Q win the first trick. However, when partner leads the suit again, your side ends up with only three tricks. Whatever you lead next, declarer wins and takes the rest of the tricks. Instead unblock the suit by overtaking partner's ♥ Q with the ♥ K. Then cash the ♥ A and lead the carefully preserved ♥ 5 back to partner's winners. Your side gets the first five heart tricks to defeat the contract.

♥ *BIDDING REVIEW* ♥

In this lesson we will summarize the responses to opening notrump bids as covered in the *Club Series* and *Diamond Series*. We will start by reviewing a useful *conventional* bid that most partnerships agree to play when responding to notrump opening bids.

The Stayman Convention

The *Stayman* convention is an artificial response of 2♣ to an opening bid of 1 NT. It is used to ask if opener has a four-card major suit. With a four-card (or longer) major suit, opener bids it at the two level. With no four-card major suit, opener makes the artificial rebid of 2♦.

The Stayman convention can also be used when responding to an opening bid of 2 NT. In this case, 3♣ is used as the Stayman convention, and opener rebids 3♥ or 3♠ with a four-card or longer major suit. With no four-card major, opener rebids 3♦.

Responding to 1 NT Opening Bids

When partner opens 1 NT, describing a balanced hand of 16–18 points, responder acts as *captain* and steers the partnership to the appropriate final contract using the following guidelines (we will look at hands of 15 or more points under slam bidding):

RESPONSES TO 1 NT OPENING BIDS	
0–7 points	• Bid 2♦, 2♥ or 2♠ with a five-card or longer suit. • Otherwise pass.
8–9 points	• Bid 2♣ (Stayman) with interest in a major suit. • Otherwise bid 2 NT (invitational).
10–14 points	• Bid 4♥ or 4♠ with a six-card or longer major suit. • Bid 3♥ or 3♠ (forcing) with a five-card major suit. • Bid 2♣ (Stayman) with a four-card major suit. • Otherwise bid 3 NT.

Responding to 2 NT Opening Bids

An opening bid of 2 NT shows a balanced hand of 22–24 points. Use the following guidelines when responding (we will look at hands of 9 or more points under slam bidding):

RESPONSES TO 2 NT OPENING BIDS	
0–2 points	• Pass
3–8 points	• Bid 4 ♥ or 4 ♠ with a six-card or longer major suit. • Bid 3 ♥ or 3 ♠ (forcing) with a five-card major suit. • Bid 3 ♣ (Stayman) with one or both four-card major suits. • Otherwise bid 3 NT.

Responding to 3 NT Opening Bids

An opening bid of 3 NT shows a balanced hand of 25–27 points. Responder does not have much room to explore. With a six-card or longer major, responder bids 4 ♥ or 4 ♠. Otherwise, responder passes. (We will look at slam bidding in a later lesson.)

♥ PLAY OF THE HAND REVIEW ♥

Developing Tricks in a Notrump Contract

When declarer needs extra tricks in a notrump contract, there are three ways in which tricks can be developed: through *promotion*, through *long suits* and through *finesses*.

In promotion declarer simply uses his high cards to drive out the opponents' higher cards, keeping in mind to *play the high card from the short side first*. For example:

DUMMY
J 10 9 3

DECLARER
Q 5

Declarer can promote two tricks in this suit by driving out the opponents' ace and king. Declarer should start by playing the queen, high card from the short side.

To develop tricks from long suits, declarer keeps playing the suit until the opponents have no cards left, even if it means giving up tricks to the opponents. You can expect the missing cards in the opponents' hands to divide in the following manner:

- *An even number of missing cards will usually divide slightly unevenly*
- *An odd number of missing cards will usually divide as evenly as possible*

For example, suppose you have the following suit:

DUMMY
K 8 4 2

■

DECLARER
A 7 6 3

There are five missing cards in the suit, an odd number, and you would expect them to divide as evenly as possible, 3–2 (three in one opponent's hand, two in the other). By playing the ace and king and giving up a trick to the opponents, you can establish a trick through length since the opponents will have no cards left in the suit.

The idea of the finesse is to try and win a trick with one of your high cards when the opponents have a higher card. You do this by *leading toward the high card* which you are hoping will win a trick. For example, consider the following suit:

DUMMY
K 3

■

DECLARER
6 4

In order to get a trick with the king, you must lead toward it from declarer's hand. If the ace is on your left, the finesse will be successful. If the ace is played, you play a small card from dummy, and the king later takes a trick. If the ace is not played, you play the king and win the trick. Of course, if the ace is on your right, the finesse will not be successful and you cannot get a trick in the suit.

If you are finessing for more than one missing card, lead toward the lower of your high cards first. Sometimes, you can afford to lead a high card to try to trap a missing card in an opponent's hand. Lead a high card *only if you can afford to have the opponents cover it with a higher card*. For example:

DUMMY
A 7 3

■

DECLARER
Q J 10

Here you can afford to lead the queen to try to trap the king on your left. If the queen is covered by the king, you will not lose any tricks. If you did not have the jack, you could not afford to lead the queen but would have to lead toward it.

♥ *SUMMARY* ♥

When your partner leads to a trick and you are the third person to play to the trick, a useful guideline is *third hand high.* You are the last player on your side to contribute a card and you want to try to win the trick for your side if possible; otherwise you want to help promote winners in your partner's hand.

You need to play *as high a card as necessary* to try to win the trick. With a choice of equal (touching) cards, play the lowest. If partner leads a high card which will win the trick, you do not need to play a higher card unless you have to unblock the suit by over-taking partner's card.

When deciding how high a card it is necessary to play as third hand, try to *keep the opponents' high cards trapped* whenever possible. If the second hand has a high card which is not played and you have both a higher card and a lower card which might win the trick, play the lower card.

♥ *GROUP ACTIVITIES* ♥

Exercise One — Third Hand High

In each of the following layouts your partner leads the 5, and the 3 is played from dummy. Which card must you play as third hand to ensure that your side gets all the tricks to which it is entitled?

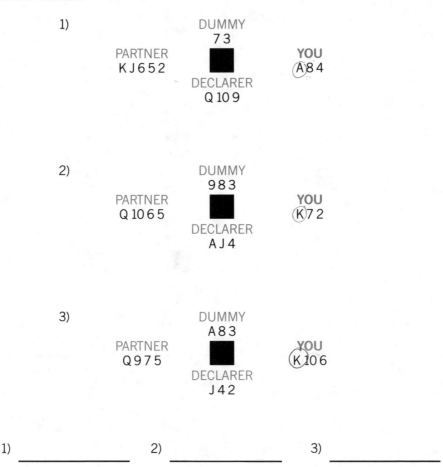

1)   DUMMY
                    7 3
PARTNER   YOU
K J 6 5 2   A 8 4
                 DECLARER
                  Q 10 9

2)   DUMMY
                    9 8 3
PARTNER   YOU
Q 10 6 5   K 7 2
                 DECLARER
                  A J 4

3)   DUMMY
                    A 8 3
PARTNER   YOU
Q 9 7 5   K 10 6
                 DECLARER
                  J 4 2

1) _____   2) _____   3) _____

Exercise Two — Only As High As Necessary

Your partner leads the 5 and the 3 is played from dummy. What card would you play? What do you expect to happen?

1)
                     DUMMY
                     A 9 3
PARTNER   ■   YOU
    5   Q J 10

2)
                     DUMMY
                     J 8 3
PARTNER   ■   YOU
    5   K Q 10

3)
                     DUMMY
                     A 6 3
PARTNER   ■   YOU
    5   K J 10

1) _____ 2) _____ 3) _____

Exercise Three — Trapping High Cards

In each of the following layouts, your partner leads the 5 and the 3 is played from dummy. Which card must you play to enable your side to eventually take the maximum number of tricks in the suit?

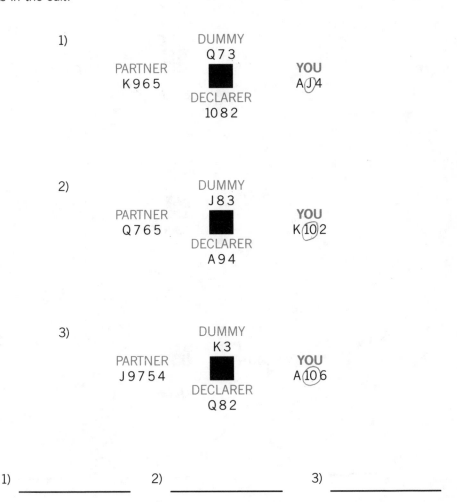

1)
    DUMMY
    Q 7 3
PARTNER   YOU
K 9 6 5   A J 4
    DECLARER
    10 8 2

2)
    DUMMY
    J 8 3
PARTNER   YOU
Q 7 6 5   K 10 2
    DECLARER
    A 9 4

3)
    DUMMY
    K 3
PARTNER   YOU
J 9 7 5 4   A 10 6
    DECLARER
    Q 8 2

1) _____ 2) _____ 3) _____

Exercise Four — When Partner Leads a High Card

In each of the following layouts, your partner leads the jack and the 4 is played from dummy. Which card must you play on the first trick? How should the defenders play the suit to get all the tricks to which they are entitled?

1)

	DUMMY	
	K 7 4	
PARTNER	■	YOU
J 10 8 5		A Q 6
	DECLARER	
	9 3 2	

2)

	DUMMY	
	Q 8 4	
PARTNER	■	YOU
J 10 9 5		A 6 3
	DECLARER	
	K 7 2	

3)

	DUMMY	
	7 5 4	
PARTNER	■	YOU
K J 10 9		A 6 3
	DECLARER	
	Q 8 2	

1) _____   2) _____   3) _____

Exercise Five — Unblocking

In each of the following examples, your partner leads the indicated card and declarer plays dummy's ace. Which card must you play to allow the defenders to take four tricks in the suit if you have the only entry outside of this suit?

1)

DUMMY
A 9 2

PARTNER
Q J 10 6 3

YOU
K 4

DECLARER
8 7 5

2)

DUMMY
A 8 3

PARTNER
J 10 9 6 5

YOU
K Q 2

DECLARER
7 4

3)

DUMMY
A 9 4

PARTNER
Q 10 7 5 2

YOU
K 8

DECLARER
J 8 6

1) _____   2) _____   3) _____

Exercise Six — Putting It Together

Your partner leads the indicated card and the 3 is played from dummy. Which card do you play in each of the following situations?

1)   DUMMY   2)   DUMMY
                  10 8 3   A 8 3
   PARTNER   ■   **YOU**   PARTNER   ■   **YOU**
      4   (K) J 5   6   Q (J) 2

3)   DUMMY   4)   DUMMY
                  A Q 3   Q 8 3
   PARTNER   ■   **YOU**   PARTNER   ■   **YOU**
     10   K J (4)   4   K J (10)

5)   DUMMY   6)   DUMMY
                   K 3   8 4 3
   PARTNER   ■   **YOU**   PARTNER   ■   **YOU**
      2   A (J) 4   Q   (K) 7

   1) _____   2) _____   3) _____

   4) _____   5) _____   6) _____

Exercise Seven — Review of Responses to 1 NT Opening Bids

Your partner opens the bidding 1 NT. What do you respond with each of the following hands?

1) ♠ 1086542
♥ 93
♦ J74
♣ 82

2) ♠ Q3
♥ J82
♦ 1075
♣ 108752

3) ♠ K6
♥ K73
♦ Q10965
♣ 975

1) __2H - TRans__   2) __P__   3) __2 N__

4) ♠ K10862
♥ A5
♦ J94
♣ K83

5) ♠ 8
♥ J108642
♦ AK7
♣ 962

6) ♠ A3
♥ 94
♦ J82
♣ KQJ742

4) __3H - TR__   5) __4D - Transfer__   6) __3 N__

7) ♠ Q1083
♥ A964
♦ A83
♣ 74

8) ♠ Q8
♥ AK62
♦ 10842
♣ 962

9) ♠ J974
♥ Q642
♦ 93
♣ 1086

7) __2C__   8) __2C__   9) __P__

Exercise Eight — Developing Tricks in Notrump Contracts

What is the maximum number of tricks you can get from each of the following suit combinations if the missing cards are favorably located? How would you plan to play the suit?

1) DUMMY
   Q 7   *2*

   DECLARER
   J 10 9 2

2) DUMMY
   A 7 5   *4*

   DECLARER
   K 8 4 3 2

3) DUMMY
   7 6 3   *3*

   DECLARER
   A Q J

4) DUMMY
   Q 7 4 2

   DECLARER
   A 8 6 3

5) DUMMY
   9 6 3

   DECLARER
   A Q 7 4 2

1) _____   2) _____   3) _____   4) _____   5) _____

98

Exercise Nine — Third Hand High

Turn up the cards on the first pre-dealt hand. Put each hand dummy style at the edge of the table in front of each player.

Dealer: North

The Bidding

What would North open the bidding? East and West pass throughout. With two four-card suits that can be bid at the one level, which does South bid? Is there still room for North to bid a suit at the one level? What does North rebid? How many points does South have? At what level does the partnership belong? Is there a Golden Fit? What does South rebid? How does the auction proceed from there? Who is declarer?

The Defense

Which player makes the opening lead? Which suit would be led? Why? Which card would be led? Which card would West play on the first trick? What would he do next?

The Play

Review the steps in declarer's PLAN. How does declarer plan to make the contract?

Exercise Ten — Trapping High Cards

Turn up the cards on the second pre-dealt hand. Put each hand dummy style at the edge of the table in front of each player.

Dealer: East

```
                    ♠ 6 5
                    ♥ 9 7 5 2
                    ♦ Q J 10 4
                    ♣ A 7 5

  ♠ Q 7 2          N           ♠ K 8 3
  ♥ Q J 3       W     E        ♥ 10 8 4
  ♦ K 7 6 2        S           ♦ A 9
  ♣ 9 8 3                      ♣ K Q J 10 4

                    ♠ A J 10 9 4
                    ♥ A K 6
                    ♦ 8 5 3
                    ♣ 6 2
```

The Bidding

What would East open the bidding? What would South do? Can West bid a suit at the one level? What would West respond? North passes. With a minimum balanced hand, what does East rebid? How does the auction proceed from there? What is the contract? Who is declarer?

The Defense

Which player makes the opening lead? Which suit would be led? Why? Which card would be led? Which card will South play if a small card is played from dummy?

The Play

Review the steps in declarer's PLAN. How does declarer plan to make the contract?

Exercise Eleven — Third Hand Not So High

Turn up the cards on the third pre-dealt hand. Put each hand dummy style at the edge of the table in front of each player.

Dealer: South

```
                    ♠ 10 9 5
                    ♥ J 7 2
                    ♦ K J 7 5
                    ♣ A Q 5
    ♠ K 8 2            N           ♠ A 7 4
    ♥ Q 9 6 3      W       E       ♥ K 10 5
    ♦ 9 6 2            S           ♦ 10 4 3
    ♣ 10 9 3                       ♣ J 7 4 2
                    ♠ Q J 6 3
                    ♥ A 8 4
                    ♦ A Q 8
                    ♣ K 8 6
```

The Bidding

What is South's opening bid? West passes. What is North's response? How does the bidding proceed from there? What is the contract? Who is declarer?

The Defense

Which player makes the opening lead? What would the opening lead be? Why? If a small card is played from dummy on the first trick, which card should East play? Why?

The Play

Review the steps in declarer's PLAN. How does declarer plan to make the contract?

Exercise Twelve — Unblocking

Turn up the cards on the fourth pre-dealt hand. Put each hand dummy style at the edge of the table in front of each player.

Dealer: West

```
                         ♠ 10 6 5 2
                         ♥ Ⓐ 6
                         ♦ 7 3 2
                         ♣ J 7 5 4
  ♠ 9 7 3          ┌─────────┐        ♠ A K Q
  ♥ 10 4 2         │    N    │        ♥ 8 7 3
  ♦ K 8 4          │ W     E │        ♦ A Q J 9
  ♣ 10 8 6 2       │    S    │        ♣ A K Q
                   └─────────┘
                         ♠ J 8 4
                         ♥ Ⓚ Q J 9 5
                         ♦ 10 6 5
                         ♣ 9 3
```

The Bidding

West and North pass. How does East describe his hand? South passes. What does West respond? How does the auction proceed from there? What is the contract? Who is declarer?

The Defense

Which player makes the opening lead? What would the opening lead be? Which card must North contribute to the first trick? Why?

The Play

Review the steps in declarer's PLAN. How does declarer plan to make the contract?

LESSON 4
Second-Hand Play

Second Hand Low
Second Hand Not So Low
Covering Honors
Bidding Review
Play of the Hand Review
Summary

Workshop Material
Group Activities

If the first card led to a trick is from your right, you are referred to as *second hand* since you are contributing the second card to the trick. The situation here is different from playing as third hand. Partner is in the enviable position of being the fourth hand, last to play to the trick. Declarer will have to play both his card and dummy's card before partner has to play. Your role as second hand is to ensure that your side does not unnecessarily spend any of its high cards in trying to win the trick.

As with third-hand play you want to keep declarer's high cards trapped whenever possible. The basic idea is expressed in the saying *"aces are meant to take kings."* In addition to winning the trick, an ace is most powerful when capturing an opponent's king at the same time. If the ace captures only small cards from the opponents, its power is lessened. Similarly, you would ideally like to use your kings to capture the opponents' queens, your queens to capture their jacks, and so forth. Of course the actual situation during a hand is seldom so ideal, but the principle is useful to keep in mind. Let's see how it can be put to use when playing second hand to a trick.

♥ *SECOND HAND LOW* ♥

One common piece of advice given for second hand play is *"second hand low."* This indicates that, with nothing else to guide you, you should play a low card to the trick. Let's see why this is often a good idea.

Conserving High Cards

Consider the following situation. Declarer leads a small card from his hand toward the dummy and you can see only the following cards in the suit:

```
              DUMMY
               Q 7 3
YOU           ■■■■■
A 9 4         ■■■■■
             DECLARER
                2
```

Should you play your ace to make sure of winning the trick? If you can see that taking your ace will clearly defeat the contract, it is likely best to take it and get on with the next hand. Otherwise follow the guideline and play second hand low, contributing the 4 to the trick. If you play the ace, declarer will play the 3 from dummy and your ace will have captured only two of declarer's small cards, leaving him with all his high cards. First, let's suppose declarer has the king and the complete layout looks something like this:

```
              DUMMY
               Q 7 3
YOU           ■■■■■   PARTNER
A 9 4         ■■■■■    J 10 6 5
             DECLARER
               K 8 2
```

If you rise with the ace on the first trick, declarer ends up with two tricks, one with the queen and one with the king. If you play low, declarer can win the first trick with dummy's queen but now his king remains trapped by your ace and partner's jack and 10. Declarer is held to one trick in the suit. Your ace is meant to take declarer's king, not the 2. Suppose we give partner the king instead of declarer.

Playing the ace on the first trick could still cost your side a trick:

	DUMMY	
	Q 7 3	
YOU		PARTNER
A 9 4		K 10 6 5
	DECLARER	
	J 8 2	

If you play the ace on the first trick, declarer will have the queen and jack left to drive out partner's king and create one trick in the suit. On the other hand, if you play second hand low, partner can capture dummy's queen with the king and your ace remains to stop declarer from getting a trick with the jack. Declarer does not get a trick in the suit. How low is low? When declarer leads the 2 toward dummy, you may be tempted to play the 9, rather than the 4, to encourage declarer to play dummy's queen. There is no need to do this, however. Declarer is surely not planning to play dummy's 7 to try to win the trick . If you waste the 9, it might later cost your side a trick. To see this, suppose you play the 9 in the previous layout, declarer plays the queen, and partner wins the king.

The remaining cards now look like this:

	DUMMY	
	7 3	
YOU		PARTNER
A 4		10 6 5
	DECLARER	
	J 8	

If partner leads the 10, declarer can cover with the jack to drive out your ace and promote his 8 into a trick since you no longer have the 9. If partner plays a small card, declarer can finesse the 8, again driving out your ace and establishing a trick in the suit. Just as aces were meant to take kings, 9's were meant to take 8's. Don't waste any of your cards when you don't have to.

Let's see the importance of second hand low in a complete hand:

Contract: 6 NT
Lead: ♦ 10

DUMMY
♠ A K J
♥ K 7 5
♦ Q 6 3
♣ A J 10 8

YOU
♠ 9 4 2
♥ A J 3
♦ 10 9 8 7
♣ 7 4 3

PARTNER
♠ 10 7 6 3
♥ 9 8 6 2
♦ 5 4 2
♣ 9 6

DECLARER
♠ Q 8 5
♥ Q 10 4
♦ A K J
♣ K Q 5 2

You start off well against the 6 NT slam by leading the ♦ 10. If you had led the ♥ A, declarer would immediately have 12 tricks. By leading a diamond, you give no help to declarer. He has three spade tricks, three diamond tricks and four club tricks and will have to get two tricks from the heart suit. Your work is not finished, however. When declarer leads a small heart toward dummy's ♥ K, you must again refrain from taking your ♥ A and play second hand low. Now your ♥ A and ♥ J have declarer's ♥ Q trapped and there is no way for him to establish a twelfth trick. Notice once again how you cannot afford to play "semi-low" by playing your ♥ J on the first trick. Declarer could then win dummy's ♥ K and use his remaining ♥ Q and ♥ 10 to drive out your ♥ A.

Making Declarer Guess

Another reason for playing second hand low is to give declarer a chance to make a mistake. Players often have difficulty defending correctly in this type of situation:

DUMMY
A Q 10
YOU
K J 5 3
DECLARER
4

When declarer leads a small card toward dummy, you may feel compelled to play the jack or king since these cards are going to be trapped anyway. You do not know what is going on in declarer's mind, however, so play second hand low and leave it to declarer to decide what to do. Declarer may have a singleton and may be planning to play the ace rather than take a finesse. Or declarer may decide to finesse the queen rather than the 10. Now your king and jack will prevent declarer from getting a third trick in the suit.

Playing low can be even more important when declarer has a complete guess. Consider the following layout:

DUMMY
K J
YOU   PARTNER
A 10 8 6 2   Q 9 5 4
DECLARER
7 3

When declarer leads a small card toward dummy, you might feel that it does not matter whether or not you play your ace since declarer is always entitled to a trick in the suit with dummy's king. Declarer, however, cannot see your cards. If you play second hand low, declarer may think that the actual layout is something like this:

DUMMY
K J
YOU   PARTNER
Q 10 8 6 2   A 9 5 4
DECLARER
7 3

In this layout, declarer should play dummy's jack, taking a finesse against your queen. Since declarer does not know which is the actual layout, play low as second hand and let declarer do the guesswork.

In situations like this, where declarer has to guess whether you or your partner holds the ace, it pays to have thought about the guideline ahead of time so that you can play second hand low without thinking too long about it. If you hesitate, pondering whether or not to take your ace, declarer won't have much of a guess left by the time you decide to play low.

Here is a similar situation where it is important to play second hand low. Second-hand play can apply whether you are on dummy's left or right. This time you are next to play when a small card is led from dummy:

```
              DUMMY
              8 6 4 3
PARTNER     ▮▮▮▮     YOU
  Q 9       ▮▮▮▮     A 10 2
            DECLARER
            K J 7 5
```

If you play low, declarer may play the jack and partner will win the queen. Declarer will later lead toward the king, and you get a second trick for your side with the ace. Even if declarer guesses to play the king the first time, your partner is still entitled to a trick with the queen, and you get a trick with the ace. In either case your side gets two tricks in the suit. Look what might happen if you play the ace when a small card is led from dummy. Declarer plays low and the remaining cards look like this:

```
              DUMMY
              8 6 4
PARTNER     ▮▮▮▮     YOU
  Q         ▮▮▮▮     10 2
            DECLARER
            K J 7
```

Declarer may choose to play the king on the next round of the suit, dropping your partner's queen. All of a sudden, your two tricks in the suit have been compressed into one.

Creating Entry Problems for Declarer

By playing second hand low, you can often create entry problems for declarer.

DUMMY
K Q 7 6 5

YOU
A 10 3

PARTNER
J 8

DECLARER
9 4 2

When declarer leads a small card toward dummy, he will have no problem establishing the suit if you take the first trick with the ace. Play second hand low and give declarer a more difficult time. He can win the first trick with dummy's queen (or king), but if he plays the remaining high card from dummy, you take the trick with the ace and your 10 is established as a winner. Instead, declarer must now get back to his hand to lead toward dummy's remaining high card, giving you only one trick with the ace. Declarer may not always have an easy entry back to his hand.

For example, here is a hand where declarer has no chance if you play second hand low:

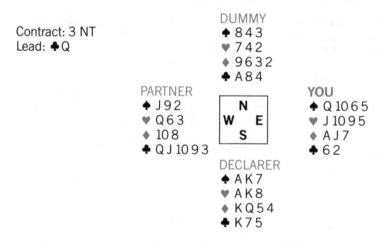

Contract: 3 NT
Lead: ♣Q

DUMMY
♠ 8 4 3
♥ 7 4 2
♦ 9 6 3 2
♣ A 8 4

PARTNER
♠ J 9 2
♥ Q 6 3
♦ 10 8
♣ Q J 10 9 3

N
W E
S

YOU
♠ Q 10 6 5
♥ J 10 9 5
♦ A J 7
♣ 6 2

DECLARER
♠ A K 7
♥ A K 8
♦ K Q 5 4
♣ K 7 5

Declarer starts with six sure tricks in his 3 NT contract, and the three remaining tricks must come from the diamond suit. Declarer would like to lead toward his king and queen twice, but he has only one entry to the dummy. Still, that will be sufficient if, when a small diamond is led from dummy, you play your ace. By playing low, you prevent declarer from taking three diamond tricks. Declarer has no other entry to dummy and will have to go down one.

♥ *SECOND HAND NOT SO LOW* ♥

As you have seen, second hand low is useful advice when you have nothing else to go on, but, as with all guidelines, there are some situations where it does not apply.

Splitting Honors

While you want to avoid wasting any of your high cards, you also want to prevent declarer from winning a trick cheaply. Consider this layout, with declarer leading low from dummy:

DUMMY
6 4 3
PARTNER · YOU
8 7 5 · K Q J 2
DECLARER
A 10 9

If you play the 2 when declarer leads a low card from the dummy, it is possible that declarer will play the 9 or 10 and win a trick to which he is not entitled. To prevent this, play one of your high cards when the suit is led. This is referred to as *splitting your honors*. You need play only as high a card as necessary to prevent declarer from winning the trick too cheaply. In the above example, you would play the jack. Declarer is then restricted to one trick in the suit.

Whether or not you need to split your honors depends on the actual layout of the suit and what declarer intends to do. Since you rarely know where all the missing cards are and cannot read declarer's mind, you have to exercise your judgment in most cases. Here is a common situation, with declarer leading a small card toward dummy:

DUMMY
A 10 4 2
YOU
Q J 6
DECLARER
3

Should you split your honors? If you do not have much else to go on, it is a good idea to split your honors to promote one trick in the suit. The complete layout may be something like this:

```
        DUMMY
        A 10 4 2
PARTNER   ■      YOU
Q J 6     ■      9 5
      DECLARER
        K 8 7 3
```

If you play the 6, declarer might decide to insert dummy's 10, which will win the trick since partner does not have a higher card. When declarer plays the ace and king, your queen and jack will fall and declarer will end up losing no tricks in the suit. By splitting your honors and playing the jack on the first trick, declarer is forced to play dummy's ace in order to win the trick. Now your queen will take a trick when declarer continues playing the suit.

In the above layout, it would not have made much difference if your partner held the king rather than declarer. Partner can let your jack win the trick. There are times, however, when you have additional information which guides you to a different decision. Suppose the bidding indicates that declarer has a five-card suit. This might be the complete layout:

```
        DUMMY
        A 10 4 2
PARTNER   ■      YOU
Q J 6     ■      K
      DECLARER
        9 8 7 5 3
```

If you split your honors, playing the jack, and declarer plays dummy's ace, partner's king will fall on the same trick. Instead of losing two tricks in the suit, declarer ends up losing only one. How could you know that this was the situation? You cannot see declarer's cards, but perhaps this is declarer's trump suit. If so he is quite likely to hold at least five cards. If declarer holds five cards in the suit, it is unlikely that he is planning to play dummy's 10 even if you do play a small card. For example, suppose this is the actual layout:

DUMMY
A 10 4 2

PARTNER   YOU
Q J 6   5

DECLARER
K 9 8 7 3

With nine cards in the combined hands, declarer is probably planning to play dummy's ace and later the king, hoping the missing cards are divided 2–2 so that he does not have to lose any tricks in the suit. So it is fairly safe not to split your honors, safeguarding against the situation where partner has the singleton king. As you can see, this situation can sometimes become a cat-and-mouse game between declarer and the defenders.

Another time not to split your honors is when there is nothing to gain and you will end up helping declarer.

DUMMY
A K 10

YOU
Q J 6

DECLARER
3

When declarer leads a small card toward dummy, you may be tempted to split your honors and play the jack. If he has an entry back to his hand, this can only help declarer. After winning the trick with dummy's king and coming back to his hand, he can lead another small card toward the ace and 10 in dummy and, whether or not you play the queen, declarer will win all three tricks. There is no reason to panic when you can see declarer will be able to win the trick with dummy's 10 if you play a low card. Remember that declarer cannot see what you hold in the suit. He may be intending to win the first trick with dummy's ace or king and now your queen and jack will prevent him from taking three tricks in the suit.

The Setting Trick

Another time to avoid automatically playing second hand low is when you can see that by winning the trick you will be able to defeat the contract. Here is an example in a complete hand:

Contract: 4 ♥
Lead: ♦ J

DUMMY
♠ K Q J 10 2
♥ Q 9 3
♦ K 7 2
♣ K 5

YOU
♠ A 8 6
♥ 8 2
♦ J 10 9 5
♣ A 10 4 2

PARTNER
♠ 7 5 4 3
♥ 6 5
♦ A Q 8 3
♣ 9 6 3

DECLARER
♠ 9
♥ A K J 10 7 4
♦ 6 4
♣ Q J 8 7

You lead the ♦ J, declarer plays dummy's ♦ K, and your partner wins the first trick with the ♦ A. Partner then plays the ♦ Q, which wins the trick, and leads a third round of diamonds, which declarer trumps. Declarer immediately leads a small spade toward dummy. Now is not the time to play low mechanically. To defeat the contract, you need to take four tricks. Your side already has two diamond tricks and you also have the ♣ A. By winning this trick with the ♠ A, you can see that you have enough tricks to defeat the contract. If you play low and let declarer win the trick with one of dummy's high spades, you may not get another chance. On this hand, declarer has a singleton spade and will end up losing just three tricks. After winning the ♠ A, don't get careless. You must immediately take the ♣ A as well. Otherwise declarer will be able to discard all his club losers on dummy's spades.

On this hand it was easy to see that taking the ♠ A would lead to declarer's defeat. It would not have been as straightforward for you if your partner rather than you held the ♠ A. You should still not let declarer slip the singleton spade by since none of the usual reasons for playing second hand low apply. You will not be saving a trick by playing low — declarer has enough high spades to drive out your ♠ A and win all the remaining spade tricks. Declarer does not have to guess which spade to play from dummy, and declarer is unlikely to have any problems with entries to his hand or the dummy with hearts as the trump suit. As a result, there is no good reason to play second hand low even if you do not hold the ♣ A.

Situations where it may be dangerous to play second hand low are quite common in suit contracts. Consider this layout of a side suit in a suit contract where declarer is leading a small card from a doubleton in the dummy:

DUMMY
7 4

YOU
A K 5

If you play low, declarer may win the trick if he has the queen. You will now get only one trick in the suit if dummy has some trumps left. It is probably best to make sure of two tricks in the suit by winning the first trick with your king. You don't want to "go to bed with" your king or your ace, especially if winning those tricks will help your side to defeat the contract.

Here is an example combining the idea of splitting your honors and taking the setting trick:

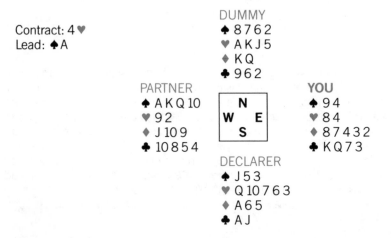

Contract: 4 ♥
Lead: ♠ A

DUMMY
♠ 8 7 6 2
♥ A K J 5
♦ K Q
♣ 9 6 2

PARTNER
♠ A K Q 10
♥ 9 2
♦ J 10 9
♣ 10 8 5 4

YOU
♠ 9 4
♥ 8 4
♦ 8 7 4 3 2
♣ K Q 7 3

DECLARER
♠ J 5 3
♥ Q 10 7 6 3
♦ A 6 5
♣ A J

Partner starts by taking the ♠ A, ♠ K and ♠ Q and then leading the ♠ 10, which declarer trumps. Declarer draws trumps by playing the ♥ A and ♥ K, then leads a small club from dummy. Here is your first chance to avoid playing second hand low. Even though you cannot see declarer's hand, split your club honors and play the ♣ Q, promoting your ♣ K into a winner. If you play low, declarer will win a trick with the ♣ J and end up making the contract. By playing the ♣ Q, you force declarer to play the ♣ A to win the trick. If declarer now plays a small diamond over to dummy's ♦ Q and leads the remaining small club, you have your second chance to avoid playing second hand low. This time win the trick with the ♣ K since it represents the setting trick. If you play low, declarer will win with the ♣ J and again make the contract.

♥ *COVERING HONORS* ♥

Another bridge maxim that requires discretion in its application is *"Cover an honor with an honor."* This implies that if declarer leads a honor you cover it with (play) a higher honor if you have one. The saying *"second hand low"* usually applies when a small card, rather than an honor, is led. To see why you would usually play a higher card in second hand when a high card is led, we need to look at the reasoning behind this advice.

Promoting Tricks

The theory behind covering an honor can be clearly seen in this example where declarer decides to lead the queen from the dummy:

DUMMY
Q 5 4
PARTNER   YOU
9 6 3 2   K J 10
DECLARER
A 8 7

If you were to play low (the 10 or the jack), declarer could play low and win the trick with dummy's queen. Declarer's ace would then give him two tricks in the suit. Instead cover dummy's queen with your king to make declarer play the ace in order to win the trick. Now your jack and 10 are promoted into the highest cards in the suit and declarer ends up with one trick. By covering the queen with the king, you made declarer use two of his high cards to capture one of yours. This in turn promoted your lower cards in the suit into winners. This is the idea behind covering an honor with an honor. You want to promote tricks for your side.

Although it is easy to see in the above layout how the jack and 10 will be promoted by covering dummy's queen, the picture may not be so clear if you do not hold these cards. Suppose these are the only cards you see when the queen is led from dummy:

DUMMY
Q 5 4
YOU
K 6 3

Should you cover with your king or play second hand low? It does not look as if there is anything to promote in your hand by covering with the king. However, there may be something in partner's hand. With nothing else to go on, cover with the king. The complete layout might look something like this:

DUMMY
Q 5 4

PARTNER ▮ **YOU**
J 10 9 2 ▮ K 6 3

DECLARER
A 8 7

By covering the queen with the king, you promote **partner's** jack and 10 into tricks for your side. Of course, declarer may have both the jack and the 10:

DUMMY
Q 5 4

PARTNER ▮ **YOU**
9 8 7 2 ▮ K 6 3

DECLARER
A J 10

If this is the case, you have still lost nothing by covering with the king. Declarer is always entitled to three tricks. If you do not cover the queen, it will win the trick and declarer can repeat the finesse by leading a small card from dummy to trap your king.

Partner does not need both the jack and the 10 to make covering the queen worthwhile. Suppose this is the layout:

DUMMY
Q 5 4

PARTNER ▮ **YOU**
10 9 8 2 ▮ K 6 3

DECLARER
A J 7

If you do not cover the queen with the king, dummy's queen will win the trick. Declarer can then lead a small card from dummy and your king is trapped. Declarer wins three tricks in the suit. If you cover with the king, however, declarer can win with the ace and take a trick with the jack, but now partner's 10 is promoted into the highest card in the suit, and declarer gets only two tricks rather than three.

Covering with the king could be important even if partner holds the ace. Suppose this is the complete layout:

DUMMY
Q 5 4

PARTNER ▮ **YOU**
A 10 8 2 ▮ K 6 3

DECLARER
J 9 7

If you play low when dummy's queen is led, partner can win the trick with ace. Declarer can later get a trick with the jack, whether or not you play your king, by leading a small card from the dummy. By covering the queen with the king, you prevent declarer from getting any tricks in the suit. Your king wins the trick and declarer's jack remains trapped by partner's ace and 10.

Here is a complete hand to illustrate the importance of covering an honor in order to promote winners for your side:

Contract: 4♠
Lead: ♦Q

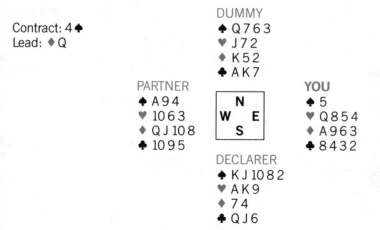

DUMMY
♠ Q763
♥ J72
♦ K52
♣ AK7

PARTNER
♠ A94
♥ 1063
♦ QJ108
♣ 1095

YOU
♠ 5
♥ Q854
♦ A963
♣ 8432

DECLARER
♠ KJ1082
♥ AK9
♦ 74
♣ QJ6

Partner leads the ♦Q, and your side takes the first two diamond tricks. When a third round of diamonds is led, declarer ruffs and starts to draw trumps. Partner wins the ♠A, and leads a club which declarer wins. Declarer draws partner's remaining trumps, takes his club tricks, and then leads the ♥J from the dummy. Here is your chance to shine by covering with the ♥Q. Declarer can win the ♥K and ♥A, but your partner's ♥10 is promoted into the setting trick.

The opportunity to cover an honor arises in a variety of circumstances. It is usually right to cover an honor if you can see your honor will be trapped anyway the next time the suit is led. For example, suppose these are the cards you see in a side suit when declarer leads the 10 from his hand:

DUMMY
A J 8 3
YOU
Q 5 2

DECLARER
10

This is your chance to cover and make declarer use both the 10 and the ace to capture your queen. If you play low, the complete layout might look like this:

DUMMY
A J 8 3
YOU   PARTNER
Q 5 2   K 9 6
DECLARER
10 7 4

If you play a small card, declarer will play a small card from dummy, and your partner will win the first trick with the king. The remaining cards will now look like this:

DUMMY
A J 8
YOU   PARTNER
Q 5   9 6
DECLARER
7 4

Your queen is now trapped by dummy's ace and jack. When declarer next leads a small card from his hand, there is no way you can prevent him from taking the rest of the tricks. If you cover the 10 with the queen originally, however, the remaining cards would look like this when declarer wins the trick with dummy's ace:

DUMMY
J 8 3
YOU   PARTNER
5 2   K 9
DECLARER
7 4

Now it is declarer's jack that is trapped by your partner's king and 9. Declarer will have to lose two tricks in the suit.

When Not to Cover

Since the idea of covering an honor with an honor is to promote tricks for your side, you do not cover when there is nothing to promote. For example, suppose the queen is led from dummy in this situation:

DUMMY
Q J 10 9
    YOU
    K 5 4 3

Since you can see the jack, 10 and 9 in the dummy, there is nothing to promote for your side by covering the queen with the king. In fact, it may cost you a trick:

DUMMY
Q J 10 9
PARTNER   YOU
8 6   K 5 4 3
DECLARER
A 7 2

If you cover the queen, declarer will win the ace and end up with four tricks in the suit. By refusing to cover each time the suit is led from dummy, declarer will get only three tricks in the suit. The situation is not so clear when there are two touching high cards in the dummy:

DUMMY
Q J 4
    YOU
    K 7 3

Should you cover the queen with the king? You can see that the jack is in the dummy, but partner may have the 10. In such situations, the guideline is to *cover the last high card* led when you have nothing else to go on. One reason for this can be see when partner holds the ace:

DUMMY
Q J 4
PARTNER   YOU
A 10 9 5   K 7 3
DECLARER
8 6 2

By letting partner win the first trick with the ace, your king remains to trap dummy's jack. Declarer gets no tricks in the suit. If you were to win the first trick with the king, declarer could later lead toward dummy's remaining jack and would get one trick whether or not partner chose to play the ace.

A more subtle reason for not covering occurs when partner has only the 10, as in this layout:

If you cover the queen with the king, declarer wins the trick with the ace and the remaining cards look like this:

Declarer can lead the 9 and partner's 10 is trapped. Whether or not partner plays the 10, declarer can take all the tricks in the suit. If you do not cover the first honor led from dummy, the remaining cards will look like this:

Declarer can no longer avoid losing a trick in the suit. If he plays dummy's jack, you cover the last high card led from dummy and promote partner's 10 into a trick. If he plays dummy's 4, you play second hand low, and whichever card declarer plays your side gets a trick. It is difficult to foresee complicated combinations such as this, but using the guideline of covering the last high card led will provide the help you need.

There are other times when you need to be careful about covering an honor with an honor, and it may be impossible to know exactly what to do without being able to see declarer's cards. This is especially true when it comes to declarer's trump suit. For example, suppose declarer leads the jack of trumps from his hand in this situation:

DUMMY
A 7 3

YOU
Q 6 2

DECLARER
J

It might be right to cover with the queen if partner has some high cards in the suit, but since this is declarer's trump suit, that is unlikely to be the case. More likely, the layout is something like this:

DUMMY
A 7 3

YOU   PARTNER
Q 6 2   8 4

DECLARER
K J 10 9 5

Why is declarer leading the jack? He does not want to lose a trick to the missing queen and is hoping that you will unthinkingly cover an honor with an honor and help him out. If you play a small card, he will likely assume that your partner has the queen and win the trick with dummy's ace. Then he will play toward his hand, intending to finesse the 10 if your partner plays a small card. Of course, if you think too long before playing a small card, declarer will no longer have to guess what to do.

Covering the jack would also be disastrous if this were the layout:

DUMMY
A 7 3

YOU   PARTNER
Q 6 2   K

DECLARER
J 10 9 8 5 4

When declarer plays dummy's ace on your queen, he will be pleasantly surprised to end up with no losers in the suit! Here is a similar situation where declarer leads the queen of trumps from the dummy:

DUMMY
Q 8 6 2

YOU
K 4

You would be disappointed if you covered the queen with the king and this was the complete layout:

DUMMY
Q 8 6 2

PARTNER
A

YOU
K 4

DECLARER
J 10 9 7 5 3

Then again it would be unfortunate if you did not cover and the layout turned out to look like this:

DUMMY
Q 8 6 2

PARTNER
J 3

YOU
K 4

DECLARER
A 10 9 7 5

Sometimes it may seem as though the game is too difficult! Is it second hand low or cover an honor with an honor? Which guideline applies? The underlying theme is that you want to cover an honor with an honor if it will promote one or more tricks for your side. The above challenge arises because you cannot look into partner's hand to see if there is something to promote. Sometimes, you have to guess and sometimes you will be lucky. Let's finish off with some straightforward examples where you have nothing else to guide you and must play after a card is led from dummy or declarer's hand:

DUMMY
7 5 **2**

YOU
K J 4

When a small card is led from dummy, conserve your high cards and play second hand low, the **4**. There is no need to help declarer out by playing either the king or the jack.

DUMMY
K J 3

YOU
A 4 2

DECLARER
6

When a small card is played toward the dummy and declarer cannot be sure which card to finesse, play the **2**, second hand low, and keep declarer guessing.

DUMMY
K Q J 3

YOU
A 10 6 5

DECLARER
7

Play low, the **5**, when declarer could be faced with entry problems. If you play the ace, declarer has three tricks, the king, queen and jack. If you play low, declarer may not have enough entries to come back and repeat the finesse. If he leads a high card from dummy, you can win the ace and restrict declarer to two tricks in the suit.

DUMMY
A 9 3

YOU
Q J 5

When a small card is led from dummy, split your honors and play the **jack**. This will prevent declarer from winning a cheap trick if he has both the king and the 10.

DUMMY
J 5 2

YOU
K 4 3

If the jack is led from dummy, cover it with the **king**, covering an honor with an honor. If a small card is led from dummy, play second hand low, the 3.

DUMMY
Q J 10 9 8

YOU
K 4 3

With nothing you can promote in your hand or partner's, play the **3**, second hand low.

BIDDING REVIEW

The opening bidder tries to describe his hand so that partner, the responder, can determine the level and the denomination in which the partnership belongs. The opening bid starts the description but responder often needs more information before deciding on the best contract. Opener's second bid, his *rebid*, is used to further describe the strength and distribution of his hand. Opener's choice of rebid will also be influenced by the bidding message given by responder's bid. Responder may have made a *signoff*, *invitational* or *forcing bid*. Opener must listen and act accordingly.

Opener's Rebid After Opening the Bidding 1 NT

By bidding 1 NT, opener has given responder a good description of both the strength and distribution of his hand. Responder is often able to make a signoff bid in partscore (2♦, 2♥ or 2♠) or in game (3 NT, 4♥ or 4♠). Responder has made the final decision for the partnership and opener must pass. If responder needs more information about opener's strength, he makes an invitational bid. For example, responder can invite game by raising to 2 NT or invite slam by raising to 4 NT. Opener has shown 16–18 points and so rejects the invitation by passing when he has the minimum of his range, 16 points, and accepts by bidding game, or slam, with a maximum, 17–18 points (17 points is on the borderline and opener could pass). If responder needs more information about opener's distribution, he makes a forcing bid. For example, responder can ask opener if he has a four-card major suit by bidding 2♣ (Stayman) or if he has three-card support for a major suit by bidding 3♥ or 3♠. Opener cannot pass a forcing response and so makes a further descriptive bid. If responder bids 2♣, opener bids a four-card major if he has one, otherwise 2♦. If responder bids 3♥ or 3♠, opener bids 4♥ or 4♠ respectively with three-card or longer support, otherwise 3 NT.

Opener's Rebid After Opening the Bidding 2 NT

The situation is similar after opening the bidding 2 NT. If responder makes a signoff bid by bidding game or slam (3 NT, 4♥, 4♠, 6 NT, etc.), opener passes. If responder invites opener to slam by bidding beyond game (4 NT, 5♥, etc.), opener accepts with the top of his range, otherwise passes. If responder makes a forcing bid such as 3♣ (Stayman) or 3♥ or 3♠ (asking for three-card support), opener makes a descriptive rebid.

Opener's Rebid After Opening the Bidding One of a Suit

An opening suit bid at the one level covers a much wider range of both strength and distribution than an opening notrump bid. Responder is not in a position to make a signoff bid (except by passing) and makes either an invitational or forcing response. In choosing his rebid, opener classifies the strength of his hand as minimum (13–16 points), medium (17–18 points) or maximum (19–21 points) and bids accordingly. As a general guideline, the more strength he has, the more (higher) he bids.

For example, responder's raise of opener's suit to the two level is an invitational bid showing support and 6–10 points. With a minimum, opener passes. With a medium strength hand, opener raises to the three level. With a maximum, opener bids game.

Similarly, a response of 1 NT is invitational, showing 6–10 points without support for opener's suit and with no other suit that can be bid at the one level. With balanced distribution, opener passes with a minimum or raises to 3 NT with a maximum (opener would open 1 NT with a medium strength balanced hand). With an unbalanced hand, opener can bid a second suit* (*jump shifting* with a maximum hand) or rebid his original suit at the two level with a minimum hand, at the three level with a medium hand and at the game level with a maximum hand.

A new suit by responder is forcing and opener cannot pass, even with a minimum hand. Opener makes the most descriptive rebid. With support for responder's suit, opener raises to the next level with a minimum hand, jumps a level with a medium hand and jumps two levels with a maximum hand. With an unbalanced hand, opener can bid a second suit* (*jump shifting* with a maximum hand) or rebid his original suit at the cheapest level with a minimum hand, jumping a level with a medium hand and jumping two levels with a maximum hand. With a balanced hand, opener rebids notrump at the cheapest level with a minimum hand and jumps a level with a maximum hand.

---

*With a minimum hand, a second suit can be bid only at the two level if it is lower-ranking than the original suit. With a medium hand, a new suit can be bid at the two level even if it is higher-ranking than the original suit.

Opener's Rebid After Opening the Bidding Two of a Suit

An opening strong two-bid is forcing to the game level, so opener continues to describe his hand with the rebid. The partnership is committed to playing at least at the game level but there may be enough combined strength to play at the slam level. Since some of the bidding room has already been used up by opening at the two level, there is no need for opener to jump again to show his strength. Opener must keep in mind that a bid of 2 NT by responder is artificial and shows a weak hand (0–5 points).

Opener's Rebid After Opening the Bidding Three of a Suit

Responder will usually pass when opener makes a preemptive bid at the three level or higher. If responder signs off in game, then opener must pass. If responder bids a new suit below the game level, however, that is still forcing and opener must make a suitably descriptive rebid.

♥ *PLAY OF THE HAND REVIEW* ♥

Leading Toward High Cards

The basic principle of the finesse is to lead toward the high card which you are hoping will win a trick:

DUMMY
K 3

DECLARER
4 2

By leading toward the king, you get a trick whenever the opponent on your left holds the ace, whether he plays it or not. With touching high cards, you may have a *repeating finesse*:

DUMMY
K Q 3

DECLARER
6 5 4

If you lead toward dummy and win the first trick with the queen (or king), you may be able to cross back to your hand with an entry in another suit to lead toward dummy's remaining honor. If the ace is on your left, you end up with two tricks. Notice how your opponent can make it more difficult for you by playing second hand low on your first lead toward dummy even when he holds the ace.

When the high cards are not touching, the general guideline is to lead toward the **lower** card first:

DUMMY
K J 3

DECLARER
6 5 4

With no other considerations you would play the jack if your left-hand opponent plays a small card when you lead toward dummy. That will give you two tricks if both the ace and the queen are on your left since you can later lead toward the king. If the jack loses to the queen, you still have a chance for one trick by leading toward the king later. The following situation, however, is a little different:

DUMMY
K J

DECLARER
4 3

When you lead a small card toward dummy, you have to guess whether to play the jack or the king unless both the ace and queen are on your left. If the queen is on your left and the ace on your right, you must finesse the jack to get one trick. If the ace is on your left and the queen is on your right, you must play dummy's king on the first trick, otherwise you will not get a trick.

Notice how your left-hand opponent makes things difficult by playing second hand low. How are you to know what to do? You might be able to deduce from the bidding which opponent is more likely to have the ace. An opponent who opened the bidding or overcalled is more likely to hold a missing ace than an opponent who passed throughout the auction. Here is another situation where you have to guess what to lead:

DUMMY
K 7 6 2

DECLARER
Q 5 4 3

It will do no good to lead toward both high cards since one of the opponents must have the ace. The best way to play this suit is to lead toward the high card that you think will win the trick. If this works, play a low card from both hands when you lead the suit a second time. Your hope is that the ace is now singleton. For example, if you think that the ace is on your left, lead toward dummy's king, playing for this layout:

DUMMY
K 7 6 2

WEST   EAST
A 10   J 9 8

DECLARER
Q 5 4 3

When you lead toward dummy, West will play the 10, and you win the trick with dummy's king. Since you now know West has the ace, it does no good to lead toward the queen. Instead, play a small card from both hands and you end up with three tricks. If East has the ace, you need to lead from dummy toward your queen originally. Of course, there is no guarantee that either opponent started with exactly a doubleton ace, but with a good guess and a little luck, who knows?

Leading High Cards

Since a defender will frequently cover an honor with an honor, you lead a high card only when you can afford to have it covered:

DUMMY
A Q 4 2

DECLARER
J 10 9 3

Here you can afford to lead the jack (or 10 or 9) to try to trap the king on your left. You do not mind if the jack is covered by the king since all your remaining cards will be promoted into winners. On the other hand, if your holding is not as strong:

DUMMY
A Q 4 2

DECLARER
J 6 5 3

You cannot afford to lead the jack since, if it is covered, the opponents' 10 will be promoted into a winner. Instead, you must lead a small card toward dummy and hope for this position:

DUMMY
A Q 4 2

WEST
K 8

EAST
10 9 7

DECLARER
J 6 5 3

You lead a small card to dummy's queen and then take the ace. After West's king falls, your carefully preserved jack prevents East from winning a trick with the 10. There are many variations of this theme, but the general idea is to consider whether or not you can afford to have the opponents cover an honor with an honor before you lead a high card. If you can't afford the cover, you may want to look for other options.

SUMMARY

When declarer leads a low card from his hand or from the dummy and you are the second person to play to the trick, a useful guideline is *second hand low*. Your partner will play last to the trick, and you do not want to waste your high cards capturing only low cards from declarer. Ideally you would like to use your aces to capture declarer's kings, your kings to capture his queens, and so forth.

There are exceptions:

• You do not want to play a low card if it will allow declarer to win a trick too cheaply. With a strong holding in the suit, you may need to *split your honors*.

• You also do not want to play second hand low if by playing high you could defeat the contract.

If declarer leads a high card, you should generally *cover an honor with an honor* if you have a higher card. You should do this, however, only if it is likely to promote a trick for your side. If declarer leads from touching high cards, you should generally wait to *cover the last high card led*.

♥ GROUP ACTIVITIES ♥

Exercise One — When Declarer Leads a Small Card

In each of the following layouts, declarer leads the 2 toward dummy. How many tricks can declarer take if you play low? How many tricks can declarer take if you play high?

1)
	DUMMY	
	Q 7 5	
YOU		PARTNER
K 8 4	■	A 10 9 3
	DECLARER	
	J 6 **2**	

2)
	DUMMY	
	A Q J	
YOU		PARTNER
K 8 4	■	10 9 7 6 5 3
	DECLARER	
	2	

3)
	DUMMY	
	A 10 9	
YOU		PARTNER
K 8 4	■	J 7 5 3
	DECLARER	
	Q 6 **2**	

1) _____   2) _____   3) _____

Exercise Two — When Dummy Leads a Small Card

In each of the following layouts, declarer leads the 2 from dummy. Which card must you play to ensure that your side gets all the tricks to which it is entitled? How do you expect declarer to play the suit?

1)

DUMMY
8 7 3 **2**

PARTNER
6

YOU
Q 9 ⑤

DECLARER
A K J 10 4

2)

DUMMY
J 8 **2**

PARTNER
A 10 6 4

YOU
Q 9 ⑤

DECLARER
K 7 3

3)

DUMMY
A 8 **2**

PARTNER
K 7 6

YOU
Q 9 ⑤

DECLARER
J 10 4 3

1) _____   2) _____   3) _____

Exercise Three — Splitting Honors

In each of the following layouts, declarer leads the 2 toward dummy. Which card must you play to ensure that your side gets all the tricks to which it is entitled?

1)
    DUMMY
    Q 9 5

YOU   PARTNER
J 10 4   A 8 7 3

    DECLARER
    K 6 2

2)
    DUMMY
    A 9 6

YOU   PARTNER
Q 10 3   8 7 4

    DECLARER
    K J 5 2

3)
    DUMMY
    K Q 9

YOU   PARTNER
J 10 4   A 7 5 3

    DECLARER
    8 6 2

1) _____   2) _____   3) _____

Exercise Four — Covering Honors

In each of the following layouts, how many tricks does declarer get if you cover with an honor when the jack is led from dummy? How many tricks does declarer get if you do not cover?

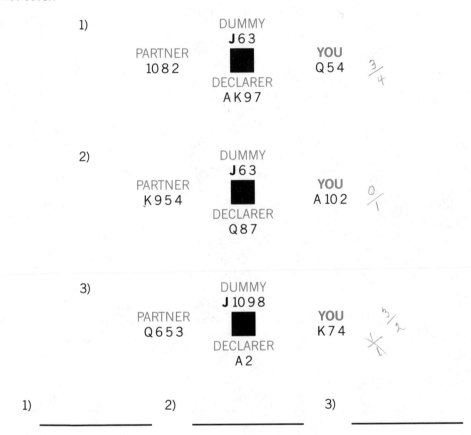

1)
DUMMY
J 6 3

PARTNER
10 8 2

YOU
Q 5 4   3/4

DECLARER
A K 9 7

2)
DUMMY
J 6 3

PARTNER
K 9 5 4

YOU
A 10 2   0/1

DECLARER
Q 8 7

3)
DUMMY
J 10 9 8

PARTNER
Q 6 5 3

YOU
K 7 4   3/2

DECLARER
A 2

1) _____   2) _____   3) _____

135

Exercise Five — Covering Second Honors

In each of the following layouts, should you play your high card when the jack is led from dummy?

1)

DUMMY
J 10 8

PARTNER
Q 9 7

YOU *No*
K 6 4 2

DECLARER
A 5 3

2)

DUMMY
J 10 3

PARTNER
K 7 6 2

YOU
Q 9 5 *No*

DECLARER
A 8 4

3)

DUMMY
J 10 3

PARTNER
7 6 5 4

YOU
K Q 9 *Yes*

DECLARER
A 8 2

1) _____   2) _____   3) _____

Exercise Six — Putting It Together

Which card do you play in each of the following situations when declarer leads the indicated card toward dummy?

1)
DUMMY
Q 8 3

YOU
A J⑤ ⬛

DECLARER
6

4)
DUMMY
Q 8 3

YOU
Ⓙ 10 9 7 ⬛

DECLARER
4

2)
DUMMY
K J 4

YOU
Q 7 ③ ⬛

DECLARER
5

5)
DUMMY
K

YOU
Ⓐ 6 4 2 ⬛

DECLARER
9

3)
DUMMY
J 8 4

YOU
K 6 ② ⬛

DECLARER
3

6)
DUMMY
A 10 3

YOU
K 7 ⑤ ⬛

DECLARER
J

1) _____

2) _____

3) _____

4) _____

5) _____

6) _____

Exercise Seven — Review of Rebids by Opener

You open the bidding 1♥ and your partner responds 1♠. What do you rebid with each of the following hands?

1) ♠ 10 8 4 2
   ♥ A K J 7 3
   ♦ K 9
   ♣ J 10

2) ♠ Q 4
   ♥ K J 10 7 3
   ♦ A 10 4
   ♣ Q J 6

3) ♠ 7
   ♥ Q J 9 7 5 3
   ♦ J 4 2
   ♣ A K J

1)   2 S

2)   1 NT

3)   2 H

4) ♠ 7 4 5
   ♥ A Q 6 4 2
   ♦ K J 6 3 2
   ♣ A

5) ♠ K Q 6 3
   ♥ A Q J 7 2
   ♦ 4
   ♣ K 9 4

6) ♠ Q 2
   ♥ A K J 8 4 3
   ♦ A 4
   ♣ 9 5

4)   2 D

5)   3 S

6)   3 H

7) ♠ K 10
   ♥ A J 10 8 2
   ♦ K Q 9
   ♣ A Q 2

8) ♠ A 4
   ♥ K Q 10 7 3
   ♦ K 5
   ♣ A K J 2

9) ♠ A J 8 4
   ♥ A K Q 7 5
   ♦ 8
   ♣ Q J 2

7)   2 N

8)

9)   4 S

138

Exercise Eight — Review of Finesses

What is the maximum number of tricks you can get from each of the following suit combinations if the missing high cards are favorably located? How would you plan to play the suit?

	1)	2)	3)	4)	5)
DUMMY:	Q J 7	7 5 4	Q J 10	Q 7 4	Q 7 5
DECLARER:	6 4 2	A J 10	A 7 5	A J 6	K 8 6

1) _____ *1*   2) _____ *2*   3) _____ *3*   4) _____ *3*   5) _____ *2*

139

Exercise Nine — Second Hand Low

Turn up the cards on the first pre-dealt hand. Put each hand dummy style at the edge of the table in front of each player.

Dealer: North

```
                        ♠ K972
                        ♥ K64
                        ♦ AQ
                        ♣ AQJ6
      ♠ AJ5                              ♠ 104
      ♥ QJ108         ┌─────────┐        ♥ A952
      ♦ 9753          │    N    │        ♦ J1064
      ♣ 108           │ W     E │        ♣ 732
                      │    S    │
                      └─────────┘
                        ♠ Q863
                        ♥ 73
                        ♦ K82
                        ♣ K954
```

The Bidding

With a balanced hand, why can North not open the bidding 1 NT? What bid would North make to open the bidding? East and West pass throughout. Does South have a suit that can be bid at the one level? What does South respond? How does North show support for South's suit and the strength of his hand? How does the auction proceed from there? Who is declarer?

The Defense

Which player makes the opening lead? What would the opening lead be? If declarer plays trump by leading a small spade toward dummy, which card does West play? Why?

The Play

Review the steps in declarer's PLAN. How can declarer avoid losing two trump tricks?

Exercise Ten — Giving Declarer a Guess

Turn up the cards on the second pre-dealt hand. Put each hand dummy style at the edge of the table in front of each player.

Dealer: East

```
                 ♠ A 9 5 4
                 ♥ 9 2
                 ♦ J 10 9 8 2
                 ♣ 10 3
  ♠ 8 3                        ♠ K J
  ♥ A K 8 6 4      N           ♥ Q J 7 5
  ♦ 6 4         W     E        ♦ K 7 3
  ♣ A Q 8 4        S           ♣ K J 9 5
                 ♠ Q 10 7 6 2
                 ♥ 10 3
                 ♦ A Q 5
                 ♣ 7 6 2
```

The Bidding

What would East open the bidding? North and South pass throughout. What does West respond? How does East show his support for West's suit and the strength of his hand? Does West have enough information to place the contract? What does West rebid? What is the contract? Who is declarer?

The Defense

Which player makes the opening lead? What is the opening lead? What will South do if a small card is played from dummy? What must North be prepared to do when West leads a spade toward dummy?

The Play

Review the steps in declarer's PLAN. How can declarer avoid a spade loser?

Exercise Eleven — Covering an Honor

Turn up the cards on the third pre-dealt hand. Put each hand dummy style at the edge of the table in front of each player.

Dealer: South

♠ 1064
♥ KQ73
♦ J7
♣ AKQJ

♠ Q93
♥ AJ108
♦ 9654
♣ 97

N
W E
S

♠ KJ852
♥ 54
♦ K2
♣ 6532

♠ A7
♥ 962
♦ AQ1083
♣ 1084

The Bidding

South and West pass. What is North's opening bid? After East passes, what does South respond? What is the contract? Who is declarer?

The Defense

Which player makes the opening lead? What would the opening lead be? Why? If a small card is played from dummy on the first trick, which card should West play? Why? If declarer leads a small diamond toward dummy, which card should East play? Which card should East play if declarer leads a diamond honor toward dummy?

The Play

Review the steps in declarer's PLAN. How does declarer plan to make the contract?

Exercise Twelve — Waiting to Cover

Turn up the cards on the fourth pre-dealt hand. Put each hand dummy style at the edge of the table in front of each player.

Dealer: West

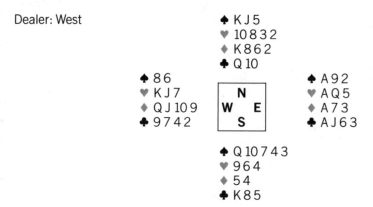

♠ K J 5
♥ 10 8 3 2
♦ K 8 6 2
♣ Q 10

♠ 8 6
♥ K J 7
♦ Q J 10 9
♣ 9 7 4 2

N
W E
S

♠ A 9 2
♥ A Q 5
♦ A 7 3
♣ A J 6 3

♠ Q 10 7 4 3
♥ 9 6 4
♦ 5 4
♣ K 8 5

The Bidding

West and North pass. Why does East not open 1 NT? What bid does East make to open the bidding? South passes. Does West have a suit that can be bid at the one level? What does West respond? North passes. How does East finish describing his strong balanced hand? South passes. What does West rebid? What is the contract? Who is declarer?

The Defense

Which player makes the opening lead? What would the opening lead be? Which card must North contribute to the first trick? Why? Should North cover if a diamond is led from dummy? Why not?

The Play

Review the steps in declarer's PLAN. How does declarer plan to make the contract?

LESSON 5
Defensive Signals

Attitude Signals
Count Signals
Suit Preference Signals
Bidding Review
Play of the Hand Review
Summary

Workshop Material
Group Activities

The defenders work as a team trying to defeat declarer's contract. They get tricks in the same fashion as declarer, developing tricks through promotion, length and finesses, and using the trump suit to ruff their opponent's winners. Unlike declarer, who can see both his hand and the dummy, the defenders cannot look into each other's hands to see their strengths and weaknesses. This is a disadvantage which they want to overcome as quickly as possible, and *defensive signals* are a way of helping them do this. By playing specific cards in certain situations, each defender can paint a picture of his hand to give partner the information needed to make an appropriate decision.

You have already seen some of the signals the defenders can give each other. By leading the top of touching honors, for example, information is passed from one defender to the other. If partner leads a queen against a notrump contract, you can assume he also has the jack, and likely the 10 as well, but not the king. If you cannot see the king in dummy or in your hand, you know declarer holds it. Notice that the specific card played by partner gives you information not only about his hand but also, by inference, about declarer's holding in the suit. This happens often enough to help you defeat the contract.

What type of information do the defenders want to give each other through their signals? The information that is of most value to partner normally falls into one of these categories:

> • **Attitude.** An *attitude signal* tells partner whether or not you like a particular suit. If he knows you like the suit, partner can lead the suit at his first opportunity. Conversely, if he knows you do *not* like a suit, he can lead a different suit when he gets the opportunity.

> • **Count.** A *count signal* tells partner how many cards you have in a suit. Since partner can see how many cards he holds and how many there are in dummy, he can determine how many cards declarer has. This can help him decide how many tricks your side can take in the suit, when to take a trick, or which cards to hold when he has to discard.

> • **Suit Preference.** A *suit preference* signal tells partner which of two suits you prefer. Again, such information will be helpful in letting partner know which suit to lead when he gets the opportunity or which cards to hold when he has to discard.

Let's take a look at how the various types of signals work and how to put them into practice.

♥ *ATTITUDE SIGNALS* ♥

You can give a signal only when you have a choice of cards to play. If partner has led a suit and you are trying to win the trick by playing third hand high, you may be forced to play your only high card and cannot give partner a signal. On the other hand, if partner or declarer is already winning the trick, you may have two or more cards which you can play to the trick which will not affect whether the current trick is won or lost. In such cases, the specific card you choose may be used to give a signal to partner. For example, consider the following situation where partner leads the 3 against a notrump contract:

DUMMY
A 7 4
PARTNER YOU
3 K 9 2

If a small card is played from dummy, you have no choice — you must play the king, third hand high, in order to win the trick for your side. On the other hand, if the ace is played from dummy, you cannot win the trick and are in a position to choose which of your cards to play. You do not want to play the king, since that card is now established as a winner, but you have a choice between the 9 and 2 . Neither is likely to have any significance as far as winning tricks is concerned, so the one you choose can be used to give partner a signal.

High Cards Encourage, Low Cards Discourage

What message do you want to give partner? One of the most important pieces of information you can give to partner is your attitude toward the suit. You give an *attitude signal* by playing a *high card to encourage and a low card to discourage*. In the above example, you like the suit that partner has led since you hold the king. You can therefore give an encouraging signal by playing the highest card you can afford, the 9, rather than the 2. Suppose we change your holding in the suit:

DUMMY
A 7 4
PARTNER 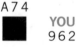 YOU
3 9 6 2

If the ace is played from dummy, you have a choice of three cards to play. With no high cards in the suit you can make a discouraging signal by playing the lowest card you can afford, the 2. Giving a discouraging signal does not stop partner from playing the suit again if he wants to. It merely suggests that you have no particular interest in the suit and, by inference, would prefer another suit.

Both partners must cooperate if the message is to be successfully communicated. One partner must be giving the appropriate signal and the other partner must be watching for it. If your partner does not bother to look to see if you played the 9 or the 2, he will not get the message. On the other hand, if you carelessly play the 2 when you want to encourage, or the 9 when you want to discourage, partner will get the wrong message. Likewise, when the roles are reversed and your partner is giving the signal, you must be watching the card he plays to see whether he likes or dislikes the suit.

Let's take a look at two hands to see how important it can be to give an appropriate encouraging or discouraging signal. We will give your partner and the dummy the identical cards in both hands but slightly change your hand and declarer's hand to show how an attitude signal can help defeat the contract in both cases. Your partner starts by leading the ♠Q against a contract of 4♥. Here is the first hand:

Contract: 4♥
Lead: ♠Q

DUMMY
♠ A 7 5
♥ J 9 4 2
♦ K Q 10
♣ K 8 3

PARTNER
♠ Q J 10 6
♥ 8
♦ A 7 6 5 3
♣ 10 9 7

YOU
♠ K 9 2
♥ Q 10 7
♦ 9 8 2
♣ J 5 4 2

DECLARER
♠ 8 4 3
♥ A K 6 5 3
♦ J 4
♣ A Q 6

Declarer wins the first trick with dummy's ♠A and starts to draw trumps by playing the ♥A and ♥K. When the trumps divide 3–1, declarer has a heart loser to go along with the two spade losers and the diamond loser. It is not all over yet, since declarer may be able to discard one of the spade losers on an extra diamond winner in dummy once the ♦A is driven out. So declarer leads the ♦J and your partner wins the ♦A.

What does he do now? There is no problem if you helped out by giving an attitude signal on the first trick by playing the ♠9. Since you encouraged by playing a high card, partner can play another spade. You will win a trick with your ♠K and partner will get a trick with the ♠J. Together with the ♦A and the ♥Q, that is enough to defeat the contract. If partner led any suit other than a spade after winning the ♦A, declarer could win and discard one of his spade losers on dummy's extra diamond winner. He would end up making the contract, losing only one spade trick, one heart trick and one diamond trick.

It looks easy enough for partner to continue leading spades after winning the ♦A. It may appear as though it does not matter whether you play the ♠9 or ♠2 on the first trick. But let's exchange a couple of cards in your hand and declarer's hand while leaving partner's hand and dummy's hand the same:

Contract: 4♥
Lead: ♠Q

DUMMY
♠ A 7 5
♥ J 9 4 2
♦ K Q 10
♣ K 8 3

PARTNER
♠ Q J 10 6
♥ 8
♦ A 7 6 5 3
♣ 10 9 7

YOU
♠ 9 8 4 2
♥ 10 7
♦ 9 8 2
♣ A Q J 2

DECLARER
♠ K 3
♥ A K Q 6 5 3
♦ J 4
♣ 6 5 4

From partner's point of view, everything looks the same. He is defending 4♥ and leads the ♠Q. Declarer wins the first trick with dummy's ♠A and plays the ♥A and ♥K to draw trumps. Next declarer leads the ♦J and partner wins the trick with the ♦A. Look what happens if partner leads another spade! Declarer wins the trick with his carefully concealed ♠K and proceeds to discard one of his club losers on dummy's extra diamond winner. He makes his contract, losing just one diamond trick and two club tricks.

Of course, you do not let partner fall into this trap. When the first trick is won with dummy's ♠A, you give a discouraging signal by playing the ♠2. When partner later wins a trick with the ♦A, your message has told him you do not like spades. Since he has no trumps and declarer has diamond winners in the dummy, the only hope for the defense is that you have some strength in the club suit. Instead of leading another spade, partner leads the ♣10 and dummy's ♣K is trapped. Your side takes three club tricks to go along with the ♦A and you defeat the contract.

It is important to see that partner has no way of knowing whether or not it is correct to lead another spade without your help. Only your attitude signal can give him the help he needs. If you were to automatically play your lowest card, the ♠2, in both cases, he would have to guess what to do later. Naturally he would go wrong about half the time. Once you and your partner start using attitude signals, you get a chance to defeat declarer in both situations.

When to Signal

Once you and your partner start signaling, you can't suddenly stop. In situations similar to those in the previous hands, partner will be expecting to see an attitude signal when he leads the suit. This means that you will have to decide whether you want to encourage or discourage when partner expects an attitude signal. Consider the following layout where partner leads the queen against a notrump contract and the ace is played from dummy:

DUMMY
A 5
PARTNER   YOU
Q   10 7 2

Since partner led the top card of a sequence, declarer must have the king. Should you give a discouraging signal to partner by playing the 2, to tell him you do not have the king? You must always consider the entire hand before deciding whether or not to encourage. If there appears to be a better suit that partner could switch to in order to defeat the contract, you should make a discouraging signal. If you cannot see anything better, you may want to encourage partner to lead the suit again. With the above holding, you probably want to encourage partner since you are holding the 10. Partner must have led the top of a broken sequence, such as Q J 9 6 4, and, if you discourage him by playing the 2, he will not want to lead the suit again, fearing that declarer has both the king and 10. Since you have the missing 10, you can give an encouraging signal by playing the highest card you can afford, the 7. This tells partner it is safe to continue leading the suit.

Here is a hand where you want to discourage partner from leading a suit again, even though you could win the next trick in the suit:

Contract: 4 ♥
Lead: ♦ A

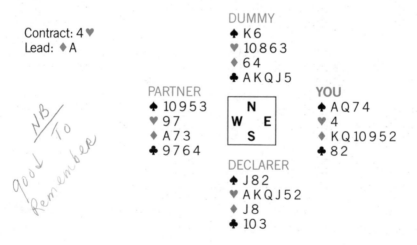

DUMMY
♠ K 6
♥ 10 8 6 3
♦ 6 4
♣ A K Q J 5

PARTNER
♠ 10 9 5 3
♥ 9 7
♦ A 7 3
♣ 9 7 6 4

```
      N
   W     E
      S
```

YOU
♠ A Q 7 4
♥ 4
♦ K Q 10 9 5 2
♣ 8 2

DECLARER
♠ J 8 2
♥ A K Q J 5 2
♦ J 8
♣ 10 3

NB/ To good Remember

The opponents arrive in a contract of 4 ♥ after you have opened the bidding 1 ♦, and your partner dutifully leads your suit. He leads the ♦A since he does not want to lead away from an ace against a suit contract. It may appear that you want to encourage partner to lead the suit again since you can win the next trick. Looking at the entire hand, however, you see that this would allow declarer to make the contract. After winning the second diamond trick, what next? If you lead a spade, declarer will get a trick with dummy's ♠K. If you do not lead a spade, declarer will discard his spade losers on dummy's club winners after drawing trumps. You can no longer defeat the contract.

Instead, you must play the ♦2, a discouraging signal, telling partner you do not want him to lead another diamond. Looking at all those club winners in dummy, partner probably will figure out that you must want him to lead a spade, trapping dummy's ♠K. If he leads a spade, you will get two spade tricks. Then you can then take your second diamond trick to defeat the contract. Of course, when you give a discouraging signal in diamonds, partner may not lead a spade, but at least you have given him a chance to find the winning defense.

How High Is High?

When giving a discouraging signal, you play the lowest card you hold in the suit, and when giving an encouraging signal, you play as high a card as you can afford. Ideally, a card lower than a 6 would usually be interpreted by partner as a discouraging card, whereas a card higher than a 6 would be seen as an encouraging card. Unfortunately, you may not always have the ideal card with which to give a clear-cut signal. Suppose this is the layout:

Partner leads the 5 and declarer wins the trick with dummy's ace. Holding the king, you would like to encourage but the highest card you can afford is the 4. You will have to play the 4 and hope partner is able to interpret that this is the highest card you could afford. Partner should notice that both the 2 and the 3 are missing, and this will give him an indication that you are making an encouraging signal.

You may also get a chance to clarify the situation later in the hand. For example, if you are discarding on another suit, you can throw the 2. Since the first card you played was the 4, partner will know that you meant that as an encouraging signal. The concept of playing a high card followed by a low card to encourage was first developed by Joseph Elwell and is called an *echo*. When you play a high card to encourage, you are starting an echo. You may or may not get an opportunity to complete the high-low echo later in the hand.

This idea can be carried over when you are trying to discourage partner. Suppose you are faced with this situation:

DUMMY
A 6

PARTNER YOU
5 9 8 7

If dummy's ace is played when partner leads the 5, the lowest card you have is the 7. Partner may be able to interpret this as a discouraging card if he can see the remaining smaller cards, but if you get an opportunity later, you can clarify the situation by playing or discarding the 8 (or 9). Since you played low-high rather than high-low, partner will know you are giving a discouraging signal in the suit.

Getting a Ruff

You usually give an encouraging signal when you have strength in the suit partner has led. In a trump contract, however, you may want to encourage partner to lead a suit in which you have shortness because you can trump declarer's winners. Let's look at an example in a complete hand:

Contract: 4♠
Lead: ♥A

DUMMY
♠ Q 10 8 7 4
♥ Q 8 3
♦ K 8 5
♣ A K

PARTNER
♠ 9
♥ A K 9 6 2
♦ 10 9 2
♣ 10 8 4 3

YOU
♠ 5 2
♥ 10 4
♦ A 7 6 4
♣ J 9 7 5 2

N
W E
S

DECLARER
♠ A K J 6 3
♥ J 7 5
♦ Q J 3
♣ Q 6

Partner leads the ♥A against declarer's 4♠ contract. Although you have no high cards in hearts, you want to encourage partner to continue leading the suit since you can trump on the third round. Play the ♥10, an encouraging card. When partner continues by leading the ♥K, you will complete your echo by playing the ♥4. Partner should realize that the reason you are encouraging him to lead hearts is that you started with two of them. When he leads the suit again, you can trump and take your ♦A to defeat the contract. Good cooperation by the defenders.

To see the importance of encouraging in this situation, let's exchange a couple of cards in your hand with those in declarer's hand:

Contract: 4♠
Lead: ♥A

DUMMY
♠ Q 10 8 7 4
♥ Q 8 3
♦ K 8 5
♣ A K

PARTNER
♠ 9
♥ A K 9 6 2
♦ 10 9 2
♣ 10 8 4 3

YOU
♠ 5 2
♥ 10 5 4
♦ A Q 7 4 3
♣ J 9 5

N
W   E
S

DECLARER
♠ A K J 6 3
♥ J 7
♦ J 6
♣ Q 7 6 2

The hands look the same to partner, but if he plays the ♥A, ♥K and another heart, declarer will make the contract. Declarer can discard a diamond loser on dummy's ♥Q and ends up losing only two heart tricks and a diamond trick. To prevent this, you must play a discouraging card, the ♥4, when partner leads the ♥A. Even if partner continues by leading the ♥K, perhaps thinking that you started with a singleton ♥4, you can clarify the situation by playing the ♥5 (or ♥10). Since you played low-high rather than high-low, partner will realize that you are not encouraging him to lead the suit again. Looking at the club winners in dummy, partner probably will lead a diamond through dummy's king, allowing you to take two diamond tricks and defeat the contract. Once again, the only way partner can distinguish between this situation and the previous one is through watching the attitude signal that you give him.

Attitude Discards

While you usually give attitude signals in the suit that is currently being played, you can also give attitude signals for other suits when you are discarding. Consider the following hand:

Contract: 1 NT
Lead: ♥ A

DUMMY
♠ 7 3
♥ 10 8 2
♦ K 10 6 2
♣ K 10 6 2

PARTNER
♠ J 9 8
♥ A K Q 6 3
♦ 8 7
♣ 9 7 4

YOU
♠ 10 6 4 2
♥ 9 5
♦ A Q 9 3
♣ J 5 3

DECLARER
♠ A K Q 5
♥ J 7 4
♦ J 5 4
♣ A Q 8

On partner's heart lead you make a discouraging signal of the ♥ 5 since you do not have any help in the suit. This does not deter partner from continuing to take his five tricks in the suit. On the third heart trick, you must decide what to discard. Stop and think about the message you want to send partner. When partner has finished taking his heart tricks, you want him to lead a diamond, since dummy's king is trapped by your ♦ A and ♦ Q, giving you two tricks in the suit. How can you get this message across to partner? Using encouraging and discouraging signals gives you a number of ways to accomplish what you want, since you will be making three discards. You could start by discarding the ♦ 9, an encouraging card in diamonds. You could follow by discarding the ♦ 3, completing the high-low echo, to confirm your interest in diamonds. Finally, you could discard a small card in one of the other suits to discourage partner from leading that suit. Alternatively, you could start by discarding the ♠ 2 to tell partner you are not interested in spades. Your next discard could be the ♣ 3 to say you are not interested in clubs. On your last discard, you could play the ♦ 9 to encourage partner to lead that suit. Whatever you choose, you should be able to get the message across to partner and defeat the contract.

Putting It Together

Here are some examples of giving attitude signals when partner makes the opening lead against a notrump contract:

DUMMY
A 7 5

PARTNER
4

YOU
Q 8 3

Partner leads the 4 and the ace is played from dummy. Play the **8**, an encouraging signal. Holding the queen, you tell partner you like the suit.

DUMMY
8 6 5

PARTNER
K

YOU
7 4

When partner leads the king and the 5 is played from dummy, play the **4**, a discouraging card. You want to tell partner you have no help for him in the suit. If you were defending a suit contract, you might play an encouraging card from your doubleton, hoping that partner would be able to give you a ruff in the suit before trumps are drawn.

DUMMY
A 3

PARTNER
K

YOU
J 5 2

When partner leads the king and the ace is played from dummy, it looks as though partner is leading from a holding headed by the king, queen and 10. The jack is therefore an important card and you want to encourage by playing the **5**, the highest card you can afford.

DUMMY
A 7 2

PARTNER
4

YOU
Q 6 3

If dummy plays the 2 on partner's lead of the 4, play the **queen**, third hand high. This is not a situation in which you can signal since you have no choice about the card to play.

COUNT SIGNALS

Not all situations require an attitude signal. Partner may already know whether or not you like a particular suit. When you do not need to give an attitude signal, you may be able to tell partner how many cards you hold in the suit. This can be a vital piece of information for partner. Once one member of the partnership knows how many cards the other holds in a suit, he can determine how many cards declarer holds, since he can see how many cards there are in his hand and the dummy. You may be able to take things further than that. Once you know how many cards declarer has in one suit, you may be able to figure out how many cards declarer has in other suits. This will be very helpful when you have to choose which suit to discard.

High-low

How do you tell partner how many cards you have in a suit? You give a *count signal* by playing *high-low to show an even numbers of cards and low-high to show an odd number of cards*. Notice that a count signal does not tell partner exactly how many cards you hold in the suit. If you play high-low, you are showing an even number of cards, which could be two, four, six or eight. Usually, partner will be able to determine exactly how many you have from other clues such as the bidding or the other cards he can see in the suit. Similarly, if you play low-high, you are showing an odd number of cards. Again, partner can hopefully tell whether you are more likely to hold three cards rather than` five or seven.

It is also important to recognize whether the situation calls for an attitude signal or a count signal. After all, a high card followed by a low card is used as an encouraging signal when showing attitude and to show an even number of cards when giving a count signal. Partner will need to know which type of signal applies. A useful guideline is that attitude signals are given priority and you *give a count signal only when attitude clearly does not apply*. A typical situation arises when declarer is playing his own long suit. There is usually no reason to show your attitude toward that suit since declarer is playing it anyway. Instead, it may be more important to tell partner how many cards you hold. This is very useful when partner is considering making a defensive *holdup play*. Let's look at an example in a complete hand:

Contract: 3 NT
Lead: ♠2

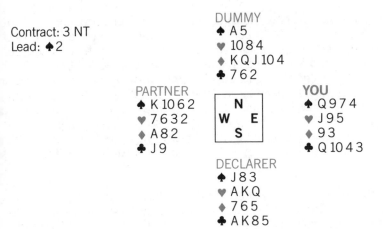

DUMMY
♠ A 5
♥ 10 8 4
♦ K Q J 10 4
♣ 7 6 2

PARTNER
♠ K 10 6 2
♥ 7 6 3 2
♦ A 8 2
♣ J 9

YOU
♠ Q 9 7 4
♥ J 9 5
♦ 9 3
♣ Q 10 4 3

DECLARER
♠ J 8 3
♥ A K Q
♦ 7 6 5
♣ A K 8 5

Partner leads the ♠2 against declarer's 3 NT contract and declarer plays dummy's ♠5. You play the ♠Q, third hand high, winning the trick and lead back a spade, returning partner's suit. Declarer is forced to win this trick with dummy's ♠A. Needing nine tricks, declarer has one sure spade trick, three heart tricks and two club tricks. The remaining tricks he needs can come from the diamond suit, once the ♦A is driven out. There is a problem, however, since there is no outside entry to dummy's diamond winners once they are established, because dummy's ♠A has already been played. Declarer will have to hope that the defenders win the first or second round of diamonds with the ♦A, leaving a small diamond in his hand as an entry to dummy's winners.

Of course, the defenders want to counter declarer's plan by holding up with the ♦A until declarer has none left, leaving the remaining diamond winners stranded in the dummy. When declarer leads a high diamond from dummy, partner does not need to win the first trick, but should he win the second trick or the third trick? He needs to know how many diamonds declarer has so that he will know when declarer has run out. Here is where you can help by giving a count signal. There is obviously no need to show attitude toward the diamond suit since that is the suit declarer is trying to establish. Instead, the specific order in which you play your cards can be used to give a count signal. With two cards in the suit, you want to show an even number by playing high-low. When the first diamond is led from dummy, play the ♦9, starting the "high" part of the signal. When the next diamond is led from dummy, you play the ♦3, completing the "low" part of the signal.

How does partner know that you have two cards in the suit rather than four or six? There are only 13 cards in the suit and partner can see five in dummy and three in his hand. Even before the suit is played, partner knows you cannot have six, since that would add up to more than 13 cards in the suit. In fact, if declarer has opened the bidding 1 NT, showing a balanced hand, he can also figure out ahead of time that you cannot have four cards in the suit since that would mean that declarer started with a singleton and would not have a balanced hand. That will be confirmed anyway when declarer plays a diamond on the second round of the suit. So when you play high-low in diamonds, partner has enough clues to determine that you must be showing exactly two cards in the suit. With five cards in dummy and three in his hand, that leaves declarer with exactly three cards in the suit.

This tells partner that he must hold up the ♦A until the third round of the suit. At that point, declarer will have no diamonds left and dummy's winners will be stranded. After winning the ♦A, partner can take his two remaining spade winners and lead a heart or a club. Declarer is left with only eight tricks, a spade trick, three heart tricks, the first two diamond tricks, and two club tricks. With careful play, the defense prevails once more.

Defeating the contract is not easy. Partner must realize the importance of holding up the ♦A. He must watch your count signal and use the information to figure out exactly when to win the ♦A. You must cooperate by realizing the need to give a count signal in the diamond suit and then by playing your diamonds in the correct order.

Was the count signal really necessary? Could partner not have held up with the ♦A as long as possible just to be sure that declarer had no diamonds left in his hand? That would have worked on this hand. Again let's change the hand slightly leaving partner's cards and the dummy's cards looking exactly the same:

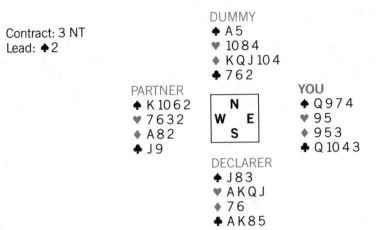

Contract: 3 NT
Lead: ♠2

DUMMY
♠ A 5
♥ 10 8 4
♦ K Q J 10 4
♣ 7 6 2

PARTNER
♠ K 10 6 2
♥ 7 6 3 2
♦ A 8 2
♣ J 9

YOU
♠ Q 9 7 4
♥ 9 5
♦ 9 5 3
♣ Q 10 4 3

DECLARER
♠ J 8 3
♥ A K Q J
♦ 7 6
♣ A K 8 5

The bidding and contract are the same, partner makes the same opening lead, and the play to the first couple of tricks goes the same way. Now, suppose partner waits until the third round of diamonds to win the ♦ A, takes his established spade winners and leads a heart or a club. This time, declarer makes the contract! He has one spade trick, four heart tricks, the two diamond tricks and two club tricks. The extra heart winner in his hand gives him enough tricks once partner ducks the first two rounds of diamonds. To defeat the contract, partner has to win the second round of diamonds with the ♦ A, restricting declarer to only one diamond trick while still stranding the remaining diamond winners in dummy.

How does partner know to win the second diamond trick rather than the third? He has to rely on your count signal to help him out. With an odd number of cards, start by playing a low diamond, the ♦ 3, when the first diamond is led from dummy. On the second round, follow with the ♦ 5 (or ♦ 9), a higher diamond. By playing low-high, you show partner an odd number of diamonds. Since it cannot be one or five, partner can figure out that you have exactly three diamonds. That leaves declarer with exactly two diamonds. By winning the second round of diamonds with the ♦ A, partner prevents declarer from getting any more tricks than he is entitled to in the suit. Again, the contract is defeated through careful defense. Partner has to trust you to give him the right information and you have to cooperate by making the appropriate signal.

Count When Discarding

You can also give count signals when discarding a suit. Of course, both you and partner must realize that the situation calls for count rather than attitude. One of the important reasons for giving a count signal is to help partner know which cards to hold on to while discarding. At least one of the defenders must hold on to enough cards in a suit to prevent declarer's little cards from becoming established through length. Here is a dramatic example:

Contract: 7 NT
Lead: ♣10

DUMMY
♠ J62
♥ J85
♦ AQ85
♣ AKJ

YOU
♠ Q103
♥ Q103
♦ 1042
♣ 10985

PARTNER
♠ 9754
♥ 97642
♦ 9
♣ 762

DECLARER
♠ AK8
♥ AK
♦ KJ763
♣ Q43

This time you will be cast in the role of the defender receiving the signals rather than sending them. The opponents reach a grand slam contract of 7 NT and you make the safe lead of the ♣10, top of a sequence, hoping that one of your queens will later take a trick to defeat the contract. Things will not be easy, however, as declarer quickly takes the first twelve tricks. There are two spade tricks, two heart tricks, five diamond tricks and three club tricks. When it comes to the last trick, declarer has only one card left in his hand. Which card are you holding on to, the ♠Q or the ♥Q?

Looking at declarer's hand, it is easy to see that you have to hold on to the ♠Q rather than the ♥Q, since declarer's last card will be the ♠8. Unfortunately, you cannot see into declarer's hand at the table. When it comes to making that crucial discard on the twelfth trick, will you be able to tell whether declarer's last card is a spade or a heart? You can be sure only if your partner is careful to provide you with the information you need and you watch the cards he plays. Partner, even with no high cards in his hand, has a key role to play for the defense. Since declarer has all the missing high cards, partner does not need to tell you his attitude toward any suit. Instead, this is a situation for count signals. Partner must realize that you will need to know what to hold on to at the end of the hand to defeat the contract.

Partner can start on the first trick, when declarer wins with one of dummy's high clubs. Partner plays the ♣2, starting to play low-high, to show an odd number. The auction and subsequent play will help you confirm that he started with exactly three clubs. This tells you that declarer also has exactly three clubs. When it comes time to find a discard, you can throw away one of your clubs without giving anything away. When declarer starts to take the diamond tricks, partner's first card will be the ♦9. This may look like the start of a high-low to show an even number but, when partner discards on the next diamond trick, you will know that he started with only one diamond and that declarer has five. The crucial information will come from partner's discards on the diamonds as declarer takes his diamond winners. He must throw a high spade and then a low spade to show an even number of spades and a low heart and then a high heart to show an odd number of hearts.

Now it is up to you to put all the information together. With partner showing an even number of spades, you can determine from the auction that he has four rather than two (giving declarer a five-card suit) or six (giving declarer a singleton), leaving declarer with exactly three. When partner shows an odd number of hearts, you can determine that he has five rather than three (giving declarer a four-card suit) or seven (giving declarer a void). This leaves declarer with exactly two hearts. When it comes down to the critical decision, you can confidently discard the ♥Q and hold on to the ♠Q, knowing that declarer started with three spades and only two hearts.

Practice Makes Perfect

Defending in this manner may seem like hard work, but it gets easier with practice. You will soon find that the necessary information can be gathered very quickly and is very helpful on most hands. Experienced defenders probably would have exchanged all the necessary information by the time the first three tricks had been played on the above hand and could defend in comfort after that point.

For example, suppose declarer wins the first club trick and then starts off by taking two diamond tricks. East plays the ♣2 on the first trick, the ♦9 on the second trick and discards the ♥2 on the third trick. Going on the assumption that declarer has a balanced hand, West will know that declarer has three clubs from partner's play of the ♣2 to the first trick and five diamonds since partner showed out on the second trick. That leaves only five cards unaccounted for. East's discard of the ♥2, showing an odd number of hearts, marks declarer with an even number, probably two, leaving room for exactly three spades. West can assume declarer has exactly 3-2-5-3 distribution and defend accordingly. Any subsequent signals by East will merely help confirm West's picture of the hand. No wonder experts always seem to know which cards to hang on to at the end of a hand!

Here are some examples to see how quickly you can get information from your partner's count signals. Declarer has opened the bidding 1 NT and has been left to play there. After winning the first trick in his hand, he is trying to establish a long suit in dummy to which there are no outside entries and you must decide how long to hold up your winner. Assuming that partner is trying to give you a count signal, let's look at how many rounds you plan to hold up in each of the following situations:

DUMMY
K Q J 10 7

PARTNER
2

YOU
A 8 4 3

DECLARER
5

Declarer leads the 5, partner plays the 2 and the king is played from dummy. Partner's 2, a low card, shows an odd number. He cannot have three, since that would give declarer a singleton. Therefore partner must have only one card. That leaves declarer with three cards and you plan to win your ace on the **third round** of the suit.

DUMMY
Q J 10 9 7 **2**

PARTNER
8

YOU
A 6 4

DECLARER
K

Declarer leads the king, partner plays the 8 and the 2 is played from dummy. Partner's 8, a high card, looks like the start of a high-low, showing an even number. If partner has two cards in the suit, declarer has two cards and you plan to win the **second round** of the suit. Of course, partner will show out on the next round if he started with a singleton 8, in which case you will know that declarer has three cards. You will have to wait until the third round before playing your ace.

DUMMY
K Q 10 5 **4**

PARTNER
7

YOU
A 6 3

DECLARER
J

Declarer leads the jack, partner plays the 7 and the 4 is played from dummy. Since you cannot see the 2, it is not clear whether partner is trying to show an even number or an odd number. If partner started with the 7 2, he is starting to play a high-low to show a doubleton. If partner started with 9 8 7, he is starting to play low-high, to show three cards. You will have to **wait** until you see partner's next card before deciding what to do. If partner has a doubleton, you will win the ace on the third round. If partner has three, declarer has only two and you will win the ace on the second round of the suit.

♥ *SUIT PREFERENCE SIGNALS* ♥

When the card you choose to play is clearly not needed for either an attitude signal or a count signal, you may be able to give partner a *suit preference signal*.

High-Low Again

A suit preference signal is used when partner will need to know which of two suits to lead when he next has the opportunity. *A high card shows preference for the higher-ranking suit and a low card shows preference for the lower-ranking suit.* This can be illustrated more clearly with the aid of a complete hand:

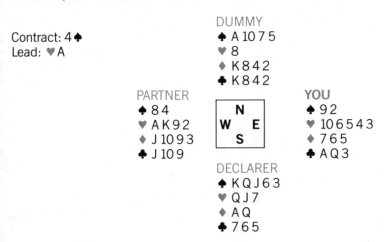

Contract: 4♠
Lead: ♥A

DUMMY
♠ A 10 7 5
♥ 8
♦ K 8 4 2
♣ K 8 4 2

PARTNER
♠ 8 4
♥ A K 9 2
♦ J 10 9 3
♣ J 10 9

YOU
♠ 9 2
♥ 10 6 5 4 3
♦ 7 6 5
♣ A Q 3

N
W   E
S

DECLARER
♠ K Q J 6 3
♥ Q J 7
♦ A Q
♣ 7 6 5

Against declarer's 4♠ contract, your partner leads the ♥A. The singleton heart accompanied by all those trumps in dummy indicates there is little future in that suit. There is not much need for you to tell partner your attitude toward hearts. Whether you like the suit or not, your side is unlikely to get more than one trick in the suit since declarer can trump his losers in the dummy. Likewise, there is not much point in using your signaling opportunity to tell partner how many cards you have in the suit. Instead, the key piece of information partner needs to know is what he should lead next.

Since attitude and count signals do not apply, this is an ideal situation to employ a suit preference signal. Partner is no longer interested in the heart suit and spades is declarer's trump suit. What partner is interested in knowing is which of the remaining two suits, diamonds and clubs, you prefer. Holding the ♣A and ♣Q, you prefer that partner lead a club, the lower-ranking of the two suits. You therefore play the ♥3, a low card as suit preference for the lower-ranking suit. Provided partner is in step with you, he will now lead the ♣J and your side will quickly take three club tricks to defeat the contract. Without the use of a suit preference signal, partner might have guessed to lead a diamond rather than a club. Declarer would win the trick and, after drawing trumps, discard one of his club losers on the extra diamond winner in dummy to make the contract.

If you held the ♦A and ♦Q instead of the ♣A and ♣Q, you would play the ♥10, telling partner you prefer the higher-ranking suit, diamonds. What if you have no preference, perhaps having high cards in both suits or neither? Play a medium-sized heart, such as the ♥5 or ♥6, to indicate no particular preference. Partner would then decide what to do next based on his holdings in the suits and the knowledge that you had no preference.

Finding an Entry

The suit preference signal is much less common than attitude and count signals since the conditions have to be exactly right. Both partners must be aware that the situation does not call for either an attitude signal or a count signal and there must be a choice between only two suits. This is sometimes the circumstance when you need to find an entry to your partner's hand. Take a look at the following layout:

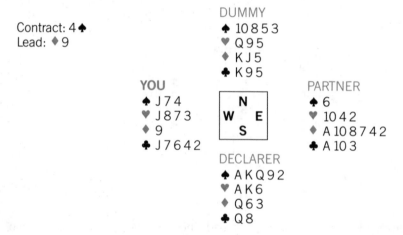

Contract: 4♠
Lead: ♦9

DUMMY
♠ 10 8 5 3
♥ Q 9 5
♦ K J 5
♣ K 9 5

YOU
♠ J 7 4
♥ J 8 7 3
♦ 9
♣ J 7 6 4 2

PARTNER
♠ 6
♥ 10 4 2
♦ A 10 8 7 4 2
♣ A 10 3

DECLARER
♠ A K Q 9 2
♥ A K 6
♦ Q 6 3
♣ Q 8

Against a strong auction to 4♠ by the opponents, you decide to lead your singleton diamond in the hope that partner can lead the suit again for you to trump. You are justly rewarded when partner wins the first trick with the ♦A and leads one back for you to trump. What now? You would like to find an entry back to partner's hand so that he can lead another diamond for you to trump, but is the best chance to lead a heart or a club?

If you and your partner are aware that this is a suit preference situation, there should be no problem. Partner should return his lowest diamond, the ♦2, to tell you that he prefers the lower-ranking suit, clubs. You lead a club to partner's ace and he leads another diamond for you to trump to defeat the contract. If partner had held the ♥A instead of the ♣A, he would have returned the ♦10, asking for the higher-ranking suit, hearts. Notice how partner must anticipate your problem before leading back a diamond for you to trump and must also recognize that there will be only two logical suits for you to choose from, hearts and clubs. If partner had no preference, he could return a medium-sized diamond and leave the decision on what to lead next up to you.

BIDDING REVIEW

Responder's role is that of captain, steering the partnership to the appropriate contract. As opener describes his hand, responder uses the information to determine the level at which the partnership belongs — partscore, game or slam — and the denomination in which the partnership should play. By the time opener has made his rebid, responder is usually in a position to place the contract.

Rebids by Responder When Opener Shows a Minimum Hand

If opener's rebid describes a minimum hand of 13–16 points, responder adds the strength of his hand to that promised by opener and bids accordingly. With 6–10, responder wants to stop in the best partscore and makes a signoff bid. With 11–12, responder wants to invite opener to game and makes an invitational bid. Opener can reject the invitation with 13–14 points and accept with the top of his minimum range, 15–16. With 13–16 points, responder makes sure the partnership gets to game by signing off in game or making a forcing bid. With 17–18 points responder invites opener to slam. With 19 or more, responder makes sure the partnership gets to slam.

Responder can use the following guidelines when choosing his rebid to make sure that opener receives the right type of message:

J.G.

RANGE	OPTIONS	MESSAGE
6–10	• Pass • 1 NT • Two-level bid of a suit already bid by the partnership	Signoff Signoff Signoff
11–12	• 2 NT • Three-level bid of a suit already bid by the partnership	Invitational to game Invitational to game
13–16	• Game (3 NT, 4♥, 4♠) • Bid of a new suit at the three level	Signoff Forcing
17–18	• Bid one level beyond game (4 NT, 5♥, 5♠)	Invitational to slam
19+	• Slam • Bid of a new suit at the three level	Signoff Forcing

OVER FOR
MORE

Rebids by Responder When Opener Shows a Medium Hand

If opener's rebid describes a medium hand of 17–18 points, responder wants to stop in partscore only when he has about 6–8 points; otherwise he wants to be in game or higher. He can use the following guidelines when choosing his rebid:

RANGE	OPTIONS	MESSAGE
6–8	• Pass • Cheapest bid of a suit already bid by the partnership	Signoff Signoff
9–14	• Game (3 NT, 4♥, 4♠) • Bid of a new suit	Signoff Forcing
15–16	• Bid one level beyond game (4 NT, 5♥, 5♠)	Invitational to slam
17+	• Slam • Bid of a new suit	Signoff Forcing

Rebids by Responder When Opener Shows a Maximum Hand

If opener's rebid describes a maximum hand of 19–21 points, the partnership is forced to at least the game level, so any bid by responder below the game level is still forcing. Responder can use the following guidelines:

RANGE	OPTIONS	MESSAGE
6–12	• Pass, if already in game • Game (3 NT, 4♥, 4♠) • Any bid other than game	Signoff Signoff Forcing
13–14	• Bid one level beyond game (4 NT, 5♥, 5♠)	Invitational to slam
15+	• Slam • Any bid other than game	Signoff Forcing

PLAY OF THE HAND REVIEW

The techniques for developing tricks in notrump are all available to declarer when he is trying to eliminate extra losers in a suit contract. In addition, declarer has the possibility of trumping losers or discarding them.

Trumping Losers

Consider the following side suit that you hold in a trump contract:

DUMMY
6

DECLARER
9 4 2

You have three losers in the suit, but since dummy has fewer cards in the suit than you do, there is the opportunity to trump losers in the dummy. To be able to trump your losers in dummy, you must first give up a trick to the opponents so that dummy is void in the suit. You must be careful to keep enough trumps in dummy to ruff your losers. In the above layout, you need two trumps in dummy to ruff two of your losers. Do not forget that the opponents may lead trumps when they get the lead, so you often have to delay drawing trumps when you are planning to trump losers in the dummy. One other thing to watch out for is the entries to your hand. After trumping one of your losers in dummy, you need an entry back to your hand to trump the second loser.

Discarding Losers

Consider the following side suit in a trump contract:

DUMMY
K Q 3

DECLARER
A 6

With only two cards in your hand, and holding both the ace and king, you have no losers in this suit. In fact, holding the queen as well, you have an extra winner in the dummy. This provides the opportunity to discard one of your losers in another suit after taking tricks with the ace and king. Here the extra winner is already established. In some cases, you will have to do the work of creating extra winners in the dummy on which you can discard your losers.

When planning to discard losers on extra winners, you must consider whether or not you can afford to draw trumps first. Whenever possible, you should draw trumps before discarding your losers to avoid the risk of having one of your winners trumped by an opponent. If you may have to give up the lead while drawing trumps, however, you must first decide whether or not you have too many *quick losers*. Quick losers are the tricks the opponents can take as soon as they get the lead. If you have too many quick losers, you will have to discard some of them before giving up the lead.

♥ *SUMMARY* ♥

Since the defenders cannot see each other's hand, they must try to communicate information about their strength and distribution through the use of defensive signals. They have the opportunity to make a signal whenever they have a choice of cards to play to a trick. The types of signals the defenders can use, in order of priority, are:

- **Attitude Signals**— When you want to tell partner whether or not you like a particular suit, *a high card is an encouraging signal, a low card is a discouraging signal*.

- **Count Signals**— When you want to tell partner how many cards you hold in a suit, *a high card followed by a low card shows an even number of cards, a low card followed by a high card shows an odd number of cards*.

- **Suit Preference Signals**— When partner will have a choice of leading one of two suits, *a high card shows preference for the higher-ranking suit, a low card shows preference for the lower-ranking suit*.

Both partners will need to be aware of which type of signal the situation calls for. While one partner is doing the signaling, the other partner must be watching the cards his partner plays in order to receive the signal.

♥ *GROUP ACTIVITIES* ♥

Exercise One — Giving an Attitude Signal

In each of the following layouts, you are defending against a notrump contract and your partner leads the king and the 3 is played from dummy. Decide whether you want to encourage or discourage. Which card do you play?

1)
    DUMMY
    7 **3**
PARTNER   ■   YOU
  K   A 8 2

2)
    DUMMY
    9 8 **3**
PARTNER   ■   YOU
  K   6 4 2

3)
    DUMMY
    9 **3**
PARTNER   ■   YOU
  K   J 7 4

4)
    DUMMY
    3
PARTNER   ■   YOU
  K   A 4 2

5)
    DUMMY
    4 **3**
PARTNER   ■   YOU
  K   8 7

6)
    DUMMY
    6 **3**
PARTNER   ■   YOU
  K   A 7

1) _____   2) _____   3) _____

4) _____   5) _____   6) _____

Exercise Two — When Partner Signals

You are defending a notrump contract with the following hand and lead the ♦Q:

```
              DUMMY
              ♠ J 3 2
              ♥ K 7 4
              ♦ A 2
              ♣ K Q 9 7 4
     YOU
     ♠ K 5 4
     ♥ 8 6 3
     ♦ Q J 10 5
     ♣ 8 5 3
```

What can you deduce about partner's hand under each of the following circumstances:

1) Declarer wins the first trick in dummy and partner plays the ♦3.
2) Declarer wins the first trick in dummy and partner plays the ♦8.
3) After winning the first trick, declarer starts taking his club tricks and partner discards the ♠6 on the third round.
4) After winning the first trick, declarer starts taking his club tricks and partner discards the ♥9 on the third round.

1) _____ 2) _____ 3) _____ 4) _____

Exercise Three — Giving a Count Signal

You are defending a contract of 6 NT holding the following hand:

♠ 9 7 6 5 2
♥ 8 7 5 3
♦ 10 6 4
♣ J

Declarer starts taking tricks in the club suit and you have to discard after the first round. With no information to give partner other than the number of cards you have in each suit, which two cards would you discard to give partner one of the following signals:

1) The number of cards you hold in the spade suit.
2) The number of cards you hold in the heart suit.
3) The number of cards you hold in the diamond suit.

1) _____ 2) _____ 3) _____

Exercise Four — Interpreting a Count Signal

You lead the ♠4 against a contract of 3 NT after an opening bid of 1 NT on your right and see the following dummy:

DUMMY
♠ A
♥ 974
♦ KQJ109
♣ J763

YOU
♠ Q8542
♥ 86
♦ A83
♣ 842

After declarer wins dummy's ♠A, he starts leading dummy's diamonds to drive out your ♦A. Which round should you take your ♦A if:

1) Partner plays the ♦7 and then the ♦4.
2) Partner plays the ♦2 and then the ♦6.
3) Partner plays the ♦5 and then discards the ♥2.

1) _____   2) _____   3) _____

Exercise Five — Giving Suit Preference

Partner leads what looks like a singleton club against declarer's contract of 4♥. After winning your ♣A, which club do you lead back for partner to ruff from each of the following hands?

1) ♠ A964   2) ♠ 765   3) ♠ 964
   ♥ 104   ♥ 104   ♥ 1043
   ♦ 765   ♦ A964   ♦ 765
   ♣ A1062   ♣ A1062   ♣ A1062

1) _____   2) _____   3) _____

Exercise Six — Putting It Together

Your hold the following hand:

♠ K92
♥ 842
♦ K763
♣ 954

During the hand, you get an opportunity to give partner a signal.

1) Which card would you play to tell partner that you would like him to lead a spade?
2) Which card would you play to tell partner that you do not like clubs?
3) Which card would you play to start to give a count signal in hearts?
4) Which card would you play to start to give a count signal in diamonds?
5) Which club could you play to tell partner that you prefer spades to hearts?

1) _____ 2) _____ 3) _____ 4) _____ 5) _____

Exercise Seven — Review of Rebids by Responder

Your partner opens the bidding 1♦, you respond 1♠ and partner rebids 1 NT. What do you rebid with each of the following hands?

1) ♠ K 10 8 6
   ♥ J 9 3 6
   ♦ 7 4
   ♣ Q 10 8 2

2) ♠ Q 9 8 3 6
   ♥ 2
   ♦ J 10 7 5 3
   ♣ K 8 5

3) ♠ J 9 8 6 5 4
   ♥ K 7 5
   ♦ 6 3
   ♣ J 7 5

1) ____P____

2) ____2 D____

3) ____2 S____

4) ♠ 10 9 7 3
   ♥ K Q 5 11
   ♦ J 9
   ♣ A J 8 2

5) ♠ K Q 10 7 6 3
   ♥ J 10+3
   ♦ A 9 7
   ♣ 9 5 3

6) ♠ A Q 8 3
   ♥ 9 3 10
   ♦ K J 8 5 2
   ♣ 7 5

4) ____2 N____

5) ____3 S____

6) ____3 D____

7) ♠ Q 10 9 3
   ♥ A 9 8 13
   ♦ K 8 3
   ♣ K J 7

8) ♠ K J 9 7 5 2
   ♥ K 6 11
   ♦ A 8 4
   ♣ 6 5

9) ♠ A J 9 7 4
   ♥ K Q 6 4 2 11+
   ♦ 3
   ♣ J 6

7) ____3 N____

8) ____4 S____

9) ____3 H____

Exercise Eight — Developing Tricks in a Suit Contract

How would you plan to make your contract of 4♠ on the following hand after the opening lead of the ♣Q? Can you draw trumps immediately?

DUMMY
♠ Q J 9 3
♥ A K 8 3
♦ 6
♣ 9 5 4 2

LEAD
♣ Q

DECLARER
♠ 10 8 6 5 2
♥ Q 2
♦ A K 5
♣ A 7 3

Exercise Nine — Giving Attitude

Turn up the cards on the first pre-dealt hand. Put each hand dummy style at the edge of the table in front of each player.

Dealer: North

```
                        ♠ 10 8 7 3
                        ♥ A K 6
                        ♦ Q J 10 2
                        ♣ K 9
        ♠ A 6          ┌─────────┐       ♠ 4 2
        ♥ 10 9 8 5     │   N     │       ♥ Q 7 2
        ♦ 9 7 3        │ W   E   │       ♦ A 6 4
        ♣ 10 7 5 2     │   S     │       ♣ A 8 6 4 3
                       └─────────┘
                        ♠ K Q J 9 5
                        ♥ J 4 3
                        ♦ K 8 5
                        ♣ Q J
```

The Bidding

What would North open the bidding? East and West pass throughout. What would South respond? How does North show both the strength of his hand and his support for responder's suit? Does South know the level at which the partnership belongs? Does South know the denomination in which the partnership belongs? What does South rebid? How does the auction proceed from there? Who is declarer?

The Defense

Which player makes the opening lead? What would the opening lead be? Which card would East play on the first trick if dummy wins the trick? Why?

The Play

Review the steps in declarer's PLAN. How does declarer plan to make the contract?

Exercise Ten — Getting a Ruff

Turn up the cards on the second pre-dealt hand. Put each hand dummy style at the edge of the table in front of each player.

Dealer: East

```
                        ♠ 10 5
                        ♥ A 10 4 2
                        ♦ 10 5
                        ♣ K J 10 9 2

   ♠ A K 8 3         N            ♠ Q 9 6 4 2
   ♥ 7            W     E         ♥ K Q 6 5
   ♦ Q 9 6            S           ♦ J 7 2
   ♣ A Q 8 6 5                    ♣ 3

                        ♠ J 7
                        ♥ J 9 8 3
                        ♦ A K 8 4 3
                        ♣ 7 4
```

The Bidding

East and South pass. What would West open the bidding? North passes. Which of his suits does East bid at the one level? Why? South passes? Counting dummy points, does West have a minimum, medium or maximum hand in support of partner's suit? What does West rebid? North passes. What does East know about West's hand? What does East rebid? What is the contract? Who is declarer?

The Defense

Which player makes the opening lead? What would the opening lead be? Which card would North play? Why? What will South lead next?

The Play

Review the steps in declarer's PLAN. How does declarer plan to make the contract?

Exercise Eleven — Giving Count

Turn up the cards on the third pre-dealt hand. Put each hand dummy style at the edge of the table in front of each player.

Dealer: South

```
                    ♠ K Q J 9
                    ♥ 9 3
                    ♦ A 7 6
                    ♣ J 10 6 5
   ♠ 7 6 3        ┌──────────┐      ♠ A 10 5
   ♥ A K 5        │    N     │      ♥ 10 7 2
   ♦ Q 8 4        │ W     E  │      ♦ K J 10 5 2
   ♣ A K Q 3      │    S     │      ♣ 8 4
                  └──────────┘
                    ♠ 8 4 2
                    ♥ Q J 8 6 4
                    ♦ 9 3
                    ♣ 9 7 2
```

The Bidding

South passes. What is West's opening bid? North passes. What does East respond? South passes. Does West accept East's invitation? How does the bidding proceed from there? What is the contract? Who is declarer?

The Defense

Which player makes the opening lead? What would the opening lead be? Which card does South play on the first trick? Why? When declarer leads diamonds, what card should South play? Why? Should North win the first diamond trick? If not, which round should North win? Why?

The Play

Review the steps in declarer's PLAN. How does declarer plan to make the contract?

Exercise Twelve — Giving Suit Preference

Turn up the cards on the fourth pre-dealt hand. Put each hand dummy style at the edge of the table in front of each player.

Dealer: West

```
                    ♠ A J 10 7 2
                    ♥ Q 8 6 4
                    ♦ 10 7
                    ♣ A K

   ♠ Q 5            ┌─────────┐        ♠ 8 4
   ♥ 9              │    N    │        ♥ A K 10 2
   ♦ K J 9 4 2      │  W   E  │        ♦ A 8 5 3
   ♣ J 9 6 3 2      │    S    │        ♣ 10 8 4
                    └─────────┘
                    ♠ K 9 6 3
                    ♥ J 7 5 3
                    ♦ Q 6
                    ♣ Q 7 5
```

The Bidding

West passes. What is North's opening bid? East passes. How does South show the support for partner's suit and the strength of his hand? West passes. What does North know about the combined strength of the hands? What does North rebid? What is the contract? Who is declarer?

The Defense

Which player makes the opening lead? What would the opening lead be? Which card does East play to the second trick? Which card does East play to the third trick? Why? Which suit does West lead to the fourth trick? Why?

The Play

Review the steps in declarer's PLAN. How does declarer plan to make the contract?

LESSON 6

Developing Defensive Tricks

Taking Sure Tricks
Promoting Tricks
Establishing Long Suits
Finessing
Trumping
Bidding Review
Play of the Hand Review
Summary

Workshop Material
Group Activities

The defenders get tricks the same way as declarer: they take their sure tricks, promote winners, establish long suits, take finesses and trump declarer's winners. They cannot see each other's hand, however, and it is sometimes more difficult for them to get the tricks to which they are entitled. They need to recognize the various possibilities, often using partner's signals to guide them. In this lesson, we look at the techniques the defenders use to get the tricks coming to them, starting with what might seem straightforward, taking their established winners.

♥ TAKING SURE TRICKS ♥

When a suit is divided evenly between the defenders' hands, there is usually no problem taking sure tricks, those that are already established as winners. The suit itself provides the necessary entries back and forth between the two hands. When the suit is unevenly divided, winners may get stranded if the defenders are not careful.

Unblocking

When declarer is faced with the problem of taking sure tricks in a suit that is unevenly divided, he follows the guideline of *playing the high card from the short side first*. This is straightforward for declarer, who can see all the cards in both his hand and the dummy, but requires some imagination from the defenders' perspective. Consider this suit layout, where partner leads the king against a notrump contract:

Through no fault of your own, the defense has a problem declarer does not face. If declarer were playing this suit, he would start by leading a small card to the ace, winning the first trick in the short side, and then leading the 6 back over to his remaining winners. Unfortunately, your partner could not see your hand when he made the opening lead and, not knowing where the ace was, made the normal lead of the top of his three touching honors. It is up to you to recover by overtaking partner's king with the ace and leading back the 6 to his established winners. In the lesson on third-hand play, we saw that this is called *unblocking* the suit. The general idea is that you want to end up with a small card, not a winner, as the last card in the suit when partner is trying to take tricks in his long suit. Once you are able to visualize the problem, it is not so difficult to come up with the solution.

Signaling

In the above layout, you could afford to overtake partner's king with your ace since your side had all of the high cards in the suit. The defenders will not always be able to afford to play two of their high cards on the same trick. Sometimes, however, it will not be necessary. Consider this layout where, once again, partner leads the king against a notrump contract:

DUMMY
10 9 6 2

PARTNER
K Q J 3

YOU
A 8 4

DECLARER
7 5

If you overtake partner's king with your ace and lead the suit back, partner will take his queen and jack, but then dummy's 10 will become established as a trick. You get only three of the four tricks to which you are entitled. You have two smaller cards to go along with your ace, so you do not need to unblock on the first trick by playing the ace on partner's king. Now that you know about attitude signals, make an encouraging signal on partner's king by playing the 8, the highest card you can afford.

Now, it is up to partner to cooperate in taking the tricks to which you are entitled. When his king wins the trick, he may be tempted to continue by leading the queen or jack. This would make it impossible for your side to take the first four tricks. Instead, seeing your encouraging 8, partner must lead a low card next, the 3, over to your ace. Since you are the shorter side, partner wants you to play your high card first. You lead back the 4 and your side quickly has the first four tricks.

Blocked Suits

It will not always be possible to unblock your sure tricks as in the earlier examples. Suppose we change the previous layout slightly:

DUMMY
10 9 6 2

PARTNER
K Q J 3

YOU
A 4

DECLARER
8 7 5

As declarer, you would have no trouble taking four tricks in this suit, but partner, with no x-ray vision available, leads the king against a notrump contract. The suit is now hopelessly blocked. If you play the ace on partner's king, declarer will eventually get a trick with dummy's 10. If you play the 4, partner can lead a small card to your ace, but you have no small cards left to lead back to partner's queen and jack.

After partner's lead of the king, the best you can usually do is to play the 4, to avoid giving declarer a trick in the suit. Although this is a small card and may look like a discouraging signal to partner, you can hope partner realizes the situation when declarer does not win the trick with the ace. If partner now plays his 3 over to your ace, you will have to try to find an entry to partner's hand in another suit.

You sometimes can recover from situations similar to this when defending against a suit contract. Consider the following hand:

Contract: 4♠
Lead: ♣K

DUMMY
♠ K Q 7 3
♥ K Q J 6
♦ 9 6
♣ J 8 5

PARTNER
♠ 10 4
♥ 9 4
♦ J 7 5 2
♣ K Q 10 7 3

YOU
♠ 9 6
♥ A 10 7 5 3
♦ 10 8 4 3
♣ A 2

DECLARER
♠ A J 8 5 2
♥ 8 2
♦ A K Q
♣ 9 6 4

Partner leads the ♣K against declarer's 4♠ contract and you are faced with a problem. It looks as though your side is entitled to three tricks in clubs as well as the ♥A, enough to defeat the contract. If you play the ♣2 on the first trick, however, the suit is blocked. Even if partner leads a small club over to your ♣A, there is no way to get back to his hand. Declarer will eventually be able to discard his club loser and make the contract. If you overtake partner's ♣K with your ♣A, dummy's ♣J could become a winner on the third trick.

Since you are defending a suit contract, however, there is a potential solution to your problem. Partner can lead another club and you can trump dummy's ♣J. Instead of taking three club tricks, you end up taking two club tricks and a trump trick! Partner will have to recognize why you overtook his ♣K with your ♣A rather than giving an encouraging signal. Only partnership cooperation can help you untangle the four sure tricks you started with against declarer's 4♠ contract.

PROMOTING TRICKS

When the defenders are trying to promote tricks by driving out declarer's high cards, they must again be aware of the problem of entries between the two hands.

More Signaling

Declarer follows the guideline of playing the high card from the short side when promoting tricks. As a defender, you may have to be careful to apply the same principle. In this example, it is on the second round that the suit may become blocked:

```
            DUMMY
             A 3
PARTNER             YOU
K Q 10 2            J 8 4
          DECLARER
           9 7 6 5
```

Partner leads the king, top of a broken sequence, against declarer's notrump contract and the ace is played from dummy. Holding the jack, you give an encouraging signal by playing the 8. If you get the lead next, lead the jack, high card from the short side, and then the 4 over to partner's winners. If partner gets the lead before you do, things will be more difficult but the same principle applies. Based on the encouraging signal, partner must lead the 2 over to your jack, playing your high card first, so that you can then lead the 4 back to his winners.

Here is a similar situation. This time, you are the defender making the opening lead against a notrump contract. We will not give you the benefit of seeing partner's or declarer's hand right away.

Contract: 3 NT
Lead: ♦ 6

```
                    DUMMY
                    ♠ A 9 4
                    ♥ K 8 3
                    ♦ 7 4
                    ♣ Q J 10 6 2
          YOU
          ♠ 8 6 2
          ♥ 7 6 4
          ♦ K 9 8 6 3
          ♣ K 5
```

You lead the ♦6, the ♦4 is played from dummy, partner plays the ♦J and declarer wins the ♦A. Declarer plays a small spade over to dummy's ♠A and then leads dummy's ♣Q, taking a finesse. After winning the ♣K, what do you lead next?

Since the ♦A has been driven out, your ♦K is established as a winner. It looks as though partner has the ♦Q, since declarer won the first trick with the ♦A. Partner would have played the ♦J if he held both the ♦Q and ♦J, since third hand plays the lower of touching cards when there is a choice. As you have the length, you want the next trick to be won from the short side. Lead the ♦3, expecting partner to have the ♦Q and hoping he has another diamond to lead back to your established diamonds.

The complete hand might look like this:

Contract: 3 NT
Lead: ♦6

DUMMY
♠ A 9 4
♥ K 8 3
♦ 7 4
♣ Q J 10 6 2

YOU
♠ 8 6 2
♥ 7 6 4
♦ K 9 8 6 3
♣ K 5

N
W   E
S

PARTNER
♠ J 10 7 3
♥ Q J 10 5
♦ Q J 2
♣ 9 7

DECLARER
♠ K Q 5
♥ A 9 2
♦ A 10 5
♣ A 8 4 3

The play of the diamond suit is the key to the defense. When you get the lead with the ♣K, if you play your ♦K and a diamond to partner's ♦Q, the suit blocks. Your side gets two diamond tricks but partner has no small card left to get to your winners. It is the play to the second diamond trick that is important. You must lead a low diamond.

More Unblocking

There are times when you need to unblock on the first trick. For example, consider this layout:

```
          DUMMY
           A 8 3
PARTNER    ████    YOU
Q J 10 6 4 ████    K 2
          DECLARER
           9 7 5
```

If partner could see your hand, he would lead a small card to your king, planning to play the high card from the short side first. However, on defense partner's normal opening lead is the queen. Whether or not declarer plays dummy's ace on the first trick, you must unblock by playing the king. The underlying theme in unblocking is that when partner has the length you *want to be left with a small card* rather than a high card as your last card in the suit. This idea can be helpful in more complicated situations such as this:

```
          DUMMY
           A 3
PARTNER    ████    YOU
K Q 10 8 4 ████    J 2
          DECLARER
           9 7 6 5
```

Partner leads the king, top of a broken sequence, against a notrump contract and declarer plays dummy's ace. If you play the 2, the remaining cards will look like this:

```
          DUMMY
            3
PARTNER    ████    YOU
Q 10 8 4   ████    J
          DECLARER
           9 7 6
```

If partner next gets the lead for your side, he can play a small card to your jack but you have no small card left to return to partner's winners. If you get the lead first, you can lead the jack, but if partner overtakes with the queen and plays the 10, declarer's 9 becomes an established winner.

Is there anything you can do? Knowing that you generally want to have a small card left rather than a high card when trying to establish partner's long suit, play the jack on the first trick, leaving this layout:

```
          DUMMY
            3
PARTNER    ████    YOU
Q 10 8 4   ████    2
          DECLARER
           9 7 6
```

If partner next gets the lead, you are no better off. He cannot take his winners without establishing declarer's 9 as a trick. The difference arises if you get the next opportunity to lead the suit. When you lead the 2, declarer's 9 is trapped. Whichever card declarer plays, your partner can take all four tricks.

Positions such as this may be difficult to foresee when you are defending. Nonetheless, they become easier to visualize once you are aware that the defenders, like declarer, must try to play the high card from the short side first when promoting tricks.

♥ *ESTABLISHING LONG SUITS* ♥

Against notrump contracts the defenders want to take tricks from their long suits just as declarer does. They are faced with the same problems. They have to be willing to lose the lead while establishing their winners and they have to be aware of the importance of having an entry to get to their established winners.

Returning Partner's Suit

When trying to establish a long suit, the defenders try to follow the same principles as declarer. That is why guidelines such as *return your partner's suit* can be useful. The defenders want to adopt a consistent approach to the defense. If one partner is trying to establish his long suit, it does not help if his partner is working at cross-purposes to try to establish his own suit. When making the opening lead against a notrump contract, partner has picked a suit to establish. Help him out by leading his suit back whenever you get the opportunity unless you can clearly see a better alternative. Here is a typical example:

Contract: 3 NT
Lead: ♠3

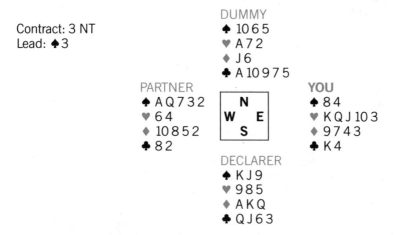

```
                    DUMMY
                    ♠ 10 6 5
                    ♥ A 7 2
                    ♦ J 6
                    ♣ A 10 9 7 5
PARTNER                              YOU
♠ A Q 7 3 2     ┌─────────┐         ♠ 8 4
♥ 6 4           │    N    │         ♥ K Q J 10 3
♦ 10 8 5 2      │  W   E  │         ♦ 9 7 4 3
♣ 8 2           │    S    │         ♣ K 4
                └─────────┘
                    DECLARER
                    ♠ K J 9
                    ♥ 9 8 5
                    ♦ A K Q
                    ♣ Q J 6 3
```

On partner's lead of the ♠3, the ♠5 is played from dummy, you play third hand high, the ♠8, and declarer wins the trick with the ♠9. Declarer then plays the ♣Q, taking a finesse which loses to your ♣K. You may have been a little disappointed to see partner's opening lead since you have such a fine heart suit. If partner had originally led a heart, you could have established four heart tricks, enough for you to defeat the contract when you won the ♣K. It may occur to you to lead a heart now, establishing four heart tricks for the defense, but this would be inconsistent with partner's line of defense. Instead, return the ♠4, partner's suit, hoping the layout is something like that on the actual hand. The spade return is the only way to defeat the contract. If you lead a heart, declarer will win the ♥A and scamper home with nine tricks.

When returning partner's suit, look at your **remaining** cards in his suit and return the card that you would normally lead in his suit: top of a doubleton, top of touching high cards or low from three or more cards (e.g., *J* 4, 9 4 *2*, *10* 9 5, Q 6 *3*).

Ducking

Consider how declarer would play the following suit if he had no entries to dummy other than the high cards in the suit:

<table>
<tr><td>·DUMMY
A K 7 5 3</td><td></td></tr>
</table>

If declarer played the ace and king and then gave up a trick, the remaining two cards in dummy would be established as winners, but would be stranded. Instead, declarer must *duck* either the first or second trick, keeping a high card in dummy as an entry. Declarer takes his losses early to retain communications between the two hands.

The defenders must employ similar tactics on the following hand. Declarer is in a contract of 3 NT after you have opened the bidding 1♠. Partner dutifully leads your suit, the ♠10, top of a doubleton:

Contract: 3 NT
Lead: ♠10

DUMMY
♠ J 8 2
♥ A 7
♦ K 8 4
♣ J 10 9 5 2

PARTNER
♠ 10 4
♥ 10 8 6 3
♦ 10 9 5 3 2
♣ K 4

YOU
♠ A K 9 7 3
♥ Q J 4 2
♦ Q 6
♣ 7 3

DECLARER
♠ Q 6 5
♥ K 9 5
♦ A J 7
♣ A Q 8 6

When declarer plays a low spade from dummy, here is your chance to shine by playing low. If you win the trick with the ♠K and play the ♠A and another spade, you will establish two more winners in the spade suit. Unfortunately, they will be stranded, since it is unlikely you can gain the lead and partner has no spades left if he gains the lead. Instead, take your losses early and duck the first spade trick. You are hoping partner will get the lead and will have a spade left to lead to your established winners. You can play the ♠9 as an encouraging signal to partner to lead the suit again if he gets an opportunity. Declarer wins the trick with the ♠Q, plays a small heart to dummy's ♥A and tries the club finesse by leading the ♣J from dummy, hoping you have the ♣K. Unluckily for declarer, your partner wins the trick with the ♣K and is now able to lead the carefully preserved ♠4 over to your spade winners. You always had to lose one spade trick. By choosing to lose it early, you left partner with a spade to return to your winners.

The need to let declarer win tricks while establishing your long suit often arises when defending a contract. Consider the following hand. Again you are defending 3 NT. This time, partner is on lead and leads the ♥4, fourth highest from his longest suit:

Contract: 3 NT
Lead: ♥4

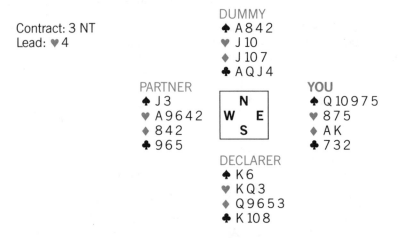

DUMMY
♠ A 8 4 2
♥ J 10
♦ J 10 7
♣ A Q J 4

PARTNER
♠ J 3
♥ A 9 6 4 2
♦ 8 4 2
♣ 9 6 5

YOU
♠ Q 10 9 7 5
♥ 8 7 5
♦ A K
♣ 7 3 2

DECLARER
♠ K 6
♥ K Q 3
♦ Q 9 6 5 3
♣ K 10 8

Declarer wins the first trick with dummy's ♥10 and, needing to promote tricks in the diamond suit to make the contract, leads dummy's ♦J which you win with the ♦K. You return partner's suit. Declarer plays the ♥Q, and now it is partner's turn to stop and think. Partner knows declarer has the ♥K since you would have played that card earlier if you held it. If he wins the ♥A and leads another heart, your last heart disappears. He establishes his remaining hearts as winners, but there will be no entry to his hand. Partner must duck the heart trick, giving declarer a second trick in the suit. When declarer leads another diamond to drive out your remaining ♦A, you still have a small heart to lead back. Partner wins declarer's ♥K with his ♥A and can now take his other two established heart winners to defeat the contract.

Notice that both defenders have to be on their toes to defeat the contract. You must continue to return partner's suit, even though declarer wins the first two heart tricks. Partner must recognize the need to duck a heart trick to preserve communication between the defenders' hands. Notice also how both defenders must be careful to hang on to all their small hearts. If declarer took his four club tricks before playing diamonds, neither defender could afford to discard a heart.

♥ *FINESSING* ♥

The defenders trap declarer's high cards using the principle of the finesse in the same way that declarer traps their high cards. The defenders have to visualize where there is an opportunity to finesse based on the cards they can see and partner's signals.

Partnership Cooperation

Let's consider how the defenders approach a finesse. You are defending against a suit contract and partner leads the ace:

DUMMY
1075
PARTNER   **YOU**
AKJ4   862
DECLARER
Q93

If partner continues by leading the king, declarer's queen will become established as a winner. First you must make use of an attitude signal and discourage partner by playing your lowest card, the 2. Partner has to recognize this as a discouraging signal and refrain from continuing to lead the suit. Instead, partner will have to *shift* to another suit, hoping to find an entry to your hand. When you do get the lead, you must cooperate by leading the original suit back, recognizing why partner did not continue leading it from his side.

Notice declarer would not have the same problem deciding how to play such a combination. Looking at both hands, he would see the need to lead the suit from your hand in order to trap the missing queen. The defenders have to work a lot harder to bring about the same result. Let's see how it might look in practice, this time putting you on lead:

Contract: 4♠
Lead: ♦A

DUMMY
♠ AQ75
♥ K75
♦ 1083
♣ A97

YOU
♠ 82
♥ 10983
♦ AKJ2
♣ J64

PARTNER
♠ K6
♥ 642
♦ 954
♣ Q10832

DECLARER
♠ J10943
♥ AQJ
♦ Q76
♣ K5

Against the 4♠ contract you lead the ♦A and partner plays the ♦4. Since you can see the ♦2 in your hand and the ♦3 in dummy, you know your partner has played his lowest diamond, a discouraging signal. It looks as if declarer must have the ♦Q. Since you want diamonds led from your partner's side in order to trap declarer's ♦Q, you must be patient and switch to another suit. Your partner's ♦4 is only an attitude signal, not a suit preference signal, so he has had no opportunity to tell you which of the other suits he prefers. That part will have to be up to you, looking at the dummy and gathering any useful information from the bidding. On this hand, it turns out not to make much difference, as long as you do not lead another diamond. Suppose you switch to the ♥10. Declarer will win in his hand and take the spade finesse, hoping you have the ♠K. Partner will win this trick and now it is up to him. He has to recognize why you did not continue leading diamonds after his discouraging signal and visualize the type of holding you must have. You must need diamonds led from his side, so he duly leads back a diamond and your patience is rewarded when you get two more diamond tricks to defeat the contract.

Here is a similar type of situation defending against a notrump contract:

Contract: 3 NT
Lead: ♦Q

```
                    DUMMY
                    ♠ K62
                    ♥ Q652
                    ♦ K8
                    ♣ QJ109

      PARTNER                      YOU
      ♠ 10985        N             ♠ AQ
      ♥ 1093      W     E          ♥ J874
      ♦ QJ97         S             ♦ 6542
      ♣ K6                         ♣ 842

                    DECLARER
                    ♠ J743
                    ♥ AK
                    ♦ A103
                    ♣ A753
```

Partner leads the ♦Q, top of a broken sequence, and declarer wins the first trick with dummy's ♦K, carefully keeping the ♦A and ♦10 in his hand. Since you have no help in the diamond suit, play a discouraging card, the ♦2. Declarer next leads dummy's ♣Q and takes a finesse, losing to partner's ♣K. Partner knows declarer holds the ♦A, since you would have won the first trick if you held that card. His problem is who holds the ♦10? Having led from a suit headed by the ♦Q and ♦J, partner has to hope you would recognize the importance of the ♦10. If you held it, you would have given an encouraging signal rather than a discouraging signal. Partner, therefore, correctly assumes declarer holds the ♦10. He realizes it would be unsafe for him to lead the suit again from his side. Instead, he must patiently switch to another suit.

On the actual hand, it does not matter which other suit he leads next, but suppose he leads a spade and you win the trick with the ♠Q after declarer plays a low spade from dummy. Things are back in your ballpark. Instead of happily taking your ♠A as well, you must ask yourself why partner did not continue leading diamonds from a suit headed by the queen and jack. When you visualize the potential problem, you can now switch back to diamonds from your side, trapping declarer's ♦10. The defense can now establish two diamond tricks to go along with their two spade tricks and their club trick.

Leading Through Strength

Another useful guideline to help the defenders visualize finessing situations is *lead through strength and lead up to weakness*. The logic behind the guideline comes from an examination of the following layout:

DUMMY
A Q 10

PARTNER
9 7 3

YOU
K J 8 5

DECLARER
6 4 2

For the defenders to get all the tricks to which they are entitled, partner needs to lead through dummy's strength, trapping dummy's high cards. Partner would also be leading up to the weakness in declarer's hand. Contrast this with having you lead the suit. You would be leading through declarer's weakness and up into the strength in the dummy, not an effective way to try for tricks in the suit. Let's look at a hand:

Contract: 2 ♥
Lead: ♦A

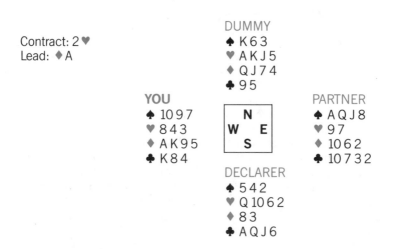

DUMMY
♠ K 6 3
♥ A K J 5
♦ Q J 7 4
♣ 9 5

YOU
♠ 10 9 7
♥ 8 4 3
♦ A K 9 5
♣ K 8 4

PARTNER
♠ A Q J 8
♥ 9 7
♦ 10 6 2
♣ 10 7 3 2

DECLARER
♠ 5 4 2
♥ Q 10 6 2
♦ 8 3
♣ A Q J 6

Against declarer's 2♥ contract, you start off leading the ♦A and get a discouraging signal of the ♦2 from partner. It does not look as though it would do any good to lead another diamond — you would only be helping declarer by establishing dummy's ♦Q and ♦J as winners. To which suit should you switch? Although you have some strength in clubs and not much in spades, you might use the guideline to help you. You want to lead through dummy's strength in spades, up to declarer's hoped-for weakness in the suit, rather than leading through dummy's weakness in clubs up to declarer's assumed strength. You do not actually know what declarer has in spades and clubs, but you can see your hand and the dummy. With that information, you try to imagine what declarer and partner might hold. On the actual hand the defense can defeat the contract if you switch to a spade. Dummy's ♠K is trapped and partner can take three spade tricks. Partner can cooperate after winning his spade tricks by leading clubs, through declarer's assumed strength, up to the weakness in dummy. You will get a trick with your ♣K to go with the three spade tricks and two diamond tricks, just enough to defeat the contract. Here is a similar example:

Contract: 4♥
Lead: ♦10

DUMMY
♠ 5 3 2
♥ K 10 7 3
♦ K Q J
♣ A J 5

PARTNER
♠ A 7 4
♥ 9
♦ 10 9 8 6 2
♣ 10 7 6 3

YOU
♠ Q J 10 9
♥ 8 5
♦ A 7 5
♣ Q 9 4 2

DECLARER
♠ K 8 6
♥ A Q J 6 4 2
♦ 4 3
♣ K 8

Partner leads the top of his diamond sequence against declarer's 4♥ contract and you win with the ♦A. Although your first consideration is to return partner's suit, you can see that dummy has nothing but winners in that suit. Instead, you want to switch to a suit that will help your side take its tricks. The spade weakness and club strength in dummy convince you to switch to a spade, through declarer's assumed strength and up to dummy's weakness. You lead back the ♠Q and declarer's ♠K is trapped. The defense quickly takes three spade tricks to defeat the contract. Spades have to be led from your side, not partner's, to trap declarer's ♠K.

♥ *TRUMPING* ♥

The defenders also take tricks in a suit contract by trumping declarer's winners when they get the opportunity. This is similar to the way declarer trumps losers in dummy.

Giving Partner a Ruff

Take a look at the following hand:

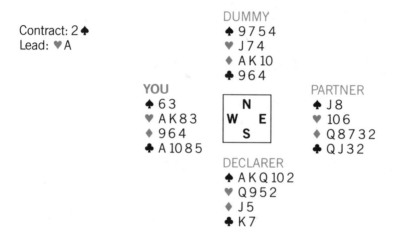

Contract: 2♠
Lead: ♥A

DUMMY
♠ 9 7 5 4
♥ J 7 4
♦ A K 10
♣ 9 6 4

YOU
♠ 6 3
♥ A K 8 3
♦ 9 6 4
♣ A 10 8 5

PARTNER
♠ J 8
♥ 10 6
♦ Q 8 7 3 2
♣ Q J 3 2

DECLARER
♠ A K Q 10 2
♥ Q 9 5 2
♦ J 5
♣ K 7

We have seen examples in previous lessons of how defenders can get ruffs. It is a combination of recognizing the possibility and making appropriate use of defensive signals. This is another example.

You lead the ♥A against declarer's 2♠ contract and partner cooperates by playing an encouraging ♥10. At this point, you do not know if partner is encouraging because he wants a ruff or because he has the ♥Q, but in either case you can continue with the ♥K and another heart. Which heart do you lead on the third round? Since you do not need to show attitude or count in this situation, the heart you choose to play should be a suit preference signal. Holding the ♣A, you prefer clubs to diamonds and therefore play the ♥3 rather than the ♥8. It turns out that partner can trump the third round. Now it is over to partner. He should interpret your ♥3 as suit preference for clubs. Even if he is not sure, the guideline of leading through strength up to weakness tells him to lead back a club rather than a diamond. Visualizing the situation, partner can lead back the ♣Q to trap declarer's ♣K. It would do no harm if you held the ♣K and declarer the ♣A instead of the actual layout.

When you win the ♣A, it is time for you to do some thinking. Both you and declarer still have one heart left while there are no hearts in either partner's hand or the dummy. Although dummy can trump hearts, you should lead another heart, hoping that partner can *overruff* if declarer trumps the heart in dummy. This proves to be the case. When you lead your remaining ♥8, declarer can trump with dummy's ♠9, but partner can over-trump with his ♠J to win the trick. The defense ends up with two heart tricks, two club tricks and the two spade tricks from partner's trumps.

Getting a Ruff

You must always be alert to the possibility of using your trumps to ruff one of declarer's winners. Take a look at the following hand where the defense must be on its toes to defeat the contract:

Contract: 4♥
Lead: ♣K

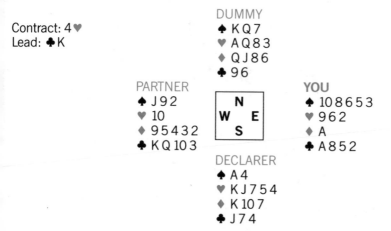

DUMMY
♠ K Q 7
♥ A Q 8 3
♦ Q J 8 6
♣ 9 6

PARTNER
♠ J 9 2
♥ 10
♦ 9 5 4 3 2
♣ K Q 10 3

YOU
♠ 10 8 6 5 3
♥ 9 6 2
♦ A
♣ A 8 5 2

DECLARER
♠ A 4
♥ K J 7 5 4
♦ K 10 7
♣ J 7 4

Partner leads the top of his touching club honors against the 4♥ contract. It might seem natural for you to encourage with the ♣8 since you have the ♣A. However, before doing so, you should be deciding on your plan to defeat the contract. It looks as if you have two club tricks and the ♦A. Where is the fourth defensive trick going to come from? With the singleton ♦A, there is the opportunity for a defensive ruff, but how can you get part-ner to cooperate? You might try playing a discouraging ♣2 on the first trick, hoping that partner will switch to a diamond. You can then win the ♦A, get back to partner's hand by leading a club to the ♣Q and partner can lead another diamond for you to trump. Partner might figure it all out, but is he really going to know to lead a diamond rather than a spade if you make a discouraging signal in clubs?

Instead, you take matters into your own hands since you can see what needs to be done. Overtake partner's ♣K with your ♣A and play your singleton ♦A. Now lead a club back to partner's ♣Q. Partner, realizing why you have gone to all this trouble, should cooperate by leading another diamond for you to ruff. Difficult perhaps, but not so hard once you consider the possibility of trumping declarer's winners and combine that with the knowledge that partner has the ♣Q when he leads the ♣K.

BIDDING REVIEW

When the opponents have opened the bidding, you can compete by making an overcall or a takeout double. When you make an overcall, you are suggesting the suit for your side. When you make a takeout double, you are asking partner to choose the suit.

Making an Overcall

When the opponents have started the auction, use the following guidelines to decide whether or not to make an overcall:

REQUIREMENTS FOR AN OVERCALL IN A SUIT
• A five-card or longer suit
• 13 or more points (less with a good suit if not-vulnerable and at the one level)

REQUIREMENTS FOR A 1 NT OVERCALL
• 16–18 points
• Balanced hand
• Some strength in the opponent's suit

Responding to an Overcall

If partner overcalls 1 NT, use the same responses as when partner opens 1 NT. If partner overcalls in a suit, use the following guidelines:

RESPONDING TO AN OVERCALL
• With a minimum hand (6–10 points):
• Pass if already at the two level
• Raise partner's suit to the two level with three-card or longer support
• Bid a new suit at the one level
• Bid 1 NT with some strength in the opponent's suit and a balanced hand
• With a medium hand (11–12 points):
• Raise partner's suit to the three level with three-card or longer support
• Bid a new suit (even if it is at the two level)
• Bid 2 NT with some strength in the opponent's suit and a balanced hand
• With a maximum hand (13 or more points):
• Raise partner's suit to game with three-card or longer support
• Bid a new suit
• Bid 3 NT with some strength in the opponent's suit and a balanced hand

Making a Takeout Double

Another way to compete is by making a takeout double. You can tell whether a double is for takeout or penalty as follows:

- If neither partner has bid anything except pass and the opponents' contract is a partscore, double is for takeout.
- If either partner has bid or the contract is game, the double is for penalty.

REQUIREMENTS FOR A TAKEOUT DOUBLE
• 13 or more points (counting dummy points)   • Support for the unbid suits

Responding to a Takeout Double

Responder must not pass partner's takeout double unless the opponent on his right bids. Choose a response using the following guideline:

RESPONDING TO A TAKEOUT DOUBLE

• With a minimum hand (0–10 points):
    • Bid a four-card or longer major suit at the cheapest level
    • Bid a four-card or longer minor suit at the cheapest level
    • Bid 1 NT
 	
 • With a medium hand (11–12 points):
    • Jump in a four-card or longer major suit
    • Jump in a four-card or longer minor suit
    • Jump to 2 NT
 	
 • With a maximum hand (13 or more points):
    • Jump to game in a four-card or longer major suit
    • Jump to 3 NT

Rebids by the Takeout Doubler

Having made a takeout double, do not bid again unless partner shows more than a minimum hand or you have more than a minimum hand. Use this guideline:

REBIDS BY THE TAKEOUT DOUBLER

- With a minimum hand (13–16 points):
  - Pass if partner bids at the cheapest level
  - Pass with 13–14 points if partner jumps a level. Bid game with 15–16 points if partner jumps.

- With a medium hand (17–18 points):
  - Raise one level if partner bids at the cheapest level
  - Bid game if partner jumps a level

- With a maximum hand (19–21 points):
  - Jump raise if partner bids at the cheapest level
  - Bid game if partner jumps a level

PLAY OF THE HAND REVIEW

An *entry* is a way of getting from one hand to the other. As declarer, you must be careful to watch for entries between your hand and the dummy when making your PLAN. You need entries to take finesses, get to your winners and so on.

Preserving an Entry

One way to conserve entries is by playing the *high card from the short side first* when taking sure tricks or promoting winners. For example:

DUMMY
A K J 2

DECLARER
Q 4

It is straightforward to take your four sure tricks in this suit if you win the first trick with the queen. You then have the 4 left in your hand to lead to dummy's winners. If you win the first trick with a high card in dummy, you create an entry problem. You cannot play another high card from dummy since your queen will have to be played on the same trick. If you lead the 2 over to your queen, dummy's last two winners are stranded unless you have an entry to dummy in another suit. Even if you do have an outside entry to dummy, it may be needed for something more important than untangling this suit. Notice how much more difficult it is for the defenders to take their tricks in this suit — they cannot see each other's hand.

Do not confuse playing the high card from the short side with this situation:

DUMMY
K 7 3

DECLARER
A 8

You only have two sure tricks and can take them in any order. This type of suit can be used for entry purposes. When making your PLAN, look to see how these entries can best be put to use.

Another way of conserving entries is by *taking your losses early* and ducking tricks to the opponents when necessary, as in this type of situation:

DUMMY
K 8 6 4 2

DECLARER
A 9 5

If the king is your only entry to dummy, you cannot afford to play it too soon if you are trying to establish winners in this suit. Either play the ace and then duck a trick to the opponents, or duck the first trick completely. If the missing cards divide 3–2, the suit is established and there is still an entry to dummy.

Creating an Entry

You may have to create your own entry when there is none readily available. For example, in this layout you can create a sure entry to the dummy through promotion:

DUMMY
K Q

DECLARER
7 5

When you lead this suit, the defenders cannot prevent you from getting to dummy, whether or not they win the first trick. On the other hand, the entry will not be so sure in this layout:

DUMMY
K 8 3

DECLARER
7 5 2

The best you can do is lead toward dummy, hoping the ace is on your left — a 50–50 chance. If you held the queen in your hand, you could try leading it first, hoping one of the opponents plays the ace, making the king a sure entry. If they can see what you are trying to do, however, they may not cooperate.

Another way to create entries is through your long suits. Consider this layout:

DUMMY
7 6 5 2

DECLARER
A K Q 3

If the missing cards are divided 3–2, you have an entry to dummy in this suit. After playing the ace, king and queen to get rid of the opponents' cards in the suit, you can play your 3 over to dummy — provided you kept a higher card in the dummy than the 2!

In a suit contract, your trump suit is often the longest suit in the combined hands and may provide a good source of entries between the two hands. When making your PLAN, decide how you want to play the trump suit to make the best use of your entries.

♥ *SUMMARY* ♥

The defenders want to develop and take their tricks using the same techniques as declarer. They are hampered by not being able to see their combined holding in each suit. However, they can overcome much of this disadvantage through the use of signals and by trying to visualize the layout of the suit based on the auction and the way the play has gone.

When taking their winners, the defenders must be careful not to block a suit when it is unevenly divided between the two hands. The shorter hand wants to have a small card, rather than a high card, as the last card left in the suit. One defender may have to *unblock* the suit by overtaking partner's high card. At other times the other defender may have to lead a small card over to the winner(s) in the short hand before taking the winners in his hand, the long hand.

The defenders must also try to maintain communication between the two hands when developing tricks. They may have to take their losses early by ducking a trick to keep an entry to the long suit and to avoid stranding their winners.

The defenders must cooperate to take finesses, trapping declarer's high cards. Each defender must try to visualize the layout of the suit to see the possibility of trapping high cards. A useful guideline is *lead through strength and lead up to weakness*. By leading through the high cards held on your left and up to the small cards held on your right, you give partner a chance to get tricks with his high cards when they are favorably placed.

♥ *GROUP ACTIVITIES* ♥

Exercise One — Taking Sure Tricks

In each of the following layouts, which card would your partner lead against a notrump contract? How would you work with partner to take all your sure tricks in the suit?

1)

DUMMY
73

PARTNER
Ⓠ J 10 4

YOU
A Ⓚ 2
A K 3
2 1

DECLARER
9865

2)

DUMMY
64

PARTNER
Ⓚ Q 10 5

YOU
A 7 2
2 1 3

DECLARER
J983

3)

DUMMY
87

PARTNER
A Ⓠ J 9 2

YOU
K 4
1 2

DECLARER
10653

1) _____ 2) _____ 3) _____

Exercise Two — Promoting Tricks

You are defending a notrump contract and lead the indicated card. Which card will partner play on the first trick? If declarer wins the first trick with the ace, which card in the suit will you lead next when you regain the lead? Why?

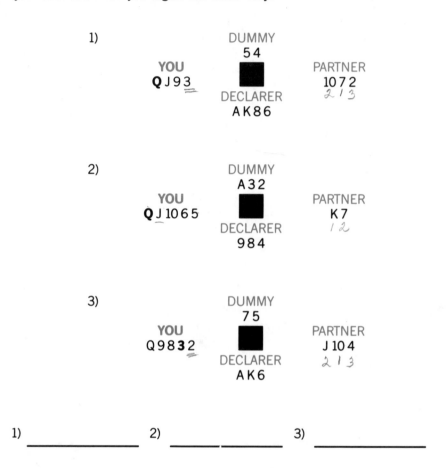

1)
                       DUMMY
                        5 4

YOU   PARTNER
Q J 9 3   10 7 2
                  DECLARER   2 / 3
                    A K 8 6

2)
                         DUMMY
                        A 3 2

YOU   PARTNER
Q J 10 6 5   K 7
                  DECLARER   1 / 2
                    9 8 4

3)
                         DUMMY
                        7 5

YOU   PARTNER
Q 9 8 3 2   J 10 4
                  DECLARER   2 / 3
                    A K 6

1) _____   2) _____   3) _____

Exercise Three — Establishing Long Suits

You are defending a notrump contract and partner leads the indicated card in a suit you have bid. If you have no entries in any outside suit, which card do you play on the first trick? Which card do you play the second time the suit is led?

1)
                    DUMMY
                    Q J 10
PARTNER   ▮   YOU
9 4   A K 8 6 3 2
                    DECLARER   2 1
                    7 5

2)
                    DUMMY
                    Q J 10
PARTNER   ▮   YOU
A 5 3   K 9 6 4 2
                    DECLARER   2 1 2
                    8 7

3)
                    DUMMY
                    K Q J
PARTNER   ▮   YOU
10 8 2   A 9 4 3
                    DECLARER   3 1 2
                    7 6 5

1) _____ 2) _____ 3) _____

Exercise Four — The Defensive Finesse

Which card would you lead against a suit contract in each of the following layouts? Which card would partner play to the first trick if a low card is played from dummy? Which defender must lead the suit next if the defenders are to take all the tricks to which they are entitled?

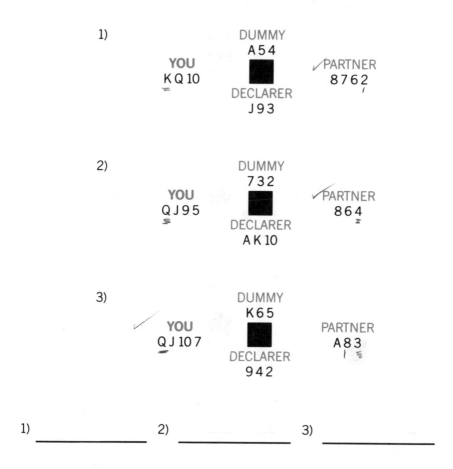

1)

DUMMY
A 5 4

YOU
K Q 10

PARTNER
8 7 6 2

DECLARER
J 9 3

2)

DUMMY
7 3 2

YOU
Q J 9 5

PARTNER
8 6 4

DECLARER
A K 10

3)

DUMMY
K 6 5

YOU
Q J 10 7

PARTNER
A 8 3

DECLARER
9 4 2

1) _____   2) _____   3) _____

Exercise Five — Leading Through Strength

In each of the following layouts, who has to lead the suit, you or your partner, in order for the defenders to get all the tricks to which they are entitled?

1)
DUMMY
7 5 3
YOU
K 8 4 2
✓PARTNER
J 10 9
DECLARER
A Q 6

2)
DUMMY
A J 10
✓**YOU**
9 7 3
PARTNER
K Q 6 4
DECLARER
8 5 2

3)
DUMMY
8 7 2
YOU
A Q 9 4
✓ PARTNER
10 6 3
DECLARER
K J 5

1) _____   2) _____   3) _____

Exercise Six — Trumping Declarer's Winners

On each of the following hands, how will the defenders cooperate to defeat declarer's 4♠ contract after the opening lead of the ♦3?

1) Contract: 4♠
   Lead: ♦3

DUMMY
♠ 10 9 6 2
♥ K 6 3
♦ K Q J
♣ K J 7

YOU
♠ J 8 5
♥ 10 7 5 2
♦ 3
♣ Q 9 8 6 5

PARTNER
♠ 3
♥ J 8 4
♦ A 10 9 6 2
♣ A 4 3 2

DECLARER
♠ A K Q 7 4
♥ A Q 9
♦ 8 7 5 4
♣ 10

2) Contract: 4♠
   Lead: ♦3

DUMMY
♠ 10 9 6 2
♥ K 6 3
♦ A K Q
♣ K 10 7

YOU
♠ A 8 5
♥ 10 7 5 2
♦ 3
♣ Q 9 8 6 5

PARTNER
♠ 3
♥ A Q 4
♦ 10 9 7 6 4 2
♣ J 4 2

DECLARER
♠ K Q J 7 4
♥ J 9 8
♦ J 8 5
♣ A 3

Exercise Seven — Review of Competitive Bidding

The opponent on your right opens the bidding 1 ♥. What do you do with each of the following hands?

1) ♠ K Q 10 8 6 2
   ♥ J 3
   ♦ A J 4
   ♣ 9 2

2) ♠ Q 10 8 3
   ♥ 2
   ♦ A Q 10 3
   ♣ K Q 7 5

3) ♠ 5 4
   ♥ 7
   ♦ A J 10 6 3
   ♣ A K J 7 5

1)   / S

2)   T.O.

3)   2 D

4) ♠ J 3
   ♥ K Q 5
   ♦ K Q J 9
   ♣ A J 9 2

5) ♠ K 7 6 3
   ♥ —
   ♦ A 9 7 5 2
   ♣ K J 9 3

6) ♠ 8 3
   ♥ A Q J 9 3
   ♦ 8 5 2
   ♣ A K 5

4)   / N

5)   2 D T.O.

6)   P

7) ♠ Q 9 3
   ♥ Q J 8
   ♦ J 8 7 4 3
   ♣ A 7

8) ♠ A J 9 2
   ♥ 8 3
   ♦ A 8 5 4
   ♣ A 6 5

9) ♠ J 4
   ♥ A J 10
   ♦ Q J 10 8 3
   ♣ A Q J

7)   2 D p

8)   T. O.

9)   / N

Exercise Eight — Watching Your Entries

How many sure entries to the dummy can you get from each of the following suits? How many entries might you get if the missing cards are favorably placed?

	1)	2)	3)	4)	5)
DUMMY:	A K J	A Q J	Q 7 6 3	9 7 4 2	A Q 9 3
DECLARER:	Q 7 3	4 3 2	A K	A K Q 3	8 7 4 2

1) _<u>3</u>_ 2) _<u>2</u>_ 3) _<u>0</u>_ 4) _<u>1</u>_ 5) _____

Exercise Nine — Taking Tricks

Turn up the cards on the first pre-dealt hand. Put each hand dummy style at the edge of the table in front of each player.

Dealer: North

```
                    ♠ K 10 7 5 3
                    ♥ J 6 4
                    ♦ K Q 9
                    ♣ A 8
    ♠ J 9 6 4          N          ♠ A
    ♥ A K 7       W        E      ♥ Q 8 5
    ♦ A J 8            S          ♦ 5 4 2
    ♣ 6 4 2                       ♣ K Q J 10 7 5
                    ♠ Q 8 2
                    ♥ 10 9 3 2
                    ♦ 10 7 6 3
                    ♣ 9 3
```

The Bidding

What would North open the bidding? How can East compete in the auction? South passes. West knows that his partner has approximately the values for an opening bid to overcall at the two level. At what level does the partnership belong? What Golden Game does West bid? How does the auction proceed from there? Who is declarer?

The Defense

Which player makes the opening lead? What would the opening lead be? Which card would South play on the first trick? Why? How will this help North?

The Play

Review the steps in declarer's PLAN. How does declarer plan to make the contract?

Exercise Ten — Maintaining Communications

Turn up the cards on the second pre-dealt hand. Put each hand dummy style at the edge of the table in front of each player.

Dealer: East

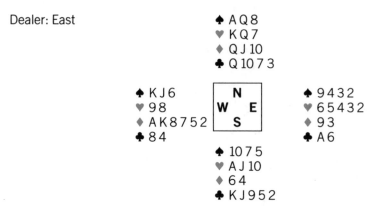

♠ A Q 8
♥ K Q 7
♦ Q J 10
♣ Q 10 7 3

♠ K J 6
♥ 9 8
♦ A K 8 7 5 2
♣ 8 4

N
W   E
S

♠ 9 4 3 2
♥ 6 5 4 3 2
♦ 9 3
♣ A 6

♠ 10 7 5
♥ A J 10
♦ 6 4
♣ K J 9 5 2

The Bidding

East and South pass. What would West open the bidding? How can North describe his hand? East passes. What does South respond to his partner's overcall? How does the bidding proceed? What is the contract? Who is declarer?

The Defense

Which player makes the opening lead? What would the opening lead be? Which diamonds does West know that his partner does not hold? Which card would West play? Why?

The Play

Review the steps in declarer's PLAN. How does declarer plan to make the contract?

Exercise Eleven — Partnership Cooperation

Turn up the cards on the third pre-dealt hand. Put each hand dummy style at the edge of the table in front of each player.

Dealer: South

```
                    ♠ 6 4 3
                    ♥ 9 4
                    ♦ K 6 4 3
                    ♣ Q 6 5 2
    ♠ 10 9 7 2        N          ♠ Q 8 5
    ♥ A J 7 6      W     E       ♥ K Q 10 8 2
    ♦ A Q 5 2         S          ♦ J 10
    ♣ 9                          ♣ A 10 4
                    ♠ A K J
                    ♥ 5 3
                    ♦ 9 8 7
                    ♣ K J 8 7 3
```

The Bidding

What is South's opening bid? With no five-card suit to overcall but with support for all the unbid suits, how does West compete? What does North do? How many points does East have? At what level does the partnership belong? What does East bid? How does the bidding proceed from there? What is the contract? Who is declarer?

The Defense

Which player makes the opening lead? What would the opening lead be? Which card does North play on the first trick? Why? What does South lead next? If North wins a trick, which suit should he lead? Why?

The Play

Review the steps in declarer's PLAN. How does declarer plan to make the contract?

Exercise Twelve — Putting Signals to Work

Turn up the cards on the fourth pre-dealt hand. Put each hand dummy style at the edge of the table in front of each player.

Dealer: West

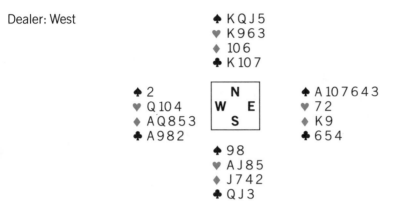

♠ K Q J 5
♥ K 9 6 3
♦ 10 6
♣ K 10 7

♠ 2
♥ Q 10 4
♦ A Q 8 5 3
♣ A 9 8 2

N
W   E
S

♠ A 10 7 6 4 3
♥ 7 2
♦ K 9
♣ 6 5 4

♠ 9 8
♥ A J 8 5
♦ J 7 4 2
♣ Q J 3

The Bidding

What is West's opening bid? Can North compete in the auction? How? What does East respond to partner's opening bid? Does South have to bid? Should South bid? What does South bid? How does the auction proceed from there? What is the contract? Who is declarer?

The Defense

Which player makes the opening lead? What would the opening lead be? Why? How does East know his partner's lead is a singleton? After winning the first trick, which card does East play to the second trick? Why? What does West lead next?

The Play

Review the steps in declarer's PLAN. How does declarer plan to make the contract?

LESSON 7
Interfering With Declarer

Defending Against Suit Establishment
Defending Against Declarer's Small Cards
Defending Against Finesses
Defending Against Declarer's Trumps
Bidding Review
Play of the Hand Review
Summary

Workshop Material
Group Activities

In the previous lesson we saw how the defenders work together to take the tricks to which they are entitled. They must also work together to try to prevent declarer from taking any tricks to which he is not entitled. In this lesson, we will look at techniques the defenders use to make it difficult for declarer to make his contract.

DEFENDING AGAINST SUIT ESTABLISHMENT

Declarer often needs to establish tricks in his long suits to make his contract. Declarer uses a combination of promotion (driving out the defenders' higher-ranking cards) and length (leading the suit until the defenders have no cards left in the suit). Once declarer has established winners in a suit, he will need an entry to get to them. The defenders cannot do anything about the cards declarer has been dealt, but they can make it as difficult as possible for declarer to establish and then get to his winners.

The Defensive Holdup Play

In previous lessons, we have looked at how the defenders can hold up their winner in a suit in order to strand declarer's winners. For example, consider this layout:

```
            DUMMY
            Q J 10 9 6
  PARTNER   ███   YOU
  7 3 2     ███   A 8 4
            DECLARER
            K 5
```

Declarer plans to promote four winners in this suit by driving out the defenders' ace. He starts by leading the king, high card from the short side. If you take the first trick with the ace, declarer has four established winners in the dummy and can use the 5 as an entry to dummy's winners once he regains the lead. To make things difficult for declarer, you can use the *defensive holdup*, refusing to take your ace until declarer has no cards left in the suit. Since you cannot see how many cards there are in declarer's hand, your partner must cooperate by giving you a count signal so that you know how long to hold up.

On the above layout, partner plays the 2 on the first trick, the start of a low-high signal to show an odd number. When you refuse to win the first trick, declarer leads the 5 to one of dummy's high cards. On this trick, partner plays the 3 (or 7), confirming that he has an odd number of cards. Since partner cannot have started with five cards in the suit, you can deduce that he has three, leaving declarer with only two. This information tells you that it is safe to win the second trick with your ace. Declarer has no small cards left as an entry to the winners. If partner had played high-low to show an even number, declarer would have started with three cards and you would need to wait until the third round to take your ace.

Of course, your holdup play will not prevent declarer from reaching dummy's winners if he has an entry in another suit, but it may inconvenience him. Declarer may have no entry in another suit or may have to use up an entry that he would rather save for other purposes. A holdup play can be quite effective, especially in a notrump contract, even when declarer does have an easy outside entry to dummy. Suppose we change the layout slightly:

DUMMY
Q J 10 9 6
PARTNER   YOU
7 5 3 2   A 8 4
DECLARER
K

If declarer leads the king and you win the first trick with the ace, declarer can use his outside entry to get to dummy's winners and take four tricks in the suit. If you hold up the ace, declarer can use his outside entry to get to dummy and lead the suit a second time, but when you now win the trick with your ace, he would need a second entry to dummy

to get back to the established winners. If declarer started with only one outside entry to dummy, your holdup play restricts him to one trick in the suit.

With the above layout, it may appear dangerous to hold up the ace in a suit contract since declarer may end up with no losers in the suit. When he goes to dummy with his outside entry and leads the suit a second time, he can trump your ace when you play it. If there is only one entry to dummy, however, sacrificing your ace may be worthwhile. If you won the ace on the first round, declarer might be able to discard up to four losers on dummy's established winners. It costs you a trick in the short run but may gain you more than one trick in the long run. You will have to judge more carefully in a suit contract whether or not to hold up your winners.

Even when declarer has an outside entry to dummy, you may be able to prevent his establishing a suit by holding up when you have two winners in the suit. Consider this layout:

DUMMY
Q J 10 9 6
PARTNER   YOU
7 5 2   A K 4
DECLARER
8 3

Suppose declarer leads the suit and you win the first trick with the king. When declarer regains the lead, he still has a small card left to lead to dummy and drive out your ace. It will do no good to hold up now since declarer still has his outside entry to dummy to get to his winners once they are establish-ed. Look at the difference if you hold up both the ace

and the king on the first trick, waiting until the second trick to win with your king. When declarer regains the lead, he has no small cards left in his hand and would have to use his only entry to dummy in order to lead the suit again and drive out your ace. Then there would be no entry left in dummy to get to the established winners. By letting declarer win the first trick, you prevent him from ever establishing any more winners in the suit.

Here is a complete hand to illustrate the possibilities for defeating a contract by holding up with two winners in a suit:

Contract: 3 NT
Lead: ♠Q

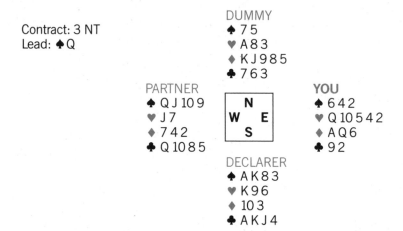

DUMMY
♠ 7 5
♥ A 8 3
♦ K J 9 8 5
♣ 7 6 3

PARTNER
♠ Q J 10 9
♥ J 7
♦ 7 4 2
♣ Q 10 8 5

YOU
♠ 6 4 2
♥ Q 10 5 4 2
♦ A Q 6
♣ 9 2

DECLARER
♠ A K 8 3
♥ K 9 6
♦ 10 3
♣ A K J 4

Against declarer's 3 NT contract, partner leads the ♠Q. Declarer has two spade tricks, two heart tricks and two club tricks. One extra trick can come from a successful club finesse or a 3–3 division of the missing clubs, but the most promising suit is diamonds. Declarer can take a finesse, hoping your partner has the ♦Q. However, even if this does not work, declarer can promote three tricks in the suit by driving out the ♦Q and ♦A. So, declarer wins the first trick with the ♠K and leads the ♦10, playing a low diamond from dummy. This is your chance to put the holdup play to work by refusing to win the first trick with the ♦Q, even though it is tempting to do so.

Let's first see what happens if you win the first diamond trick with the ♦Q. You lead back a spade to drive out declarer's remaining ♠A (declarer could also win any other return in his hand). Declarer leads another diamond to dummy to drive out your ♦A. It is too late to hold up. Dummy still has the ♥A as an entry. Declarer ends up with three diamond tricks to go with his other six sure tricks, enough to make the contract.

Instead, let declarer win the first diamond trick. Declarer will lead another diamond to dummy's ♦J (or ♦9 or ♦8), hoping that his finesse has been successful. You can win this trick with the ♦Q and lead back a spade. Now declarer is helpless. He can win the spade trick and use dummy's ♥A as an entry to lead another diamond and drive out your ♦A, but there will be no entry left to get to dummy's established winners. Declarer's only chance is to use dummy's ♥A as an entry to try the club finesse, hoping that you have the ♣Q and the suit divides 3–3. When this fails, he is defeated. Declarer ends up with only two spade tricks, two heart tricks, the initial diamond trick and two club tricks. You defeat the contract by two tricks.

There are many opportunities to make declarer's life difficult by holding up your winners. Here is a typical layout:

```
              DUMMY
             A J 10 9 6 5
  PARTNER      ███      YOU
    8 2                 K 7 4
            DECLARER
              Q 3
```

Trying to establish winners in this suit, declarer leads the queen and plays a low card from dummy. This would be successful if your partner held the king since declarer's queen would win the trick and he could repeat the finesse. It would also be successful if you won the first trick with the king since the remaining cards in dummy would be winners and declarer would have a small card left to get to them. If declarer has no outside entries to the dummy, you can limit him to one or two winners by holding up the king. When his queen wins the first trick and he leads another small card toward dummy, declarer will be faced with a dilemma. He can win the trick with dummy's ace to guarantee two tricks in the suit. If, however, your partner holds the king, declarer can finesse dummy's jack (or 10 or 9), and if partner's king next falls under the ace, declarer ends up with six tricks. In the actual layout if declarer takes a finesse, you can now win the king. Since the suit is blocked declarer will not get any more tricks.

Notice that partner clarifies the layout of the suit for you by giving a count signal when the queen is led. He plays the 8, starting a high-low, to show an even number. The situation becomes a little more exciting if this is the complete layout:

```
              DUMMY
             A J 10 9 6 5
  PARTNER      ███      YOU
    8 4 2               K 7
            DECLARER
              Q 3
```

When declarer plays the queen, partner signals with the 2, to show an odd number. Assuming partner has three cards, that leaves declarer with two. Do you hold up on the first trick? If it takes you too long to decide, you are better off to win the first trick with the king. Otherwise, declarer may assume that you are thinking about whether or not to hold up your king and he may play dummy's ace on the second round of the suit, ending up with all the tricks! If your nerves are strong and you do not take too long to think about it, you can risk playing a small card. If declarer repeats the finesse, confident that your partner has the king, your holdup play will be successful and will limit declarer to one trick in the suit. What if declarer goes up with the ace on the second round of the suit? You win some and you lose some — this time you would lose.

Attacking Entries

Another way for the defenders to make life difficult for declarer is by driving out his entries before he is ready to use them. Take a look at this hand:

Contract: 3 NT
Lead: ♥ J

DUMMY
♠ A 5
♥ 7 4 2
♦ J 5 4
♣ K J 10 9 3

PARTNER
♠ 10 6 4
♥ J 10 9 8
♦ 9 6 3
♣ 8 6 2

YOU
♠ K Q 9 3
♥ A 5
♦ 10 8 7 2
♣ A 7 5

DECLARER
♠ J 8 7 2
♥ K Q 6 3
♦ A K Q
♣ Q 4

Partner leads the ♥ J against declarer's 3 NT contract. You play the ♥ A, third hand high, since you know that declarer holds the ♥ Q. Declarer may or may not hold the ♥ K, depending on whether partner has led from the top of a sequence or the top of an interior sequence. Before automatically returning partner's suit, however, you need to consider the whole picture. Looking at dummy you can see that declarer will probably try to establish the club suit by driving out your ♣ A and use the ♠ A as an entry to the established winners. You can foil this plan by leading the ♠ K (or ♠ Q) to remove dummy's entry before declarer is ready to use it. Declarer can win with dummy's ♠ A and lead a club to his ♣ Q and the ♣ 4 back to one of dummy's high clubs. You hold up your ♣ A, watching partner's count signal to see on which round you should win the trick. When partner shows three clubs, you win the second round and declarer is held to one club trick rather than the four tricks he would get if you left the ♣ A as an entry to dummy.

Leading back the ♠K was not too difficult when you were looking at the ♠Q as well and could see that you were also promoting a trick for yourself. Let's look at the layout of the spade suit by itself:

DUMMY
♠ A 5
PARTNER   YOU
♠ 10 6 4   ♠ K Q 9 3
DECLARER
♠ J 8 7 2

The lead of the ♠K actually costs a trick since declarer can win dummy's ♠A and lead toward his ♠J for a second trick. The sacrifice of one trick is worthwhile, however, since you prevent declarer from getting four club tricks. Suppose declarer holds the ♠Q:

DUMMY
♠ A 5
PARTNER   YOU
♠ 10 6 4   ♠ K 9 8 3
DECLARER
♠ Q J 7 2

It would still be worthwhile leading back the ♠K to drive out dummy's ♠A, even though declarer gets tricks with both the ♠Q and ♠J. Notice that the half-hearted attempt of leading a small spade would not work. Declarer could win with the ♠Q or ♠J, keeping the ♠A in dummy. By leading the ♠K, you are certain of driving out dummy's ♠A. Of course, you may not hold the ♠K. In that case, you would have to lead back a small spade hoping that partner can drive out dummy's entry. For example:

DUMMY
♠ A 5
PARTNER   YOU
♠ K 10 6   ♠ 9 8 4 3
DECLARER
♠ Q J 7 2

When you lead back a small spade, declarer cannot prevent your partner from driving out dummy's ♠A.

In addition to driving out declarer's entries, the defenders can sometimes prevent declarer from creating an entry. Consider this layout:

DUMMY
♠ Q 6 5
PARTNER   YOU
♠ 10 9 8 2   ♠ A 7 4
DECLARER
♠ K J 3

If declarer needs to create an entry to dummy, he might try leading the king, and then the jack, from his hand. If you win either the first trick or second trick with your ace, dummy's queen will become an entry. By refusing to win either the first or second trick, declarer cannot get to dummy in this suit. Partner should be helping you out by playing high-low to give you a count signal. If partner has four cards, declarer has three and you must wait until the third round to win the trick.

Here is a more complicated example combining the holdup play with denying declarer an entry:

Contract: 3 NT
Lead: ♠J

DUMMY
♠ A 7 5
♥ J 5 2
♦ 8
♣ Q J 9 7 5 2

PARTNER
♠ J 10 9 8
♥ 8 4
♦ J 10 7 4
♣ A 8 4

YOU
♠ 4 3 2
♥ A 10 9 6
♦ Q 9 5 2
♣ K 6

DECLARER
♠ K Q 6
♥ K Q 7 3
♦ A K 6 3
♣ 10 3

Partner leads the ♠J and the defenders will have to cooperate carefully to defeat the contract. Declarer wins the first trick with the ♠Q, keeping the ♠A in the dummy, and leads the ♣10, planning to establish the extra tricks he needs in the club suit. Partner must do his part by playing low, holding up his ♣A. Since declarer has an entry to dummy, you cannot afford to win the first club trick either, but must let declarer win. It may seem difficult to leave yourself with the singleton ♣K, but it is unlikely that declarer has the ♣A since he probably would have played it earlier. Declarer leads another club and partner must play low again, letting you win the trick with the ♣K, otherwise your side's ♣A and ♣K would fall on the same trick! When you win the ♣K, you return a spade, partner's suit. It does declarer no good to win in his hand, since he has no clubs left to play. Suppose he wins dummy's ♠A and leads another club to establish the suit. Partner wins with the ♣A and leads another spade to drive out declarer's remaining ♠K. Declarer now leads a crafty ♥Q from his hand. If you win the ♥A, dummy's ♥J will become an entry. So you must let declarer's ♥Q win the trick. If declarer continues by leading the ♥K, you must let him win this trick also. If instead declarer leads a small heart toward dummy's ♥J, you must win this trick, preventing him from ever reaching the stranded clubs in the dummy. With careful cooperation between the defenders, declarer ends up with only three spade tricks, two heart tricks, two diamond tricks and one club trick — one trick short of making his contract.

♥ *DEFENDING AGAINST DECLARER'S SMALL CARDS* ♥

Declarer can get tricks from a long suit by continuing to play it until the defenders have no cards left in the suit. The defenders must be careful not to make declarer's task any easier by throwing away the cards that would prevent him from establishing the suit.

Discarding

You are often faced with the problem of which suit to discard when you cannot follow suit to the current trick. In choosing your discard, you must be careful not to present declarer with a trick to which he is not entitled. Any time declarer has a long suit in either his hand or the dummy, there is the possibility of a small card in that suit becoming a winner. The defenders have to guard against this by making sure that at least one member of the partnership keeps the same length in the suit as declarer. Since you are not able to see into partner's or declarer's hand, it will not always be apparent which suit you must guard against. In some situations, however, it is obvious that you cannot afford to discard from a particular suit since partner cannot protect it. Consider this layout:

DUMMY
A K Q 10
    YOU
    J 4 3 2

Whatever cards partner holds, only you can prevent declarer from getting four tricks in this suit. If you discard one of your cards, declarer can play the ace, king and queen and his 10 will become a trick.

DUMMY
A Q 6 5
    YOU
    7 4 3 2

The situation can be a lot less obvious if we change the layout to something like this:

DUMMY
A Q 6 5
PARTNER   YOU
J 10 8   7 4 3 2
DECLARER
K 9

It does not look as though your four small cards are of much use, but discarding one of them would give declarer a trick if this is the complete layout of the suit:

If you discard a card in the suit, declarer will play the king and then the 9 over to dummy's ace and queen. Dummy's remaining 6 will have become a winner. You must tenaciously hold on to all four of your cards in the suit to prevent declarer from getting an extra trick. You need to keep the same number of cards as dummy. If declarer discards one of dummy's cards in the suit, then you can safely discard one of your cards. The situation can be even more difficult when it is declarer who holds the length in the suit, since you cannot see the hidden cards.

For example, suppose this is the layout:

DUMMY
6 5 2
PARTNER   YOU
Q 9   10 7 4 3
DECLARER
A K J 8

Looking at three small cards in dummy, it may not seem that there is much to guard against. Discarding a small card, however, is doubly dangerous. First, it will cost a trick even if declarer chooses to finesse his jack, losing to partner's queen. When declarer later takes his ace and king, your 10 will fall and declarer's 8 will become a trick. Worse, declarer may assume from your discard that you do not have the queen to protect and may play the ace and king, rather than taking the finesse, ending up with all four tricks in the suit!

Without seeing declarer's hand, how are you to know that you must hold on to all your cards in a suit such as this? One place from which you get information about declarer's hand is through the bidding. Suppose the auction proceeds as follows:

NORTH (DUMMY)	EAST (**YOU**)	SOUTH (DECLARER)	WEST (PARTNER)
		1♠	Pass
2♣	Pass	2♦	Pass
3♠	Pass	4♠	Pass
Pass	Pass		

Partner leads the ♥J and you see the following cards when dummy arrives:

Contract: 4♠
Lead: ♥J

DUMMY
♠ A 8 3
♥ Q 7 3
♦ 6 4 3
♣ A J 4 2

LEAD
♥ J

YOU
♠ 9 2
♥ A K 4
♦ 10 7 5 2
♣ K Q 10 3

Declarer plays a small heart from dummy and you let partner's ♥J win the trick. Partner leads another heart and you take the ♥K and ♥A as declarer follows suit both times. Needing only one more trick to defeat the contract, you lead back the ♣K. Declarer plays the ♣7, partner plays the ♣9, and declarer wins the trick with dummy's ♣A. Declarer then plays three rounds of trumps, the ♠A, ♠K and ♠Q. On the third round of trumps you discard a small club. Declarer leads two more spades. Partner discards the ♣5 and ♣6 while declarer discards a small club and a small diamond from dummy. You can afford to discard your ♣10 on the fourth round of spades, but what do you discard on the fifth round? These are the remaining cards:

DUMMY
♦ 6 4
♣ J 4

YOU
♦ 10 7 5 2
♣ Q

One of your cards must go. Which one? If you recall the bidding, declarer bid diamonds at his second opportunity in the auction. It looks as if declarer's last four cards are diamonds, so you must discard the ♣Q, even though it is a winner. Declarer cannot have any clubs left. If you discard a diamond, declarer makes the contract since the complete hand looks like this:

Contract: 4♠
Lead: ♥ J

DUMMY
♠ A 8 3
♥ Q 7 3
♦ 6 4 3
♣ A J 4 2

PARTNER
♠ 10 6 5
♥ J 10 9 6
♦ J 8
♣ 9 8 6 5

YOU
♠ 9 2
♥ A K 4
♦ 10 7 5 2
♣ K Q 10 3

DECLARER
♠ K Q J 7 4
♥ 8 5 2
♦ A K Q 9
♣ 7

If you ever discard a diamond, declarer takes four diamond tricks to go along with the five spade tricks and ♣A. The key clues came from the auction and partner's play to the club suit. Declarer opened the bidding 1♠, showing a five-card suit, and later bid diamonds to show four of them. Once he shows up with three hearts, there is room left for only one club. You must grimly hold on to all four of your diamonds, since partner will be unable to guard the suit.

Where else do your clues come from? Sometimes you can tell a lot from the way declarer is playing the hand. At other times, partner can help you out. Did you notice that partner played high-low in the club suit on the above hand? This could not be attitude, since you can see all the high club cards. It must be a count signal to show an even number of clubs. This confirms the fact that partner started with four clubs while declarer started with only one.

You have to keep both your ears and eyes open when trying to determine which suit you can safely discard. You cannot afford to be left holding on to your high cards in one suit while declarer is taking tricks with small cards in the suit which you discarded.

DEFENDING AGAINST FINESSES

Another way declarer takes tricks is by using the finesse. You can make it difficult for the declarer by not disclosing the location of the cards that he is looking for unless you have to. Remember that declarer cannot see the cards in your hand or your partner's.

Ducking

In the lesson on second hand low, you have already seen how playing a low card, rather than your high card, can create a problem for declarer. For example:

```
            DUMMY
             K J
  YOU                  PARTNER
 A 9 6 5 4            Q 10 7 2
          DECLARER
            8 3
```

If declarer leads a small card toward dummy, you must play a low card to leave him with a guess. When you duck, declarer does not know whether to play dummy's king or jack in order to get one trick from the suit.

Similarly, you should usually play low when declarer leads a small card in this situation:

```
            DUMMY
            K Q 5
  YOU                  PARTNER
 A 9 6 4             J 10 7
          DECLARER
            8 3 2
```

Declarer can win the first trick with dummy's queen (or king) but may have difficulty finding an entry back to his hand so that he can repeat the finesse.

You can also make things difficult for declarer by not taking your trick when declarer's finesse is actually going to lose. Let's change the above layout slightly, putting you on the other side:

DUMMY
K Q 5

PARTNER   YOU
J 10 7   A 9 6 4

DECLARER
8 3 2

When declarer leads a small card to dummy's queen, you should be in no hurry to win the first trick with your ace. If you play a small card, declarer may think your partner has the ace and use up one of his entries to come all the way back to his hand and lead toward dummy again. The second time, his finesse is unsuccessful. If you had won the first time, revealing the situation, declarer might have been able to direct his efforts (and entry) to better use.

DUMMY
K Q 10

PARTNER   YOU
J 7 5   A 9 6 4

DECLARER
8 3 2

If we change the layout slightly, giving dummy the 10, it is even more important that you let declarer win the first trick.

If declarer starts this suit by playing a small card to dummy's queen and you win the trick with the ace, the remaining cards look like this:

DUMMY
K 10

PARTNER   YOU
J 7   9 6 4

DECLARER
8 3

If declarer needs two tricks from this suit, he will lead from his hand next time and finesse dummy's 10, trapping your partner's jack. You have forced him to find the winning play. If you duck your ace the first time, declarer will be faced with a problem when he crosses back to his hand and plays another small card toward dummy. When partner follows with another small card, he will have to guess whether to play dummy's king (correct if partner started with the ace) or dummy's 10 (correct if you started with the ace).

Here is a complete hand showing how declarer can be led astray when you do not let him know that a finesse is going to lose:

Contract: 2 ♠
Lead: ♥ K

DUMMY
♠ 8 3
♥ A 8 6 5
♦ 9 4 2
♣ A J 6 5

YOU
♠ K 10 5
♥ K Q 10 9
♦ J 7 6
♣ Q 8 2

PARTNER
♠ 7 4
♥ 7 4 2
♦ A Q 10 5
♣ K 10 7 3

DECLARER
♠ A Q J 9 6 2
♥ J 3
♦ K 8 3
♣ 9 4

Against declarer's 2 ♠ contract, you lead the ♥ K. Declarer wins with dummy's ♥ A and sees that he has a spade loser, a heart loser, three diamond losers and a club loser. He can make the contract if either the spade or the diamond finesse works. Suppose he starts by playing a small spade toward his hand, finessing the ♠ J, hoping that your partner holds the ♠ K. If you win this trick with the ♠ K, declarer is left with little choice. He will have to use his other entry to dummy, the ♣ A, to lead toward the ♦ K. This time he will be successful and make the contract.

Look at the difference if you let the ♠ J win the first trick. It will look to declarer as if the spade finesse is working. He may use his remaining entry to dummy to lead another spade to his ♠ Q, repeating the finesse. This time, you win the trick with the ♠ K. Now declarer has no entry left to enter dummy and lead toward his ♦ K. Provided you and your partner are careful not to give declarer a free finesse by leading diamonds for him, he will have to lead them from his hand and lose all three diamond tricks. He will go down one trick in a contract he could have made. Next time, declarer will be a little more wary when his first finesse seems to have worked — but he still will not know for sure whether you are just leading him on.

Covering

You generally wait to cover the last honor led from dummy when declarer is finessing. There are times, however, when you can give declarer a more difficult time by covering. First, look at this layout:

If declarer leads the queen from dummy, planning to finesse, you give him an easy time if you play the 10. The queen will win the trick, and now that the 10 has appeared declarer can repeat the finesse, losing no tricks in the suit. If you cover the queen with the king, declarer is faced with a problem.

These are the remaining cards:

You can see that declarer should play dummy's jack next, dropping your 10, but it is not so obvious for declarer. If he thinks your partner has the 10, he may finesse dummy's 9, losing a trick to your 10.

You have to visualize the problem you will create for declarer by covering. Here is a different type of opportunity:

Normally, you do not cover if there is nothing to promote in the partnership hands, but if there is no outside entry to the dummy, you can block the suit by covering the first or second round. If declarer wins with dummy's ace, he ends up with only three tricks in the suit. If you waited to play your king until the third round of the suit, declarer can take all five tricks with no problem.

♥ *DEFENDING AGAINST DECLARER'S TRUMPS* ♥

Declarer plays in a trump contract expecting to take advantage of his trump suit by ruffing your winners, for example. The defenders have to try to counter declarer's plans, using the trump suit to their advantage whenever possible.

Leading Trumps

In the lesson on opening leads against suit contracts, you saw examples where the auction indicated that an initial trump lead might prevent declarer from ruffing losers in the dummy. The auction is not always so informative, but it may still not be too late to lead trumps once the opening lead has been made. Consider this hand:

Contract: 2♠
Lead: ♦ K

```
                        DUMMY
                        ♠ J 5
                        ♥ J 9 7 4 2
                        ♦ J 6
                        ♣ Q J 8 5
          YOU                            PARTNER
          ♠ 6 4 2       ┌─────────┐      ♠ 8 7
          ♥ Q 8 5       │    N    │      ♥ K 6 3
          ♦ K Q 10 5    │  W   E  │      ♦ A 7 4 2
          ♣ A 10 2      │    S    │      ♣ K 7 4 3
                        └─────────┘
                        DECLARER
                        ♠ A K Q 10 9 3
                        ♥ A 10
                        ♦ 9 8 3
                        ♣ 9 6
```

Declarer is in 2♠ and you start by leading the ♦ K. Partner plays an encouraging ♦ 7, to show the ♦ A, and it is time to pause. With only two diamonds in dummy, your side will not be able to take more than two diamond tricks unless you can get rid of dummy's trumps. Declarer is unlikely to help you out by drawing trumps himself if he has more than two diamonds. Instead, he will probably want to ruff one of his losers in the dummy. It is up to you to prevent this by shifting to a trump. When you lead a spade, declarer can win and lead a diamond, to make dummy void, but you can win and lead another trump. There are no trumps left in dummy and declarer will end up losing three diamond tricks, two club tricks and a heart trick. You started leading trumps just in time.

Overruffing

One way to stop declarer from trumping losers in the dummy is by trumping higher than the dummy. Look at this hand:

Contract: 4 ♥
Lead: ♠ A

DUMMY
♠ 10 8 3 2
♥ 9 7 6
♦ 9 2
♣ A K 6 3

PARTNER
♠ A K Q J 5
♥ 4 2
♦ Q 10 7 3
♣ Q 10

YOU
♠ 9 6
♥ 10 8 3
♦ J 6 5
♣ 9 8 7 4 2

DECLARER
♠ 7 4
♥ A K Q J 5
♦ A K 8 4
♣ J 5

Your partner leads the ♠ A, ♠ K and ♠ Q to the first three tricks. You follow suit on the first two rounds but must find a discard on the next round. It does not look as though you need all your small clubs and it seems straightforward to discard one, but look what happens. Declarer trumps the third round of hearts and, with diamond losers in his hand, plays the ♦ A and ♦ K and leads another diamond and trumps in dummy. Declarer can then draw trumps and make the contract, losing only two spade tricks and a diamond trick.

To prevent this result, discard a diamond, not a club, on the third round of spades. When declarer tries to trump a diamond loser in dummy, you can overtrump. Declarer ends up losing two diamond tricks. Notice how partner helped you out by leading the third round of spades, allowing you to discard a diamond. Partner had to visualize the possible advantage of leading another high spade, even though he knew declarer would be able to trump the trick.

The Uppercut

Sometimes the defenders can cooperate to create a trump trick out of thin air. Here is an example:

Contract: 4 ♠
Lead: ♦ A

DUMMY
♠ 10 8 6 4
♥ A K
♦ J 8 7
♣ A K Q J

YOU
♠ J 5
♥ 10 6 4 2
♦ A K Q 5
♣ 9 4 2

PARTNER
♠ Q
♥ J 9 8 3
♦ 9 4 3
♣ 10 8 7 5 3

DECLARER
♠ A K 9 7 3 2
♥ Q 7 5
♦ 10 6 2
♣ 6

You quickly take the first three diamond tricks against declarer's 4♠ contract as everyone follows suit. At this point, the situation looks hopeless for the defense. Declarer has no losers left in hearts, diamonds or clubs and it does not look as though he can lose any trump tricks. All is not quite over, however, if the defenders cooperate. With nothing better to do, you can lead your last diamond, even though all the other players are void in the suit. Declarer plans to trump with one of the small spades in his hand and then draw trumps, but this is where partner can cooperate. He can see no real use for his ♠Q, unless it can help promote a trump trick for your side. He trumps with the ♠Q, knowing that declarer can overtrump. Look at the devastating result for declarer. He has to overtrump with the ♠K to win the trick. When he next plays the ♠A, you play your ♠5 and your ♠J has been promoted into the setting trick. Because this play is like hitting declarer on the jaw, it is often called an *uppercut*. The defenders have again cooperated to use declarer's trump suit against him.

BIDDING REVIEW

There are large bonuses in the scoring for bidding and making slam contracts. To bid a slam, you and your partner need to have enough combined strength and must find a suitable denomination in which to play the contract.

The Strength Required for a Slam

As when deciding whether the partnership belongs in partgame or game, one partner must add the points promised by his partner to those in his own hand to determine if there is enough combined strength, using the following guideline:

STRENGTH REQUIRED FOR SLAM
• Small Slam (12 tricks): 33 or more points • Grand Slam (13 tricks): 37 or more points

The Denomination for Slam

Since the same number of tricks are required for a slam in any denomination, the partnership should generally look for a *Golden Fit* of eight or more cards in any suit. If a suitable trump fit cannot be found, then the partnership should play in notrump.

If there is enough combined strength and a suitable fit has been found, then you can bid a slam directly (more sophisticated methods will be discussed in the *Spade Series*).

Here are some examples. Suppose your partner opens the bidding 1 NT (16–18 points):

♠ —
♥ A 9 3
♦ K Q 10 8 6 5 2
♣ A J 3

With 14 HCPs plus 3 points for the seven-card suit, there should be at least 33 combined points (16+17= 33). Partner must have at least two diamonds, so there is a *Golden Fit*. Respond 6♦.

♠ K 9 3
♥ A 10 8
♦ A K 7 5
♣ A 10 7

With 18 HCPs, there is a minimum of 34 points (16+18) and a maximum of 36 points (18+18) in the combined hands. You have no methods to find out if partner has four or more diamonds so simply bid the most likely slam, 6 NT.

♠ A J 8 3
♥ K J 7 5
♦ A 9 4
♣ A 7

You have 17 HCPs, enough for a small slam. There may be a Golden Fit in either hearts or spades and you can find out by using the Stayman convention. Bid 2♣. If partner rebids 2♥ or 2♠, you can bid slam in that suit. If partner rebids 2♦, denying a four-card major suit, you can bid 6 NT.

Inviting Slam

When you know the denomination you want to play in but are not sure if there is enough combined strength for slam, you invite partner to bid slam by bidding one level beyond game. Partner will accept if he is at the top of his range but pass if he has minimum values. For example, suppose partner opens 2 NT (22–24):   20 - 21

♠ K 10 9
♥ Q 9 3
♦ J 10 9 5
♣ A 6 4

With 10 HCPs, there may not be enough for slam if opener has only 22 points (10+22=32), but there will be enough if opener has a maximum (10+24=34). Invite partner to slam by bidding one level beyond game, 4 NT.

♠ A J 9 7 4 2
♥ Q 3
♦ J 9 5
♣ 7 4

With 8 HCPs plus two points for the six-card suit, you have enough to invite slam. Since there must be a Golden Fit in spades, invite slam by bidding one level beyond game, 5♠.

♥ *PLAY OF THE HAND REVIEW* ♥

As we have seen, while declarer is trying to develop the extra winners he needs to make the contract, the defenders are doing their best to stop him. When declarer puts his PLAN together, he has to watch out for the opponents.

The Holdup Play

Just as the defenders hold up to try to strand declarer's winners, declarer must hold up to disrupt the defenders' communications. This is the classic example:

```
                    NORTH
                   (DUMMY)
                     8 3
      WEST            ██            EAST
    K Q J 10 9        ██            7 6 4
                    SOUTH
                  (DECLARER)
                     A 5 2
```

West leads the king against your notrump contract. If you must let the opponents win one or more tricks while developing the winners you need, you need to hold up your ace twice so that East has no cards left in the suit. If West does not have an outside entry, then it is safe to let East win a trick. On the other hand, it is still dangerous to let West win a trick. West has become the *dangerous opponent*.

In one sense, you have an easier time than the defenders when holding up since you can see both your hands. You do not need signals to tell you how many cards are in partner's hand. On the other hand, you do not know how the missing cards are divided. If they are divided 5–3, as in the above layout, then East has no cards left. If they are divided 4–4, East will still have a card left. The only time you can be certain is when one defender shows out of the suit. The defenders' bidding and signals will sometimes give you the clues you need to decide how long you need to hold up.

Avoiding the Dangerous Opponent

When one opponent is dangerous and the other is not, you want to avoid giving up the lead to the dangerous opponent. An opponent who can take enough winners to defeat your contract is dangerous. An opponent who is in a position to trap one of your high cards is also dangerous. For example, consider this layout:

```
                        NORTH
                       (DUMMY)
                        K 8 3
        WEST           ████████        EAST
        Q J 10 9       ████████        A 6 4
                        SOUTH
                      (DECLARER)
                        7 5 2
```

West is the dangerous opponent, since he is in the position to lead the queen, trapping dummy's king. East is not dangerous since he cannot lead the suit without giving you a trick with dummy's king.

When one opponent is dangerous and the other is not, you want to try to lose a trick to the non-dangerous opponent if one must be lost. For example, suppose West is the dangerous opponent and you need to develop an extra trick from this layout:

```
                        NORTH
                       (DUMMY)
                       K 10 8 3
        WEST           ████████        EAST
        Q 6 2          ████████        J 4
                        SOUTH
                      (DECLARER)
                        A 9 7 5
```

It will do no good to play the ace, the king and then give up a trick — West, the dangerous opponent, will win the third round. Instead lead a small card toward dummy. It will do West no good to play his queen, since you can win dummy's king and take all the tricks. When West plays a small card, play dummy's 8 or 10, letting East win the trick. When you regain the lead, you will get three tricks from the suit without having to give up the lead to West.

♥ *SUMMARY* ♥

The defenders want to develop their own tricks, but they also want to prevent declarer from developing his tricks whenever possible. The defenders must watch to see what declarer is trying to do and look for ways to thwart his plans.

When declarer is trying to develop tricks in a long suit, the defenders can make use of the *holdup play*, refusing to take their winner(s) until declarer's winners are stranded. The defenders can also *attack declarer's entries* to try to drive them out before declarer is ready to use them.

When discarding, the defenders must be careful to prevent declarer from winning undeserved tricks with his small cards. In general, the defenders must work together so that at least one of them keeps enough cards in each suit to prevent declarer's small cards from becoming established. The defenders will have to share the responsibility, with one defender guarding a suit that the other defender cannot protect. Since declarer's cards are hidden, they must listen to the bidding and watch each other's signals for clues as to which cards to keep.

When declarer is taking finesses, the defenders should avoid taking their winners before they have to, keeping declarer in doubt as to the location of the missing cards.

When defending trump contracts, the defenders must look for ways to prevent declarer from ruffing his losers in dummy, either by leading trumps or being in a position to over-trump the dummy. The defenders should also look for opportunities to promote tricks for their side whenever possible.

♥ *GROUP ACTIVITIES* ♥

Exercise One — The Defensive Holdup

In each of the following layouts, declarer has no entries to the dummy other than the cards in the suit. To limit declarer to the minimum number of tricks, which cards would you and partner play on the first trick if declarer leads the 10? Which cards would you play on the second trick if declarer leads a small card to dummy's queen?

1)
DUMMY
K Q J 9 8

PARTNER
7 3
1 2

YOU
A 4 2
2 1

DECLARER
10 6 5

2)
DUMMY
K Q J 9 8

PARTNER
A 4 2
2 1

YOU
7 6 3
2 1

DECLARER
10 5

3)
DUMMY
A Q J 9 2

PARTNER
8 6
1 2

YOU
K 7 4 3
2 1

DECLARER
10 5

1) _____   2) _____   3) _____

239

Exercise Two — Attacking Entries

In each of the following layouts, you are on lead. Which card would you lead to prevent declarer from later using this suit as an entry to the dummy?

1)

DUMMY
A 7

PARTNER
10 8 3

YOU
K J 4 2

DECLARER
Q 9 6 5

2)

DUMMY
K 7 3

PARTNER
10 9 8 4

YOU
A 6 2

DECLARER
Q J 5

3)

DUMMY
K Q 2

PARTNER
8 7 5

YOU
A J 10 4

DECLARER
9 6 3

1) _____   2) _____   3) _____

Exercise Three — Watching Your Discards

In each of the following layouts, how many tricks does declarer get if you discard a small card in the suit? How many tricks does declarer get if you do not discard any cards in the suit?

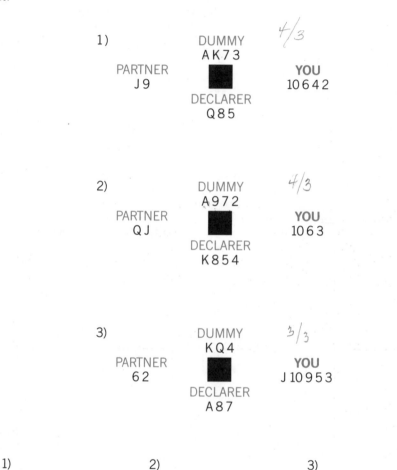

1)   DUMMY   4/3
             A K 7 3
PARTNER   YOU
   J 9   10 6 4 2
             DECLARER
             Q 8 5

2)   DUMMY   4/3
             A 9 7 2
PARTNER   YOU
   Q J   10 6 3
             DECLARER
             K 8 5 4

3)   DUMMY   3/3
             K Q 4
PARTNER   YOU
   6 2   J 10 9 5 3
             DECLARER
             A 8 7

1) _____   2) _____   3) _____

Exercise Four — Practicing Counting

Suppose you can see the following cards in dummy and your own hand:

```
DUMMY
♠ 10 7 5 3
♥ A 6 2
♦ K 9 6 2
♣ 7 5
            YOU
            ♠ K 8 6
  ┌───────┐ ♥ J 8 7 3
  │   N   │ ♦ 10 3
  │ W   E │ ♣ Q 9 6 2
  │   S   │
  └───────┘
```

1) How many spades does declarer have if partner shows out (discards) on the second round?
2) If partner is known to have one spade, five hearts and four diamonds, how many clubs does he hold?
3) Given partner's distribution as above, what is declarer's exact distribution?
4) From the above information, which suit should you be careful not to discard?

5S, 1H, 3D, 4C

1) _____ 2) _____ 3) _____ 4) _____

C suit

Exercise Five — Defending Against Finesses

In each of the following layouts, you are defending a notrump contract and declarer leads a small card toward dummy's jack. Which card should partner play and which card should you play to give declarer the most difficulty in the suit?

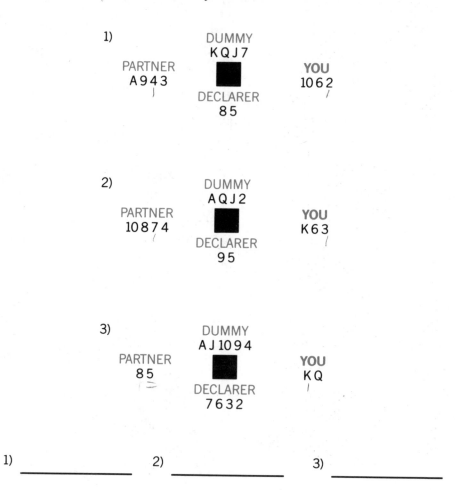

1) DUMMY
    K Q J 7
PARTNER   YOU
A 9 4 3   10 6 2

DECLARER
8 5

2) DUMMY
    A Q J 2
PARTNER   YOU
10 8 7 4   K 6 3

DECLARER
9 5

3) DUMMY
    A J 10 9 4
PARTNER   YOU
8 5   K Q

DECLARER
7 6 3 2

1) _____   2) _____   3) _____

243

Exercise Six — Defending Against Trump Suits

On the following hand, how can the defenders defeat declarer's 2 ♠ contract after West leads the ♥ Q?

Contract: 2 ♠
Lead: ♥ Q

DUMMY
♠ J 7 3
♥ 5 2
♦ K 9 7 2
♣ K 6 4 3

YOU
♠ K 9 5
♥ Q J 10 8
♦ Q 8 6
♣ J 9 7

```
    N
W       E
    S
```

PARTNER
♠ 6 4
♥ A K 6
♦ J 10 5 3
♣ A 10 8 2

DECLARER
♠ A Q 10 8 2
♥ 9 7 4 3
♦ A 4
♣ Q 5

___

Exercise Seven — Review of Slam Bidding

20-21

Your partner opens the bidding 2 NT showing a balanced hand of 22—24 points. What do you respond with each of the following hands?

1) ♠ 8 6 2
    ♥ K J 3
    ♦ A 8 4 2
    ♣ 9 6 2

2) ♠ Q 10 8
    ♥ 9 6 2
    ♦ K 6 3
    ♣ K Q 7 5

3) ♠ A 4 2
    ♥ J 7 3
    ♦ J 10 6 3
    ♣ A Q 5

1) _____3 N_____

2) _____4 N_____

3) _____6 N_____

4) ♠ A J 3
    ♥ K Q 5
    ♦ Q J 9
    ♣ K 10 9 2

5) ♠ 7 6 3
    ♥ Q
    ♦ A J 9 7 5 2
    ♣ K 9 7

6) ♠ K 10 9 8 6 3 2
    ♥ 10 9
    ♦ 5 2
    ♣ A 5

4) _____4 NT_____

5) _____6 NT_____

6) _____6 S_____

7) ♠ K Q 9 3
    ♥ J 8
    ♦ J 8 7 4
    ♣ A 7 3

8) ♠ 9 2
    ♥ A Q J 4 3
    ♦ A 8 5
    ♣ 7 6 5

9) ♠ K J 8 4
    ♥ A J 10 3
    ♦ J 8 3
    ♣ 7 2

7) _____3C_____

8) _____5 H_____

9) _____3C_____

Exercise Eight — Watching Out for the Opponents

You are declarer on the following hand in a contract of 3 NT. West leads the ♥5 and East plays the ♥K on the first trick. Where are your extra tricks going to come from? What is the danger? Which card do you play on the first trick? Why?

Contract: 3 NT
Lead: ♥5

DUMMY
♠ K Q J
♥ 10 8 4
♦ Q J 10 7
♣ A 9 6

♠ 9 3
♥ J 9 7 5 2
♦ A 6 3
♣ J 5 3

```
    N
W       E
    S
```

♠ 10 8 6 4 2
♥ K 6
♦ K 8
♣ Q 7 4 2

DECLARER
♠ A 7 5
♥ A Q 3
♦ 9 5 4 2
♣ K 10 8

Exercise Nine — The Defensive Holdup

Turn up the cards on the first pre-dealt hand. Put each hand dummy style at the edge of the table in front of each player.

Dealer: North

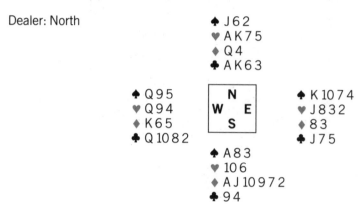

♠ J62
♥ AK75
♦ Q4
♣ AK63

♠ Q95	N	♠ K1074
♥ Q94	W E	♥ J832
♦ K65	S	♦ 83
♣ Q1082		♣ J75

♠ A83
♥ 106
♦ AJ10972
♣ 94

The Bidding

What would North open the bidding? East and West pass throughout the auction. At what level does South know the partnership belongs? Is there a Golden Fit in a major suit? What does South respond? How does the auction proceed? Who is declarer?

The Defense

Which player makes the opening lead? What would the opening lead be? Which card would West play on the first trick if a low card is played from dummy? What would West do next? Which card would West play if the first trick is won in dummy? Which suit must the defenders try to stop declarer from establishing?

The Play

Review the steps in declarer's PLAN. How does declarer plan to make the contract?

Exercise Ten — Discarding Carefully

Turn up the cards on the second pre-dealt hand. Put each hand dummy style at the edge of the table in front of each player.

Dealer: East

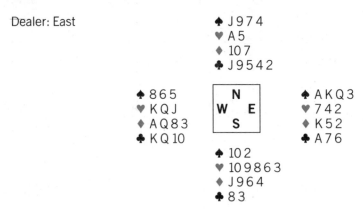

The Bidding

What would East open the bidding? North and South pass throughout. What does West know about the minimum combined strength of the partnership hands? At what level does the partnership belong? Is there any known Golden Fit? What does West respond? How does the auction proceed from there? What is the contract? Who is declarer?

The Defense

Which player makes the opening lead? What would the opening lead be? Which suit must South guard? Which suits can North guard? How can North get clues as to which cards to discard and which cards to keep?

The Play

Review the steps in declarer's PLAN. How does declarer plan to make the contract?

Exercise Eleven — Making Declarer Guess

Turn up the cards on the third pre-dealt hand. Put each hand dummy style at the edge of the table in front of each player.

Dealer: South

♠ A J 8 6 2
♥ K Q 7
♦ A Q
♣ A 8 5

♠ 9
♥ J 8 3
♦ J 10 9 6 3
♣ 9 6 4 2

N
W   E
S

♠ 10 3
♥ A 6 5 4
♦ 8 5 4 2
♣ J 10 3

♠ K Q 7 5 4
♥ 10 9 2
♦ K 7
♣ K Q 7

The Bidding

What is South's opening bid? East and West pass throughout. How many points does North have in support of South's suit? At what level does the partnership belong? In which denomination does the partnership belong? What does North respond? How does the bidding proceed from there? What is the contract? Who is declarer?

The Defense

Which player makes the opening lead? What would the opening lead be? What possibilities can East see for a second defensive trick? What does East plan to do if a heart is led to dummy? Why? Which suit must West avoid discarding?

The Play

Review the steps in declarer's PLAN. How does declarer plan to make the contract?

Exercise Twelve — A Trump in Time

Turn up the cards on the fourth pre-dealt hand. Put each hand dummy style at the edge of the table in front of each player.

Dealer: West

```
                      ♠ 743
                      ♥ QJ75
                      ♦ KQ106
                      ♣ K9
      ♠ KJ952      ┌─────────┐      ♠ Q108
      ♥ A8         │    N    │      ♥ K963
      ♦ 982        │  W   E  │      ♦ J5
      ♣ A75        │    S    │      ♣ J642
                   └─────────┘
                      ♠ A6
                      ♥ 1042
                      ♦ A743
                      ♣ Q1083
```

The Bidding

What is West's opening bid? North and South pass throughout the auction. Can East support partner's suit? What does East respond? How does the auction proceed from there? What is the contract? Who is declarer?

The Defense

Which player makes the opening lead? What would the opening lead be? Which card would South play on the first trick? Why? After seeing the dummy, what does North lead next? Why? How can South cooperate? What must South be careful to do if declarer leads a second diamond from dummy? Why?

The Play

Review the steps in declarer's PLAN. How does declarer plan to make the contract?

LESSON 8
Making a Plan

The Defenders' Plan
Before the Opening Lead
After the Opening Lead
Bidding Review
Play of the Hand Review
Summary

Workshop Material
Group Activities

In the previous lessons we have looked at the various techniques the defenders have available and how they can work together to take their tricks and prevent declarer from taking his tricks. A number of guidelines have been developed to help the defenders handle situations where they are not sure of the best play. Now it is time to put it all together and see how the defenders go about making a plan to defeat declarer. Having a plan will help the defenders decide when to apply a guideline such as "return partner's lead" and when to step outside it to try something different.

♥ THE DEFENDERS' PLAN ♥

The defenders ideally want to make their plan in the same fashion as declarer. They have to go through the same four steps:

1. *Pause to consider your objective*
2. *Look at your winners and losers*
3. *Analyze your alternatives*
4. *Now put it together*

The disadvantage the defenders have is that they cannot see each other's hand. Nonetheless, the idea of making a plan is still important. The defenders have to be more flexible than declarer, modifying their plan as the hand goes along and they get more information about their combined holdings. Let's start by going through the basic planning steps and seeing how they can be applied.

Step One — The Objective

The defenders' basic objective is to defeat the contract whenever possible. The objective can be put into concrete terms in the same fashion that declarer determines how many winners he needs in a notrump contract or how many losers he can afford in a suit contract. The defenders consider how many tricks they need to defeat the contract. For example, when declarer is in a 2♠ contract, he can afford five losers. The defenders need to find six tricks to come out on top.

Determining your objective may seem like a trivial task, but you should not ignore it in favor of considering the best way to handle an individual suit.

Step Two — Counting Tricks

Declarer's next step is to count his winners or losers to see how far he is from his objective. Declarer does this by looking at his combined holding in each suit. The defenders, unable to see each other's holding, do not have it so easy. Suppose these are the defenders' hands:

YOU	PARTNER
♠ A K 6 4	♠ Q J 7 3
♥ A Q	♥ 5 4
♦ J 8 5 4	♦ 10 9 2
♣ 9 6 2	♣ 8 7 5 3

If you are defending a notrump contract, you can see immediately that you have two spade winners and a heart winner. You would not be able to tell right away that your side also has two more sure tricks in spades. Hopefully, as the play progresses you will be able to find that out. For example, partner may be able to make an encouraging signal in spades.

If you are defending a heart contract, it is less obvious how many tricks you have. The only trick you are sure to get is the ♥A. The number of spade tricks depends on how the missing spades are divided. Looking at the combined hands, the best you could hope for is that missing spades are divided 3–2 and you can take two tricks before declarer is able to trump in his hand or the dummy. If the missing spades are divided 4–1, you will get only one trick, and if they are divided 5–0, there are no sure tricks for the defense.

If you are unable to see partner's hand, how would you know you can expect to take no more than two spade tricks? Often the auction will give you the clues you need. If your side has bid and raised a suit, you can generally expect that you have at least eight of them between you and are unlikely to take more than two tricks against a suit contract, even when you have all the top cards in the suit. The fewer cards you have in a suit, the more likely it is that your high cards will take tricks.

The best you can do before seeing the dummy is estimate the number of tricks you are likely to have. With the above hand, you know you will get at least one heart trick if hearts is the trump suit. However, if the opponent on your right (South) bid hearts first, you might expect him to have the ♥K in which case you will get tricks with both the ♥A and ♥Q. You will not know for sure when making the opening lead, but you will be waiting anxiously to see dummy. If the ♥K does not appear in the dummy, you can be confident about taking two heart tricks.

As a defender, you must be patient when trying to count your tricks. You can come up with an initial estimate, but may have to adjust your estimate when dummy appears and as the play progresses.

Step Three — The Alternatives

Once declarer has determined the number of winners he requires and the number he has, or the number of losers he can afford and the number he has, his next step is to look at the alternatives available for establishing extra winners or eliminating excess losers. He looks at each combined suit in turn and analyzes the possibilities. The defenders want to take the same approach, looking to see where they can develop additional tricks.

As you have seen in earlier lessons, the defenders use exactly the same techniques as declarer for developing tricks. They can promote winners, establish long suits, take finesses and trump their losers. Again, they are hampered by the inability to see their combined holding in a suit. That is why they often have to fall back on general guidelines: leading the fourth highest of their longest and strongest suit against notrump contracts; leading the top of touching high cards against suit contracts; playing second hand low and third hand high; covering an honor with an honor; leading through strength.

Once dummy appears, however, the defenders gain the advantage of seeing the location of half of declarer's cards. By visualizing the layout of the missing cards, a defender can often see possibilities for developing tricks. As play progresses, more information comes to light. The defenders can signal each other, and the line of play chosen by declarer will provide clues to the location of the missing cards.

Once more, the defenders must be patient about analyzing their alternatives. They will have to revise their earlier thoughts as each card is played. For example, suppose you start off an opening leader with this hand, defending against a spade contract:

♠ 9 6 3
♥ Q J 10
♦ A Q 6
♣ Q 9 5 2

It looks as though you have one sure trick, the ♦ A. Where can other tricks come from? The heart suit offers the possibility of promotion. If declarer holds the ♥ A and ♥ K, you may be able to drive them out and promote a winner for your side. If partner has the ♥ K, the promotion idea will work that much more quickly. There is also the possibility that partner has the ♥ A and you will be able to trap the ♥ K if it turns up in dummy. The diamond suit has the possibility of providing two tricks especially if declarer has the ♦ K, provided you do not lead the ♦ A initially. You will have to wait until partner, or declarer, leads the suit. On the other hand, if partner has the ♦ K, you may want to lead the suit as soon as you get the opportunity so that you can take your winners before declarer discards his diamond losers on another suit. The club suit offers some potential as well. If partner has some strength in the suit, you may be able to establish one or more winners by leading that suit.

Often the auction will have provided some clues. If partner has bid clubs, you might expect to be able to take or establish winners in that suit by leading a club. If declarer has bid diamonds, you would expect him to have the ♦ K and would want to wait to trap it. With no information to go on, you would probably choose to lead the ♥ Q and wait to see what further information you can get. Suppose this dummy comes down:

DUMMY
♠ K 8 5
♥ K 9 3
♦ 7 4 2
♣ A 8 6 3

YOU
♠ 9 6 3
♥ Q J 10
♦ A Q 6
♣ Q 9 5 2

Having led the ♥ Q, you are about to get some additional information. If declarer wins the first trick with the ♥ A, you know that your only possibility to promote a trick in the suit is by driving out dummy's ♥ K. On the other hand, if declarer plays a small heart from dummy and your ♥ Q wins the first trick, it would be reasonable to assume that partner has the ♥ A and dummy's ♥ K is trapped. By continuing to lead hearts, you may be able to get one or two more tricks for the defense, depending on how many hearts declarer has. You still do not know where the ♦ K is, but at least you know it is not in dummy. Perhaps partner will be able to clarify the situation later, either by giving an encouraging or discouraging signal, or by leading the suit from his side. The possibilities in the club suit are also not clear, but you can see that partner cannot have both the ♣ A and ♣ K. You will have to watch as the play develops to see whether this suit represents a potential source of tricks for the defense or for declarer.

Step Four — Putting it Together

The final step in declarer's plan is to choose from among the alternatives the one most likely to succeed and put everything together into an integrated plan. Declarer must be careful to watch his entries, using them wisely, and to watch out for the opponents, anticipating the damage they might do if they gain the lead.

The defenders need to put their plan together in a similar fashion. For example, to develop tricks in a suit, the suit may have to be led from a particular side. The defenders have to use their entries wisely. They also have to be aware of what declarer may do when he gets the lead, such as discarding or trumping his losers. The defenders have to coordinate their efforts, since there are two of them, each with his own version of the plan. This is both a disadvantage and an advantage. Sometimes, two heads are better than one!

You have already seen examples of how the defenders cooperate when executing their plan. A guideline such as "return partner's suit" helps point you in the right direction, even when you cannot be sure of exactly what partner has in mind. A guideline such as "lead through strength" helps to get a suit led from the appropriate side. Hopefully, as the play develops, the individual plans made by the defenders will merge into a single unified plan, with both defenders focusing their efforts in the same direction.

As the defensive plan takes shape, you need to rely less on the guidelines. The overall plan has priority, and you may find that you need to override a particular guideline when the situation warrants it. Returning partner's suit may not be the way to defeat the contract, you may have to play second hand high or third hand low to give the defense its best chance.

BEFORE THE OPENING LEAD

While it is difficult to make a complete plan before you have even seen the dummy, going through the steps is still worthwhile. It will help you pick out the situations where the standard guidelines may not apply.

Defending a Notrump Contract

Suppose the auction proceeds as follows:

NORTH	EAST	SOUTH	WEST
(DUMMY)	(PARTNER)	(DECLARER)	(YOU)
		1 NT	Pass
3 NT	Pass	Pass	Pass

The bidding has not given you much information and you have to find an opening lead from the following hand:

♠ K J 9 5 3
♥ A 8
♦ A 6
♣ Q 10 8 5

Knowing the guideline "fourth highest from your longest and strongest", you might immediately lead the ♠ 5. It is good practice, however, to go through the planning steps first. This first step is to consider your objective. To defeat three notrump, you need to take five tricks. The next step is to see how many tricks you have. There are two sure tricks, the ♥ A and ♦ A, so you will need to find three more to reach your objective. The third step is to consider the alternatives for developing the extra tricks you need. Any of the suits might provide the tricks you require and, without seeing partner's hand or the dummy, you cannot be sure which suit will work out best. You do know that a good source of tricks is often the longest combined suit in the combined partnership hands. With no other information to go on, that makes spades a most attractive possibility. You may change your mind later if, for example, partner turns up with a singleton spade, but you cannot see a better alternative. The last step is to put everything together. You plan to lead a small spade, hoping partner will have some help in the suit. You also plan to use the ♥ A and ♦ A as entries to help you establish the suit and then take your winners. So, your plan leads you back to the conclusion that your opening lead should be the ♠ 5.

Here is the complete deal:

Contract: 3 NT
Lead: ♠5

DUMMY
♠ Q 6
♥ Q J 7
♦ K J 7 5
♣ J 6 4 3

YOU
♠ K J 9 5 3
♥ A 8
♦ A 6
♣ Q 10 8 5

PARTNER
♠ 10 8 4
♥ 10 9 6 3
♦ 9 4 2
♣ 9 7 2

DECLARER
♠ A 7 2
♥ K 5 4 2
♦ Q 10 8 3
♣ A K

Declarer wins the first trick with dummy's ♠Q and, needing to develop some extra winners, leads a small diamond to his ♦Q. Having seen the dummy, there is nothing to make you revise your original plan. You win the ♦A and continue to establish your spade suit, leading the ♠K (or ♠J) to drive out declarer's ♠A. Declarer has only two spade tricks, three diamond tricks and two club tricks to take, so he will have to lead a heart to try to establish the other winners he needs. You win the ♥A, your second entry, and take three spade tricks to defeat the contract.

Even though you do not have much to guide you before making your opening lead, you can see that it is possible to visualize how the play is likely to go and make a plan. This hand turned out much the way you expected. Now, suppose the auction goes exactly the same way, but we move a couple of cards around in your hand:

♠ 9 8 5 4 3
♥ A 8
♦ A 6
♣ K Q J 10

You go about making your plan in the same manner. You need five tricks to defeat the contract and you start with the same two sure tricks. Where can the additional tricks come from? Spades is your longest suit and you may be able to establish the tricks you need in that suit. You must look at all the alternatives, however, and this draws your attention to the club suit. By leading the ♣K, you will be able to drive out the ♣A and promote three winners in the suit. Putting those tricks together with your two aces will give you enough tricks to reach your objective. Leading a spade may or may not achieve your objective. Leading a club is a sure thing. By making a plan before making the opening lead, you come to the conclusion that the ♣K is a better lead than your fourth highest spade, even though spades is your longest suit.

Let's look at the complete deal:

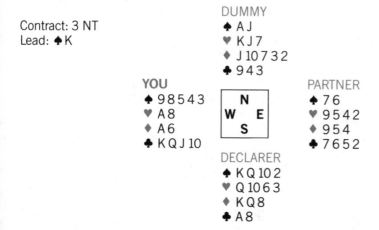

Contract: 3 NT
Lead: ♠K

DUMMY
♠ A J
♥ K J 7
♦ J 10 7 3 2
♣ 9 4 3

YOU
♠ 9 8 5 4 3
♥ A 8
♦ A 6
♣ K Q J 10

PARTNER
♠ 7 6
♥ 9 5 4 2
♦ 9 5 4
♣ 7 6 5 2

DECLARER
♠ K Q 10 2
♥ Q 10 6 3
♦ K Q 8
♣ A 8

When you lead the ♣K, declarer has no chance. After winning the ♣A, he will have to lead a diamond to establish the tricks he needs. You win the ♦A and take your club winners and the ♥A. If you led a spade originally, declarer would win dummy's ♠A and lead a diamond to drive out your ♦A. Now it would be too late to lead a club. Declarer has four spade tricks, four diamond tricks and the ♣A, enough to make the contract.

Defending a Suit Contract

Making a plan before making the opening lead can be equally effective against a suit contract. Suppose the auction proceeds as follows:

NORTH (DUMMY)	EAST (PARTNER)	SOUTH (DECLARER)	WEST (YOU)
	1♥	1♠	Pass
3♠	Pass	4♠	Pass
Pass	Pass		

You have to make the opening lead with the following hand:

♠ 7 5
♥ J 10 7
♦ 8 6 5
♣ 10 9 7 5 2

"Lead partner's suit" jumps out as the guideline to apply, but first go through the planning steps. You will need four tricks to defeat the contract. You do not appear to have any, so it looks as though they will have to come from partner. What are the possibilities? Partner is likely to have some strength in hearts, since he bid the suit. You may be able to help him establish some tricks in the suit by leading a heart. Nothing else looks more appealing, so you end up leading the ♥J, top of touching cards in partner's suit.

Here is the complete deal:

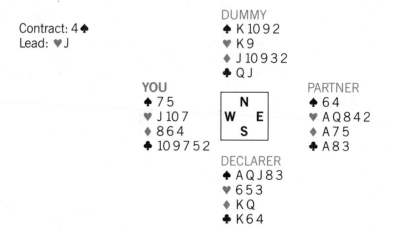

Contract: 4♠
Lead: ♥J

DUMMY
♠ K 10 9 2
♥ K 9
♦ J 10 9 3 2
♣ Q J

YOU
♠ 7 5
♥ J 10 7
♦ 8 6 4
♣ 10 9 7 5 2

PARTNER
♠ 6 4
♥ A Q 8 4 2
♦ A 7 5
♣ A 8 3

DECLARER
♠ A Q J 8 3
♥ 6 5 3
♦ K Q
♣ K 6 4

Your lead of the ♥J easily defeats the contract. Dummy's ♥K is trapped. Partner gets two heart tricks and the ♦A and ♣A, enough to defeat the contract. If you led another suit, declarer would make the contract. Partner would be unable to trap dummy's ♥K by leading from his side and would get only his three aces. Declarer would be able to discard his other heart losers. Leading partner's suit turned out to be the winning defense. Now, let's have the auction go the same way, but change your hand slightly:

♠ 7 5
♥ J 10 7 6 5
♦ 8
♣ 10 9 7 5 2

Again your objective is to take four tricks and you do not have any sure tricks in your hand. Since partner opened the bidding 1 ♥, the heart suit is again a possible source of tricks. This time, however, you have five of them. Partner is also showing at least a five-card suit. The opponents have at most three between them, so one opponent can have no more than a singleton heart. At best, your side will get one trick from the suit. Are there any alternatives? You have a singleton diamond and, if you lead it, partner may be able to win the trick and lead one back for you to trump. If you can get back to partner's hand, you may even be able to get a second ruff. That looks like a more promising plan than leading the ♥J.

You lead the ♦8 and this is the complete deal:

Contract: 4♠
Lead: ♦ 8

DUMMY
♠ K 10 9 2
♥ K 9
♦ J 10 9 3 2
♣ Q J

YOU
♠ 7 5
♥ J 10 7 6 5
♦ 8
♣ 10 9 7 5 2

PARTNER
♠ 6 4
♥ A Q 8 4 2
♦ A 7 5
♣ K 8 3

DECLARER
♠ A Q J 8 3
♥ 3
♦ K Q 6 4
♣ A 6 4

Partner will have to cooperate, but your unusual lead of a diamond, rather than his suit, should tip him off to the winning defense. He wins the first trick with the ♦A and leads one back for you to ruff. He should lead back the ♦7, a suit preference signal for the higher-ranking suit. You now return a heart. Partner must be careful to win this trick and lead his last diamond for you to ruff, rather than trying to take a second heart trick. With careful cooperation, the partnership has found the only defense to defeat the contract. If you had not taken the time to make a plan beforehand, you might have been lulled into following the general guideline to lead partner's suit.

♥ AFTER THE OPENING LEAD ♥

After the opening lead has been made, both defenders can see the dummy and adjust their plan accordingly. The further the play progresses, the more information they will have and the more accurate their plan will become. Here are some examples.

A Shift in Time

This time, you are East and the auction goes as follows:

NORTH	EAST	SOUTH	WEST
(DUMMY)	(**YOU**)	(DECLARER)	(PARTNER)
		1♠	Pass
2♣	Pass	2♠	Pass
4♠	Pass	Pass	Pass

Partner leads the ♦5 and this is the complete hand:

Contract: 4♠
Lead: ♦5

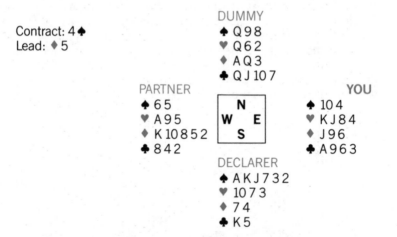

```
                      DUMMY
                      ♠ Q98
                      ♥ Q62
                      ♦ AQ3
                      ♣ QJ107
        PARTNER       ┌─────────┐      YOU
        ♠ 65          │  N      │      ♠ 104
        ♥ A95         │ W    E  │      ♥ KJ84
        ♦ K10852      │  S      │      ♦ J96
        ♣ 842         └─────────┘      ♣ A963
                      DECLARER
                      ♠ AKJ732
                      ♥ 1073
                      ♦ 74
                      ♣ K5
```

Declarer wins the first trick with dummy's ♦Q, draws trump by playing the ♠A and ♠K and then leads the ♣K, on which your partner plays the ♣2. Since partner obviously does not need to show attitude toward clubs, the ♣2 must be a count signal, showing an odd number, likely three. Declarer started with only two clubs, but there is not much point in holding up your ♣A, since there are plenty of entries to dummy. After winning the ♣A, it may be tempting to lead back a diamond, following the guideline to "return partner's suit." You should have been busy revising your plan, however.

You need four tricks to defeat the contract and can see only one for sure, the ♣A. Where are the others to come from? You might be able to establish a trick in diamonds by driving out dummy's ♦A but, even if declarer started with a diamond loser, he can probably discard it on one of dummy's established club winners. The only hope is in the heart suit. Can you visualize a layout of the suit which will let you take three tricks?

If partner has the ♥A, you can lead a small heart to his ♥A and he can lead one back, trapping dummy's ♥Q. Since that is your only hope, you win the ♣A and return the ♥4, forgetting about partner's original suit. Hopefully, partner is busy planning too and can see that the only way to defeat the contract is to take three heart tricks quickly. After winning the ♥A, he leads back the ♥9 and declarer is defeated. If you had returned partner's suit after winning the ♣A, declarer would have discarded two heart losers on dummy's extra club winners and ended up making an overtrick.

Shifting from one suit to another in order to take your winners before declarer can discard his losers is an important consideration in your plan. Let's put you back on opening lead after the auction has gone as follows:

NORTH (DUMMY)	EAST (PARTNER)	SOUTH (DECLARER)	WEST (**YOU**)
	Pass	1♠	Pass
2♣	Pass	2♠	Pass
4♠	Pass	Pass	Pass

You lead the ♥A and this is the complete layout:

Contract: 4♠
Lead: ♥A

DUMMY
♠ Q 7 2
♥ 10 6 5
♦ K 5
♣ A K Q 10 8

YOU
♠ 10 6
♥ A K J 9 3
♦ 10 8 6 2
♣ 9 3

PARTNER
♠ 9 4
♥ 7 4 2
♦ A Q 9 3
♣ 7 5 4 2

DECLARER
♠ A K J 8 5 3
♥ Q 8
♦ J 7 4
♣ J 6

You need four tricks. It is not clear how many heart tricks you can take, but after seeing the dummy and partner's first card, the picture becomes clearer. Partner plays the ♥ 2 on the first trick, a discouraging card, apparently denying the ♥ Q. Partner is unlikely to have exactly two hearts since he might have encouraged, hoping to get a ruff. Partner could also have a singleton heart, so you continue with the ♥ K. When declarer's ♥ Q appears, the layout of the heart suit becomes evident. You could continue by leading the ♥ J, making declarer trump, but you must first consider your plan. You have taken two tricks and two more are needed to defeat the contract. Partner may have a trump trick, but he will get that without your help.

The only other possibility appears to be diamonds. If partner has tricks in diamonds, they may disappear if you do not lead one now. Declarer may be able to discard his diamond losers on dummy's extra club winners after drawing trumps. In order to achieve your objective of defeating the contract, you must shift to a diamond. On the actual hand, partner is able to take two diamond tricks, trapping dummy's ♦ K, and you defeat the contract. If you led anything else, declarer would draw trumps and take the rest of the tricks. You may have been lucky to find partner with the ♦ A and ♦ Q, but if you had not thought about your plan, even that fortunate holding would not have been enough.

Giving the Right Signal

Making a plan will often help you choose the appropriate signal to give partner when you have the opportunity. Consider this hand:

Contract: 2 ♠
Lead: ♥ A

DUMMY
♠ Q 7
♥ 10 8 7
♦ A Q 8
♣ K Q J 8 4

PARTNER
♠ J 6 5
♥ A K J 6
♦ 7 4 3
♣ 9 6 3

YOU
♠ 9 3
♥ Q 9 2
♦ K J 9 5
♣ A 7 5 2

DECLARER
♠ A K 10 8 4 2
♥ 5 4 3
♦ 10 6 2
♣ 10

Partner leads the ♥ A after the bidding has gone:

NORTH (DUMMY)	EAST (**YOU**)	SOUTH (DECLARER)	WEST (PARTNER)
1♣	Pass	1♠	Pass
1 NT	Pass	2♠	Pass
Pass	Pass		

Looking at the ♥ Q in your hand, it would seem natural to make an encouraging signal with the ♥ 9, but first you must consider your plan. To defeat 2♠, you need to take six tricks. It looks as though you may be able to get three heart tricks to go along with your ♣ A, but where are the other tricks going to come from? Looking at your diamond holding, there is the possibility of two diamond tricks, provided the suit is led from partner's side, through dummy's strength. How can you get partner to lead a diamond? Not by encouraging in the heart suit! Instead, play the ♥ 2, a discouraging signal. On seeing this card, partner may not be certain what to do, but it does not look as though leading a club will help the defense establish tricks. Hopefully partner will also realize that the defenders will need some tricks from the diamond suit and use this opportunity to lead one, through dummy's strength, to help you out.

If partner leads a diamond, the defenders can prevail. If declarer plays dummy's ♦ A and leads the ♣ K to drive out your ♣ A, you can lead a heart over to partner and he can lead another diamond through, trapping dummy's ♦ Q. You end up with three heart tricks, two diamond tricks and a club trick. It does no good for declarer to finesse dummy's ♦ Q. You win the ♦ K, lead a heart over to partner and he leads another diamond, establishing

265

your ♦J as a trick. Neither does it do any good for declarer to play the ♦8 when your partner leads one. You win the trick with the ♦J, lead back a heart, and partner leads another diamond to set up the second diamond trick for the defense.

If you played an encouraging heart on the first trick, partner would take the ♥K and lead another heart to your ♥Q. Now it is too late to lead diamonds. Declarer will drive out your ♣A and discard his diamond losers on dummy's ♣Q and ♣J, making an overtrick.

Sometimes, you have to do the exact opposite to the above example. You may need to play an encouraging card when you have no interest in the suit partner has led. Suppose the auction goes this way:

NORTH (DUMMY)	EAST (**YOU**)	SOUTH (DECLARER)	WEST (PARTNER)
		1♠	Pass
3♠	Pass	4♠	Pass
Pass	Pass		

Partner leads the ♥J and this is the complete deal:

Contract: 4♠
Lead: ♥J

```
                       DUMMY
                       ♠ 9 7 4 2
                       ♥ A K 5
                       ♦ A 7 3
                       ♣ A 8 6
    PARTNER                           YOU
    ♠ A Q J        ┌──────────┐      ♠ 5
    ♥ J 10 9 4     │   N      │      ♥ 8 7 2
    ♦ Q 6 4        │ W   E    │      ♦ 10 9 5 2
    ♣ Q 9 5        │   S      │      ♣ 10 7 4 3 2
                   └──────────┘
                       DECLARER
                       ♠ K 10 8 6 3
                       ♥ Q 6 3
                       ♦ K J 8
                       ♣ K J
```

Declarer wins dummy's ♥A and leads a spade toward his ♠K. After winning the first spade trick, what does partner do next? Partner can see that he has three spade tricks and needs to find one more to defeat the contract. If you gave a discouraging signal on the first heart trick by playing the ♥2, he will know the extra trick will have to come from either diamonds or clubs. He may lead one of these suits, hoping that you have the king, or at least the jack, and that he can establish a trick before all the trumps are gone and declarer can discard any loser in the suit.

Looking at the actual deal, it is fatal for the defense if partner leads either a diamond or a club. If he leads a diamond, declarer will get a trick with the ♦J. If he leads a club, declarer will get a trick with the ♣J and be able to discard his diamond loser on dummy's ♣A. The only safe defense is for partner to take his spade winners and lead another heart. Declarer will eventually have to lose another trick due to the unfavorable lie of the missing queens. Partner may decide to defend this way by himself, but you can help him out. Instead of playing a discouraging card on the first trick, play an encouraging card, the ♥8 (or ♥7). It is not that you like hearts so much, it is that your plan does not indicate anything better for partner to lead.

Working Together

Although each partner's plan may be vague to start with, the direction will become clearer as the play progresses. Eventually, the two separate plans should merge into one. Take a look at this hand, where the auction has gone as follows:

NORTH (DUMMY)	EAST (PARTNER)	SOUTH (DECLARER)	WEST (YOU)
		1♥	Pass
2♥	Pass	Pass	Pass

Contract: 2♥
Lead: ♦10

On opening lead, you do not have much to go on. You know you need six tricks to defeat 2♥, but it is hard to say where they are all going to come from. One possibility is the ♠A and ♠Q. You probably can get two tricks if either partner or declarer has the ♠K. If declarer has it, you will have to wait for partner or declarer to lead the suit. In the meantime, you start off by leading the ♦10, top of your sequence, hoping partner has some help in the suit so you can establish some tricks.

Partner is in a similar position to you before dummy comes down. He is uncertain where all the tricks are going to come from. Once he sees the dummy and your opening lead, however, things start to pick up. He can see that your lead has trapped dummy's ♦K and

♦ J, since he holds the ♦ A and ♦ Q. If declarer does not have a singleton or doubleton diamond, it may be possible to get three tricks from that suit. What possibilities are there for more tricks? You may have a trump trick or the ♣ A. Those you are likely to get anyway. Looking at the spade weakness in dummy, however, there is the possibility of trapping high cards in declarer's hand, provided the suit is led from his side.

Suppose declarer puts dummy's ♦ J on your ♦ 10 and partner wins the trick with the ♦ Q. He now leads back the ♠ 10, leading through strength and up to the weakness in dummy. Declarer plays the ♠ J and you win the trick with the ♠ Q. Now things are starting to come into focus and the defense is shifting into high gear. You can lead back the ♦ 9, trapping dummy's ♦ K. When partner wins the ♦ A, he leads back another spade, trapping declarer's ♠ K. The defense ends up taking the first six tricks, three diamond tricks and three spade tricks. After the opening lead, the opportunities for the defenders became clearer and clearer.

On the above hand, both defenders followed the guideline of "leading through strength". Sometimes your defensive plan will show that it is time to lead right into strength.

Suppose the auction goes like this:

NORTH	EAST	SOUTH	WEST
(DUMMY)	(**YOU**)	(DECLARER)	(PARTNER)
1 ♥	Pass	1 NT	Pass
Pass	Pass		

Partner makes the opening lead of the ♣ J and this is the full deal:

Contract: 1 NT
Lead: ♣ J

DUMMY
♠ K Q 6
♥ J 10 9 8 5
♦ K J 10
♣ K 8

PARTNER
♠ J 10 9 4
♥ A 7 6 4
♦ 8 6
♣ A J 5

YOU
♠ 8 3 2
♥ K 3
♦ A Q 7 4 2
♣ 10 7 2

DECLARER
♠ A 7 5
♥ Q 2
♦ 9 5 3
♣ Q 9 6 4 3

Declarer wins the first trick with the ♣ A and leads the ♥ Q. Partner and dummy play low hearts and it is up to you. You consider holding up the first round, but there appear to be enough entries to dummy for declarer to establish the suit, so you win the ♥ K. What next? Your plan says you need seven tricks. Where are they coming from? You may be able to establish some tricks in spades, the suit partner led, depending on how many he has. It looks as though partner has the ♥A and declarer is planning to drive it out to establish winners in the suit. Partner may come up with a trick or two in clubs, but by that time, declarer will probably have enough winners to make the contract.

It looks as if you need some tricks from the diamond suit. Holding the ♦A and ♦Q, you would usually want partner to lead the suit through dummy's strength, but you have no time to wait. Lead back a small diamond, into dummy's strength, letting dummy win a trick with the ♦10. Declarer will lead another heart to drive out partner's ♥A and establish three winners in the suit. Now it is up to partner. He must assume that you have a good reason for leading back a diamond, rather than a spade. Cooperating with your plan, even though he cannot see your hand, partner leads back a diamond, enabling you to take four diamond tricks. Together with the two heart tricks and partner's ♣A, you just manage to defeat the contract.

Giving the Defensive Plan Priority

Here is an example of ignoring the principle of "second hand low." South opens 1 NT and is raised to 3 NT by North. Partner leads the ♥Q and this is the complete layout:

Contract: 3 NT
Lead: ♥Q

```
                    DUMMY
                    ♠ K64
                    ♥ K73
                    ♦ 964
                    ♣ A952
   PARTNER                        YOU
   ♠ J5          ┌─────────┐      ♠ Q10972
   ♥ QJ1085      │ N       │      ♥ 64
   ♦ K3          │ W    E  │      ♦ A85
   ♣ Q743        │    S    │      ♣ 1086
                 └─────────┘
                    DECLARER
                    ♠ A83
                    ♥ A92
                    ♦ QJ10072
                    ♣ KJ
```

Declarer wins the first trick with dummy's ♥K and leads a diamond from dummy. If you instinctively follow by playing the ♦5, second hand low, declarer makes the contract. How do you know that this is the time to play "second hand high"? You have to be busy making your plan. You can see only one sure trick for the defense, the ♦A. Partner's lead of the ♥Q, however, gives you some valuable information. It looks as though partner has led from a long suit headed by a sequence. This should be a good potential source of tricks for the defense, hopefully enough to defeat the contract. When putting your plan together, is there any problem? Just as declarer has to be careful to watch his entries when making a plan, so must the defenders. While partner may be able to establish his suit when he next gets the lead, he may have no entry left. It will do no good if you get the lead — partner's winners will be stranded.

To prevent this, you have to use your entry first to establish partner's winners, saving partner's entry to get in and take his winners. Play the ♦A right away and lead another heart, establishing the suit. When declarer tries to establish the winners he needs in the diamond suit, partner will get a trick with the ♦K and take his heart tricks, defeating the contract.

If you played a low diamond on the first trick, declarer would play a high diamond, driving out partner's ♦K. He could lead another heart to drive out declarer's ♥A, but it would do no good. Declarer can drive out your ♦A and you have no hearts left to lead. Declarer ends up with two spade tricks, two heart tricks, three diamond tricks and two club tricks, making the contract.

Normally, you do not want to let declarer trump losers in the dummy. Here is a hand to show that there are times when you must actually force declarer to ruff in the dummy in order to defeat the contract. Here is the complete deal:

Contract: 6♥
Lead: ♠A

DUMMY
♠ 3
♥ A 9 3
♦ A K Q J 8
♣ A Q J 7

YOU
♠ A K 8 5
♥ K 4 2
♦ 10 4 3
♣ 8 6 4

PARTNER
♠ 10 7 6 4 2
♥ 7
♦ 9 6 5
♣ 10 9 3 2

DECLARER
♠ Q J 9
♥ Q J 10 8 6 5
♦ 7 2
♣ K 5

The opponents have a long auction to 6♥. Holding the ♠A and ♠K, as well as the ♥K, you might think of doubling the contract. If you do, you had better be careful while defending it. You start off by leading the ♠A, hoping to take two quick spade tricks, but the sight of dummy forces you to abandon your original plan. The singleton spade in dummy makes it appear you are not going to get a second trick in that suit. In addition, the ♥A has shown up in dummy, leaving your ♥K in danger of being trapped. Is there anything you can do to find the second trick you need?

The answer is to lead your ♠K, even though declarer can trump it in dummy. The advantage of this play is that declarer will be left with only two hearts in dummy and will no longer be able to trap your ♥K. When he leads the ♥Q from his hand, you will refuse to cover, and eventually you will take the setting trick with the ♥K. It is always a good feeling to defeat an opponent's slam contract.

BIDDING REVIEW

When both sides are in the auction, it is not always possible to make the ideal bid. The opponents' bidding often takes away the room you need to describe your hand. In such situations, you may have to make the best bid possible, rather than the best possible bid. Competition gives an added element of excitement to the auction.

When an Opponent Overcalls

Suppose your partner opens the bidding 1 ♦ and you hold the following hand:

♠ K 10 6 3
♥ J 6 4
♦ 10 8
♣ A 9 6 3

With 8 HCPs, you plan to respond 1 ♠, bidding a new suit at the one level. If the opponent on your right overcalls 1 ♥, no harm has been done. You can still respond 1 ♠. The opponent's bid has not interfered with your natural response. On the other hand, if the opponent overcalls 1 ♠, rather than 1 ♥, you cannot make your normal response. On this hand, however, you have a suitable alternative. You can respond 1 NT, showing partner that you have 6–10 points. Things are more difficult if the opponent overcalls 2 ♦. You do not have enough strength to bid at the two level. Instead, you will have to pass. This is not ideal because partner does not know you have some strength. The auction is not over, however. Partner still has another chance to bid if he has more than a minimum hand — you may still get an opportunity to describe your hand.

The Penalty Double

One bid that becomes available when the opponents interfere with your auction is the penalty double. A double is for takeout only if your partner has not already made a bid in the auction. For example, suppose your partner opens the bidding 1 ♥ and you have the following hand:

♠ A J 8 3
♥ 8
♦ K J 10 6 4
♣ Q 10 3

If the opponent on your right overcalls 2 ♦, this is a good hand to make a penalty double. With partner having the strength for an opening bid, it is very unlikely that the opponents can make a contract of 2 ♦. Your double tells partner you would like to defend the hand for penalties. You are not concerned about warning the opponents that they are in trouble. It does not look as though they have any better place to play the contract.

When an Opponent Makes a Takeout Double

If an opponent doubles your partner's bid for takeout, it does not take up any room in the auction. The easiest thing to do is to continue making your natural bids as though nothing happened. In the *Spade Series*, we will look at the use of the *redouble after an opponent has doubled*. For now, bidding naturally will suffice.

Competing for Partscore

When both sides are bidding and the strength is fairly evenly divided, you will often be faced with having to choose between the following actions:

- Pass, planning to defend against the opponents' contract
- Bidding higher, hoping to buy the contract or to push the opponents even higher

For example, suppose partner opens the bidding 1 ♥ and you hold the following hand:

♠ 7 4
♥ A 9 6 3
♦ K 10 8 6 5
♣ 9 5

If the opponent on your right overcalls 1 ♠, you would raise to 2 ♥, hoping to play there if partner has a minimum hand. If the opponent on your left bids 2 ♠, however, and partner and the overcaller both pass, you are faced with a decision. You can pass and defend 2 ♠, hoping to defeat that contract, or you can bid on to 3 ♥, hoping to make that contract or push the opponents up to 3 ♠. With good support for your partner and little defense against a spade contract, you should bid 3 ♥ on the actual hand. Partner will know that you are just competing. You limited your hand to 6–10 points when you raised to 2 ♥ originally.

PLAY OF THE HAND REVIEW

When declarer is putting his plan together in a suit contract, one of the key considerations is how to handle the trump suit. Declarer must decide whether to draw trumps right away or to delay drawing trumps while dealing with other priorities.

Drawing Trumps

You generally want to draw trumps as soon as possible to avoid having the opponents trump any of your winners. If you do not need your trumps for any other purpose, you should draw trumps when:

- You do not have more losers than you can afford.
- You have more losers than you can afford but can draw trumps without giving up the lead to the opponents.
- You have more losers than you can afford but there are not too many quick losers if you have to give up the lead while drawing trumps.

For example, consider the following hand. You are playing in a 4♠ contract and the opening lead is the ♦J:

```
                    DUMMY
                    ♠ K 9 6 2
                    ♥ A K 10 7
                    ♦ 6 5 2
      LEAD          ♣ Q 6
      ♦ J
                    DECLARER
                    ♠ Q J 7 5 3
                    ♥ Q 9
                    ♦ A K 7
                    ♣ 9 3 2
```

You have a spade loser, a diamond loser and three club losers. You will have to give up the lead to draw trumps because the opponents have the ♠A. You have only three quick losers, however — the ♠A and two club tricks. It is safe to start drawing trumps. Once the opponents' trumps are gone, you plan to discard a diamond loser on dummy's extra heart winner and trump a club loser in the dummy. If you tried to discard your diamond loser before drawing trumps, an opponent might trump one of your heart tricks. Now you could no longer make the contract.

Delaying Drawing Trumps

You will have to delay drawing trumps when:

- You may have to give up the lead and have too many quick losers.
- You need the trumps for other purposes, such as trumping losers or for entries.
- You need to get to the other hand so that you can take a finesse in the trump suit to avoid a loser.

Consider the following hand in a contract of 4♠, with the opening lead of a club:

```
                        DUMMY
                        ♠ K 9 3
                        ♥ A K 7 5
                        ♦ 10 5
        LEAD            ♣ K 8 4 2
        ♣ J
                        DECLARER
                        ♠ A Q J 7 5
                        ♥ 8 4 3
                        ♦ J 6 3
                        ♣ A 7
```

There is a heart loser and three diamond losers. You can eliminate one of the diamond losers by ruffing in dummy. You need only one trump to ruff your loser, but you cannot afford to draw even one round. You will have to give up the lead twice to make dummy void in diamonds so that you can trump your loser. The opponents may try to foil your plan by leading trumps when they get in. You must therefore lead a diamond immediately after winning the first club trick. The opponents can lead trumps twice, but you will still have one left in dummy to ruff your loser.

♥ **SUMMARY** ♥

Each defender makes a plan, going through the same steps as declarer:

1. **P**ause to consider your objective.
2. **L**ook at your winners and losers.
3. **A**nalyze your alternatives.
4. **N**ow put it together.

Since the defenders cannot see their combined holding in each suit, it is sometimes difficult to determine where their tricks are going to come from. Nonetheless, making a plan will often point them in the right direction and, as the hand progresses, the plan will become more concrete. The defenders try to work together, giving each other information through their signals and trying to visualize how they can help each other. They both want to end up working on the same plan.

♥ *GROUP ACTIVITIES* ♥

Exercise One — Before Dummy Comes Down

You (West) are on lead with the following hand:

     ♠ 10 9 8 3
     ♥ K 5
     ♦ A Q 3
     ♣ J 6 4 2

The auction has gone:

NORTH (DUMMY)	EAST (PARTNER)	SOUTH DECLARER)	WEST (YOU)
		1 ♥	Pass
2 ♣	Pass	2 ♦	Pass
2 ♥	Pass	4 ♥	Pass
Pass	Pass		

How do you plan to defeat the contract? What is your opening lead?

Exercise Two — After Dummy Comes Down

You (East) are defending a contract of 4♠ after the bidding has gone:

NORTH	EAST	SOUTH	WEST
(DUMMY)	(**YOU**)	(DECLARER)	(PARTNER)
1♦	Pass	1♠	Pass
1 NT	Pass	4♠	Pass
Pass	Pass		

Partner leads the ♥2 and dummy is put down:

Contract: 4♠
Lead: ♥2

DUMMY
♠ K 5
♥ 10 7 5
♦ K Q J 7
♣ A J 7 3

YOU
♠ 8 4 2
♥ A 9 6 4
♦ A
♣ 10 8 6 5 2

How do you plan to defeat the contract?

277

Exercise Three — Competitive Bidding

Your partner opens the bidding 1 ♥ and the opponent on your right overcalls 2 ♣. What do you bid on each of the following hands?

1) ♠ A 9 3	2) ♠ K J 6 4	3) ♠ A 10 7
♥ K 8 6	♥ 8 4	♥ K 6
♦ 10 7 6 2	♦ Q 7 2	♦ A J 8 7 4
♣ J 9 4	♣ J 8 6 3	♣ 9 4 2

1) ___2 H___   2) ___P___   3) ___2 D___

4) ♠ J 6 2	5) ♠ K 10 3	6) ♠ A J 10 7 3
♥ K Q 7 2	♥ 4	♥ 10 3
♦ A 10 7 6 2	♦ Q 10 6 2	♦ A Q 8 7 4
♣ 4	♣ A Q J 9 3	♣ 9

4) ___3 H___   5) ___Dbl.___   6) ___2 S___

Exercise Four — Drawing Trumps

How do you plan to play the following hand in a contract of 6 ♣ after an opening lead of the ♥ K?

```
                        DUMMY
                        ♠ K 9
                        ♥ A 9 6 4
                        ♦ A Q 7
         LEAD           ♣ 10 9 6 3
         ♥ K
                        -DECLARER
                        ♠ A Q J 5
                        ♥ J 7
                        ♦ 8
                        ♣ K Q J 8 5 2
```

Exercise Five — Making a Plan

Turn up the cards on the first pre-dealt hand. Put each hand dummy style at the edge of the table in front of each player.

Dealer: North

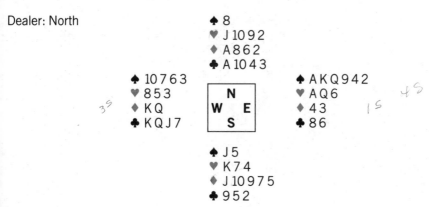

Dummy layout:

North
- ♠ 8
- ♥ J 10 9 2
- ♦ A 8 6 2
- ♣ A 10 4 3

West
- ♠ 10 7 6 3
- ♥ 8 5 3
- ♦ K Q
- ♣ K Q J 7

East
- ♠ A K Q 9 4 2
- ♥ A Q 6
- ♦ 4 3
- ♣ 8 6

South
- ♠ J 5
- ♥ K 7 4
- ♦ J 10 9 7 5
- ♣ 9 5 2

The Bidding

North and South pass throughout the auction. What would East open the bidding? How does West plan to show support for partner's major with 12 dummy points? How does the auction proceed? What is the contract? Who is declarer?

The Defense

Which player makes the opening lead? What would the opening lead be? After seeing the dummy, how does North plan to defeat the hand?

The Play

Review the steps in declarer's PLAN. How does declarer plan to make the contract?

Exercise Six — Finding a Shift

Turn up the cards on the second pre-dealt hand. Put each hand dummy style at the edge of the table in front of each player.

Dealer: East

The hand diagram:

```
                    ♠ 10 6
                    ♥ A K Q 10
                    ♦ 10 7 3
                    ♣ 9 7 4 3
  ♠ A Q J 9 5 3    ┌─────────┐    ♠ K 8
  ♥ J 8            │    N    │    ♥ 9 6 5 4
  ♦ K 6            │  W   E  │    ♦ A Q J 5
  ♣ J 10 6         │    S    │    ♣ K 8 2
                   └─────────┘
                    ♠ 7 4 2
                    ♥ 7 3 2
                    ♦ 9 8 4 2
                    ♣ A Q 5
```

The Bidding

What would East open the bidding? North and South pass throughout. What does West respond? How does East describe his hand with his rebid? What level does West know the partnership belongs in? Is there a *Golden Fit*? What does West rebid?

The Defense

Which player makes the opening lead? What would the opening lead be? What is North's original plan. What further information does North have after the first trick? After the second trick? Which cards might partner hold to defeat the contract?

The Play

Review the steps in declarer's PLAN. How does declarer plan to make the contract?

Exercise Seven — Making Use of Signals

Turn up the cards on the third pre-dealt hand. Put each hand dummy style at the edge of the table in front of each player.

Dealer: South

```
                    ♠ A K
                    ♥ K J 10 6 5
                    ♦ Q 10 3
                    ♣ K Q J

   ♠ J 10 9 6 3   ┌─────────┐   ♠ Q 8 2
   ♥ A 9 3        │   N     │   ♥ 7 4 2
   ♦ 7 4          │ W     E │   ♦ A K J 9
   ♣ 9 5 2        │   S     │   ♣ 7 6 4
                  └─────────┘
                    ♠ 7 5 4
                    ♥ Q 8
                    ♦ 8 6 5 2
                    ♣ A 10 8 3
```

The Bidding

South and West pass. Why can North not open 1 NT? What does North bid? East passes. Without support for opener's suit and no suit to bid at the one level, what does South respond? West passes. How does North show his maximum strength and balanced distribution? How does the bidding proceed from there? Who is declarer?

The Defense

Which player makes the opening lead? What would the opening lead be? Does East like the suit partner led? How does East plan to defeat the contract? What signal does East give on the first trick?

The Play

Review the steps in declarer's PLAN. How does declarer plan to make the contract?

Exercise Eight — The Lesser of Evils

Turn up the cards on the fourth pre-dealt hand. Put each hand dummy style at the edge of the table in front of each player.

Dealer: West

```
                          ♠ K6        14⁺
                          ♥ A9542
                          ♦ A43
                          ♣ K64
        ♠ J9742        ┌─────────┐    ♠ A103
        ♥ 6            │   N     │    ♥ K73
        ♦ J72          │ W     E │    ♦ 10986
        ♣ J1093        │   S     │    ♣ A85
                       └─────────┘
                          ♠ Q85
                          ♥ QJ108    3 4
                          ♦ KQ5
                          ♣ Q72
```

The Bidding

West passes. What is North's opening bid? East passes. How does South show his support for partner's major and the strength of his hand? West passes. What does North rebid? How does the auction proceed from there? Who is declarer?

The Defense

Which player makes the opening lead? What is East's plan? What would the opening lead be? Does West like the suit partner has led? Does West prefer another suit? Which card would West play on the first trick? Why? When East regains the lead, how does he plan to defend? Why?

The Play

Review the steps in declarer's PLAN. How does declarer plan to make the contract?

Exercise Nine — Third Hand Not So High

Turn up the cards on the fifth pre-dealt hand. Put each hand dummy style at the edge of the table in front of each player.

Dealer: North

♠ 84
♥ 972
♦ A863
♣ KQ86

♠ K1095
♥ AQ3
♦ Q104
♣ 954

N
W   E
S

♠ QJ73
♥ KJ8
♦ KJ75
♣ AJ

♠ A62
♥ 10654
♦ 92
♣ 10732

The Bidding

North and South pass throughout. What would East open the bidding? At what level does West know the partnership belongs? Is there a *Golden Fit* in a major suit? How can West find out? What does East rebid? What does West rebid? How does the auction proceed from there? What is the contract? Who is declarer?

The Defense

Which player makes the opening lead? How might South plan to get a second trick from the trump suit? What would the opening lead be? How does North know that his partner is unlikely to have a singleton diamond? How does North plan to defeat the contract? Which card would North play on the first trick? Why?

The Play

Review the steps in declarer's PLAN. How does declarer plan to make the contract?

Exercise Ten — Working Together

Turn up the cards on the sixth pre-dealt hand. Put each hand dummy style at the edge of the table in front of each player.

Dealer: East

```
                    ♠ Q J 10
                    ♥ K 3 2
                    ♦ Q 10 7 5
                    ♣ K 9 4

     ♠ K 8 6 5 2    ┌─────────┐    ♠ A 9 3
     ♥ 10 6 4       │    N    │    ♥ 9 8 5
     ♦ 8 3          │ W     E │    ♦ A 6 2
     ♣ J 8 6        │    S    │    ♣ 10 5 3 2
                    └─────────┘
                    ♠ 7 4
                    ♥ A Q J 7
                    ♦ K J 9 4
                    ♣ A Q 7
```

The Bidding

East and West pass throughout. What does South open the bidding? What does North respond? How does the auction proceed from there? What is the contract? Who is declarer?

The Defense

Which player makes the opening lead? How does West plan to defeat the contract? What would the opening lead be? Which card does East play to the first trick? How does East plan to defeat the contract? Which card does East return? Which card does West play? Why? Does East plan to hold up if declarer leads diamonds?

The Play

Review the steps in declarer's PLAN. How does declarer plan to make the contract?

Exercise Eleven — Trump Promotion

Turn up the cards on the seventh pre-dealt hand. Put each hand dummy style at the edge of the table in front of each player.

Dealer: South

```
                        ♠ 10 9 8 6 5 2
                        ♥ 6 4 2
                        ♦ K Q
                        ♣ K Q

        ♠ J 7 3              N              ♠ 4
        ♥ A Q 8 5       W         E         ♥ J 10 9 7
        ♦ 10 8 3            S              ♦ 9 7 6 4
        ♣ A 7 5                             ♣ 9 8 4 2

                        ♠ A K Q
                        ♥ K 3
                        ♦ A J 5 2
                        ♣ J 10 6 3
```

The Bidding

What is South's opening bid? East and West pass throughout. Does North know if there is a *Golden Fit*? At what level does the partnership belong? What does North respond? How does the bidding proceed from there? What is the contract? Who is declarer?

The Defense

Which player makes the opening lead? What would the opening lead be? How many defensive tricks can West see? What possibilities are there for defeating the contract? What is West's plan?

The Play

Review the steps in declarer's PLAN. How does declarer plan to make the contract?

Exercise Twelve — Second Hand High

Turn up the cards on the eighth pre-dealt hand. Put each hand dummy style at the edge of the table in front of each player.

Dealer: West

```
              ♠ 10 8 3
              ♥ Q J 10 7 3
              ♦ J 7 2
              ♣ K 7

♠ A K 5          N          ♠ Q 6 2
♥ 9 6 5 2    W       E      ♥ A K
♦ A K 6          S          ♦ 10 5 3
♣ Q 10 4                    ♣ J 9 8 5 2

              ♠ J 9 7 4
              ♥ 8 4
              ♦ Q 9 8 4
              ♣ A 6 3
```

The Bidding

What is West's opening bid? North and South pass throughout the auction. What does East respond? How does the auction proceed from there? What is the contract? Who is declarer?

The Defense

Which player makes the opening lead? What would the opening lead be? How does South plan to defeat the contract? What does South plan to do when he gets the lead? If declarer leads a club, which card should South play? Why?

The Play

Review the steps in declarer's PLAN. How does declarer plan to make the contract?

APPENDIX
Glossary of Terms
Answers to Exercises

GLOSSARY OF TERMS

Attitude Signal — An attitude signal gives your partner advice on whether or not to lead or continue a particular suit. It is partner's option to follow this advice as he sees fit. (Page 146)

Blocked — A situation in which entry problems within a particular suit make it difficult or impossible to take winners or possible winners in that suit. (Page 8)

Broken Sequence — A sequence in which you have the top two cards but are missing a card before the next highest card (K Q 10 or Q J 9, for example). (Page 12)

Captain — The partner who knows more about the combined hands and is responsible for directing the partnership to its contract. Usually the responder is the captain. (Page 55)

Combined Hands — The cards making up both hands belonging to one partnership. (Page 112)

Combined Points — The total number of points belonging to a partnership. (Page 234)

Convention — A bid that conveys a meaning other than that which would normally be attributed to it. (Page 56)

Count Signal — A count signal tells partner how many cards you have in a suit. (Page 146)

Dangerous Opponent — A defender is dangerous if he can, or might, be able to lead a card that will set your contract. (Page 236)

Defensive Signals — Specific cards played by the defenders in certain situations by which each defender can paint a picture of his hand to give partner the information needed to make an appropriate decision. (Page 146)

Discarding a Loser — Getting rid of a card in a player's hand that could lose a trick to the opponents. (Page 83)

Distribution — The number of cards held in each suit by a particular player or by a partnership; the number of cards held in a particular suit by a partnership. (Page 22)

Drawing Trumps — The playing of trumps until there are none in the opponents' hands. (Page 39)

Duck — To play a low card and surrender a trick which could be won, with the object of preserving an entry or of shutting out an opponent's suit. (Page 17)

Entry — A card that provides a means of winning a trick in a particular hand. (Page 4)

Equals (Play from) — When holding cards of equal rank in a suit, it is often important which card is chosen to be played to a particular trick. A defender's card may provide partner with important information, or it may deceive the declarer. (Page 75)

Finesse — An attempt to win a trick with a card that does not rank as high as one held by the opponents. (Page 16)

Forcing (Bid) — A bid that requires partner to bid again (unless the opponent calls first). (Page 45)

Fourth Highest — The fourth highest card of a long suit, starting at the top and counting down (e.g., K 5 4 **3** 2). (Page 3)

High-Low (Signal) — The order of playing cards so that a higher card is played first followed by a lower card (the 5 followed by the 3, for example) expressing the desire for partner to continue the suit or suggesting an interest in that suit being played when partner obtains the lead. It also may suggest an even number of cards in the suit. (Page 151)

Hold-up (Play) — Refusing to take a winner at your first opportunity with the intention of removing one opponent's link cards in that suit. (Page 8)

High-Card Points (HCPs) — The points given to the four honor cards. Ace — 4; King — 3; Queen — 2; Jack — 1. (Page 22)

Interior Sequence — A sequence in which the top card of the suit is not part of the sequence (K J 10 or A 10 9, for example). (Page 12)

Invitational (Bid) — A bid that invites partner to bid again. (Page 87)

Link — A card which can be led to a winner (entry) in the opposite hand. (Page 17)

Long Suit — A suit in which four or more cards are held. (Page 3)

Lose Control — A situation in which declarer has no trumps left to prevent the defenders from taking their winners. (Page 45)

Loser — A card in a player's hand that could lose a trick to the opponents. (Page 38)

Low-High (Signal) — A low card followed by a higher card (the 3 followed by the 5, for example), indicating an odd number of cards in the suit or a lack of interest in the suit. (Page 152)

MUD — A lead convention in which the original lead from three small cards is the middle one, followed in play by the higher. The acronym comes from the first letters of middle, up, down, the order in which the cards are played. (Page 59)

Natural Trump Trick — Trick in a trump suit which will eventually be a winner. For example, when a defender holds Q J 10 9 in the trump suit, he has two natural trump tricks when declarer holds the ace and king. (Page 44)

Opening Lead — The card led by declarer's left-hand opponent after the bidding has ended. (Page 2)

Opponents' Suit — A suit held or bid by one or both of the opponents. (Page 196)

Overruff — To trump higher than the opponent on one's right after a non-trump suit has been led. (Page 195)

Overtake — To play a higher card than the one already played by partner for entry reasons. (Page 76)

Partner's Suit — The suit bid or rebid by your partner. (Page 4)

Passive Lead — An opening lead which is unlikely to hurt the defending side, but is not expected to have a positive value. In certain situations a trump lead may be passive. (Page 48)

Preemptive (Bid) — A bid made to interfere with the opponents' auction. It usually is made with a long suit and a weak hand. (Page 23)

Quick Loser — A quick loser is one that will be lost as soon as you give up the lead. (Page 167)

Redouble — A bid made after the opponents have doubled. Originally it was used to increase the scoring value of overtricks or undertricks. In modern bidding methods it can be used for other purposes. (Page 271)

Ruff — Playing a trump on a trick when you are void in the suit led. (Page 38)

Sacrifice — A bid made without the intention of fulfilling the contract but of preventing the opponents from playing and making their contract. The assumption is that you will lose fewer points by going down in your bid than the opponents would have received for making their contract. (Page 16)

Second Hand — The second player to play to a trick after the lead is made. (Page 6)

Shift — To lead a suit other than that previously led. (Page 38)

Short Suit — In an original hand of thirteen cards, a suit containing three cards or fewer. (Page 7)

Signoff (Bid) — A bid that asks partner to pass. (Page 124)

Splitting Honors — Playing one of two honors which are in sequence. Playing the king or queen from a holding of the K Q 6, for example. (Page 110)

Spot (Cards) — Cards ranking below the jack — from the 10 down to the 2. (Page 3)

Stranded — Winners that cannot be taken because there is no entry to them. (Page 8)

Stayman (Convention) — An artificial response of 2♣ to an opening bid of 1 NT (or 3♣ in response to a 2 NT opening) asking opener to bid a four-card major suit if he has one, and otherwise to bid 2♦. (Page 87)

Stronger Suit — A suit which has equal length to another suit but has more high card strength. (Page 5)

Suit Preference (Signal) — A device in defensive play whereby a player may indicate a desire to have his partner lead one suit rather than another, when his partner has a choice. (Page 146)

Sure Trick — A trick that can be taken without giving up the lead to the opponents. (Page 2)

Third Hand — The partner of the leader to a trick. (Page 72)

Top of Nothing — The highest ranking card of three or more low cards. (Page 59)

Top of a Sequence — The highest ranking card in a sequence. (Page 28)

Touching Honors — Two or more honors in sequence. In a holding of Q J 10 7, the first three are touching honors. (Page 7)

Trap (a high card) — A position where a high card cannot win a trick because the opponent next to play has a higher card. (Page 9)

Unbid Suit(s) — A suit or suits not bid by a partnership during the auction. (Page 6)

Unblocking — Playing or discarding a high card during the play in order to get rid of it to allow the opposite hand to take tricks in the suit. (Page 102)

Uppercut — A ruff, usually by a defender, aimed at promoting a trump trick for partner. (Page 233)

ANSWERS TO EXERCISES

Lesson One: Opening Leads Against Notrump Contracts

Exercise One
    1) Heart   2) Spade   3) Diamond   4) Club

Exercise Two
    1) Jack, the top of a doubleton
    2) Queen, top of a sequence
    3) Five, low from three cards not headed by touching high cards

Exercise Three
    1) Jack, top of a three-card sequence; you expect to take three tricks; partner plays the ace only when dummy's king is played.
    2) Queen, top of a broken sequence; you expect to take three tricks; the suit has to be led by partner the second time in order to trap declarer's 10.
    3) Jack, top of an interior sequence; you expect to take four tricks; if dummy's king wins the first trick, the suit has to be led by partner the second time in order to trap declarer's queen.
    4) King, top of a three-card sequence; you expect to take five tricks; partner has to overtake your king with the ace (or overtake your queen with the ace on trick two) and lead back the suit.

Exercise Four
    1) The 7 (or 2); you expect to take three tricks; the suit has to be led by partner the second time in order to trap declarer's 10.
    2) The 3; you expect to take three tricks; partner has to return the suit.
    3) The 3 (or 2); you expect to take five tricks; you must overtake partner's honor card in order to take the lead and play the rest of your winners in the suit.

Exercise Five
    1) ♥4   2) ♦Q   3) ♠6

Exercise Six
    1) ♦2   2) ♦J   3) ♣K

Exercise Seven
    1) 1♠   2) 1 NT   3) 1♦
    4) 2 NT   5) 2♠   6) 3♦

Exercise Eight
  Declarer needs nine tricks and has five. Four more tricks can be promoted in diamonds. Declarer has to make sure to leave the ♣A in the dummy as an entry to the diamonds once they are established. He also has to play the ♦K first, high card from the short side.

Exercise Nine
  The bidding
  - North opens the bidding 1 ♦.
  - East bids 1 NT and South passes.
  - West has 10 total points — 9 HCPs plus 1 for the five-card suit.
  - The partnership belongs in game.
  - There is no *Golden Fit* so West responds 3 NT.
  - All players pass and the contract is 3 NT.
  - East is the declarer.

  The defense
  - South leads partner's suit, the ♦9.
  - North plans to drive out declarer's ♦A and ♦K and take three promoted diamond tricks along with the two club winners to defeat the contract.

  The play
  - Declarer needs nine winners and has six sure tricks. Declarer plans to promote the club suit into three winners by driving out the ♣A and ♣K, hoping the defenders do not collect their diamond tricks before he has a chance to follow through with his plan.

Exercise Ten
  The bidding
  - South opens with 1 ♦ and North responds 1♠.
  - South rebids 1 NT showing a balanced, minimum hand.
  - The partnership belongs in game. Since there is no *Golden Fit*, North rebids 3 NT.
  - All players pass and South is the declarer.

  The defense
  - West leads the ♥J, the top of touching honors from an interior sequence.
  - East knows declarer has the ♥Q because of West's lead of the ♥J.
  - East has to play the ♥A on the ♥J and return a heart so that declarer's ♥Q is trapped. The defenders take four heart tricks and the ♣A.

  The play
  - Declarer needs nine tricks. He has four spade tricks and five diamond tricks — as soon as he gets the lead. The defenders, however, can take four heart tricks and a club trick before declarer gets a chance.

Exercise Eleven
  The bidding
  - West opens 2 NT.
  - East responds 3 NT.
  - Everyone passes, 3NT is the final contract and the declarer is West.

  The defense
  - North leads a low heart since he does not have a three-card or longer sequence.
  - The defenders lose the first trick but have four heart winners and a club winner ready to take. Eventually declarer has to give South the lead with the ♣A. South will have to have kept a heart to get back to North's winners and North will have to have kept all of his hearts.

  The play
  - After taking the first heart trick, declarer has eight tricks and needs to promote a club in order to make the contract. The defenders get the lead and can take their heart tricks before declarer can promote enough winners in the club suit.

Exercise Twelve
  The bidding
  - North opens the bidding 1♦.
  - East has no five-card suit to overcall and cannot make a takeout double without support for the unbid suits and so passes.
  - South bids 1♥.
  - North bids 1 NT.
  - The contract belongs in a game so South bids 3 NT.
  - All pass and North is the declarer in 3 NT.

  The defense
  - East leads the ♣2, the unbid suit.
  - If a different suit were chosen declarer would win the trick and have time to drive out the ♦A to make the contract.

  The play
  - Declarer starts with five tricks and plans to promote four winners in the diamond suit before the defenders establish enough club tricks to defeat the contract.

Lesson Two: Opening Leads Against Suit Contracts

Exercise One
1) Against a notrump contract, you sacrifice one trick but develop three winners in the process. Against a suit contract, the trick is sacrificed in vain.
2) Against a notrump contract you promote two tricks for your side, but at the same time declarer also gets two tricks. In a way, you are helping declarer develop an extra trick. Against a suit contract it is a good idea to lead the suit to get the tricks that are coming to you.
3) You give up a trick by leading the suit, but against notrump you have a chance of developing four tricks in return. Against a suit you give declarer a trick he could not get for himself and gain nothing.
4) You hope to develop two tricks against a notrump contract and one trick against a suit contract. This type of suit is a good choice to lead against either notrump or a suit.

Exercise Two
1) You are hoping for a ruff by leading the singleton diamond.
2) You have natural trump tricks, so leading the club for a ruff would gain nothing. Leading the ♦ Q could promote a diamond trick for your side.
3) By leading a diamond, you could force declarer to use his trumps. One of your trumps could be promoted into a winner if you end up with more trumps than declarer.

Exercise Three
Possible suit distribution for dummy and declarer might be:

1) DUMMY	2) DUMMY	3) DUMMY
♠ x x x	♠ —	♠ x x x
♥ x x	♥ x x x x	♥ x x x
♦ x x x x	♦ x x x x x	♦ x x
♣ x x x x	♣ x x x x	♣ x x x x x
DECLARER	DECLARER	DECLARER
♠ x x	♠ x x x x x	♠ x x x x x
♥ x x x x x	♥ x x x x	♥ x x
♦ x x x x	♦ x x	♦ x x
♣ x x	♣ x x	♣ x x x x

On the first two hands, a trump lead is a good idea. On the third hand, you are better off to find another lead.

Exercise Four

1) Club	2) Diamond	3) Heart	4) Club or Spade

Exercise Five

1) Lead low against a notrump contract and the ace against a suit contract.
2) Lead the jack against a notrump contract. If you decide to lead the suit against a suit contract, the ace is safer.
3) Lead low against a notrump contract and the king against a suit contract.

Exercise Six

1) ♦ Q	2) ♦ A	3) ♦ 3
4) ♦ 6	5) ♦ K	6) ♠ 3

Exercise Seven

1) 1♥—Pass; 2♥—2 NT; 3♥—Pass.
2) 1♥—1♠; 2♥—2♠; 3♥—Pass.
3) 1♥—3♥; 2♥—3♥; 3♥—Pass.

Exercise Eight

You can afford three losers and have six. Two spade losers can be trumped in the dummy and one of the club losers can be discarded on the extra diamond winner in dummy. Declarer cannot draw trumps before eliminating the losers since he would have to give up the lead and the defenders would take enough tricks to defeat the contract. Win the ♣A, cash the ♠A, trump a spade, cross to the ♦Q, trump a second spade and cash the ♦A and the ♦K, discarding a losing club.

Exercise Nine

The bidding
- North would open the bidding 1♦.
- East overcalls by bidding 1♥.
- South bids 1♠ and North rebids 2♠ to show support.
- With 13 points South knows the partnership belongs in game.
- Since there is a *Golden Fit*, South rebids 4♠.
- All players pass and the final contract is 4♠ by South.

The defense
- West leads the ♥2, partner's suit.
- East plans to take two heart tricks and two diamond tricks to defeat the contract.

The play
- Declarer has two more losers than he can afford. He can try the heart finesse and/or plan to promote an extra diamond winner in dummy on which to discard a heart loser. The club loser can be trumped in dummy. After the heart lead, however, the defenders can take four tricks giving declarer no opportunity to try to make the contract.

Exercise Ten
The bidding
- East opens the bidding 1 ♥.
- West raises to 2 ♥ showing 6–10 points.
- East rebids 4 ♥, showing maximum values.
- All players pass and East is declarer in 4 ♥.

The defense
- South leads the ♦ K, top of a strong sequence.
- If South chose the longest suit, spades, it would give up a trick since declarer would no longer have a spade loser and would make the contract.

The play
- Declarer has one more loser than he can afford. He could take the spade finesse, hoping to eliminate the spade loser.

Exercise Eleven
The bidding
- North opens the bidding 1 ♣.
- South responds 1 NT.
- North rebids his second suit, 2 ♥, which South prefers.
- All players pass and the final contract is 2 ♥ by North.

The defense
- East leads a trump because dummy is likely short in spades, and it is likely that declarer will want to trump his spade losers in the dummy.
- When East gets the lead he plans to lead another trump. West can help by leading a trump after winning the ♥ A.

The play
- Declarer, with two losers to eliminate, plans to give up a spade trick and trump two spade losers in the dummy.

Exercise Twelve
The bidding
- West opens the bidding 1 ♣.
- East responds 3 ♣, a limit raise.
- West rebids 4 ♣.
- All players pass and West is in a final contract of 4 ♣.

The defense
- North leads the ♦ 9, hoping that South has some strength and can give him a ruff.
- South wins the ♦ A and leads a diamond back for North to trump. South leads another diamond after getting the lead with the ♣ A.

The play
- After driving out the ♠A, declarer plans to draw trumps, and then promote the diamond suit by driving out the ♦A. At first declarer expects to lose the ♠A and ♦A. If, however, trumps cannot be drawn quickly enough, the defenders may trump some of declarer's winners.

Lesson Three: Third-Hand Play

Exercise One
    1) Ace   2) King   3) King

Exercise Two
    1) 10, only as high as necessary. If the 10 wins the trick, partner will know that you also have the queen and the jack. If declarer wins the trick with the king, partner might also suspect that you have the jack and perhaps the queen.
    2) 10, trapping dummy's jack. If partner has the ace, the 10 will win the trick. If declarer has the ace and wins the trick, your king and queen will have been promoted into winners.
    3) King, third hand high. If you don't play third hand high, declarer may win the trick with the queen.

Exercise Three
    1) Jack   2) 10   3) 10

Exercise Four
    1) 6, to let partner's jack win the trick. Partner can lead the suit again and dummy's king remains trapped. The defenders get all the tricks in the suit.
    2) 6, keeping dummy's queen trapped, even though you know declarer has the king. Partner will have to lead the suit again to trap dummy's queen.
    3) Ace, to prevent declarer from getting a trick with the queen. Lead the suit back, trapping declarer's queen. The defenders can take all of the tricks in the suit.

Exercise Five
    1) King   2) King or Queen 3) King

In all examples you want to have a low card left to lead back to partner's length in the suit. You want to unblock the suit.

Exercise Six
    1) King   2) Jack   3) 4
    4) 10   5) Jack   6) King

Exercise Seven
    1) 2♠   2) Pass   3) 2 NT
    4) 3♠   5) 4♥   6) 3 NT
    7) 2♣   8) 2♣   9) Pass

Exercise Eight
1) Two. Play the suit twice, driving out the ace and king to promote two winners. Play the queen, high card from the short side, first.
2) Four. Play the suit five times, giving one trick to the opponents so that you can collect four tricks.
3) Three. Take a repeated finesse against the opponent on your right.
4) Three. Lead toward dummy's queen and get an extra trick through length assuming the suit is divided 3–2.
5) Four. Take the finesse with the queen and hope the suit is divided 3–2 so that you also get two extra tricks through length.

Exercise Nine
The bidding
- North opens the bidding 1♣.
- South responds 1♥.
- Yes. North rebids 1♠.
- South has 13 high card points and knows there are enough points for game. The partnership has a fit in spades and so South rebids 4♠.
- The final contract is 4♠ and North is the declarer.

The defense
- East leads the ♦3, fourth best from the unbid suit.
- West plays the ♦A, third hand high and returns the ♦J, top of his remaining doubleton.

The play
- Declarer can afford three losers in 4♠ and has one too many. Declarer plans to discard one of the diamond losers on dummy's extra heart winner. After an opening diamond lead and a diamond return, however, the defenders get three diamond tricks before declarer has a chance to discard a loser.

Exercise Ten
The bidding
- East opens the bidding 1♦.
- South overcalls 1♠.
- With a minimum balanced hand, West bids 1 NT.
- All players pass.
- The final contract is 1 NT by West.

The defense
- North leads the ♠6, top of doubleton in partner's suit.
- South will play the ♠9, as high a card as necessary while still keeping dummy's ♠K trapped.

The play
- Declarer needs seven tricks and has only three sure tricks. Four more tricks can be developed in clubs after the opponents' ♣A is driven out. Declarer will have to keep the ♦A in dummy as an entry to the clubs in case the opponents hold up their ♣A.

Exercise Eleven
The bidding
- South opens the bidding 1 NT.
- North responds 3 NT.
- All players pass and the final contract is 3 NT by South.

The defense
- West leads the ♥3, fourth highest from the longest suit.
- East should play the ♥10 to keep dummy's ♥J trapped by his ♥K.

The play
- Declarer needs nine tricks and starts with eight sure tricks. The additional trick required can be developed in the spade suit through promotion by driving out the opponents' ♠A and ♠K.

Exercise Twelve
The bidding
- East describes his hand by bidding 3 NT.
- All players pass and East is the declarer in a contract of 3 NT.

The defense
- South leads the ♥K.
- North must contribute the ♥A and return a small heart to get back into South's hand. Otherwise the suit is blocked.

The play
- Declarer needs nine tricks and has nine — as soon as he gets the lead. Meanwhile, the defenders may have taken enough tricks to defeat the contract.

Lesson Four: Second-Hand Play

Exercise One
1) If second hand plays low, declarer takes no tricks because your king keeps his jack trapped and partner's ace keeps the queen trapped. If second hand plays high, declarer gets one trick with either his queen or jack.
2) Play low and declarer gets two tricks since he cannot repeat the finesse to trap your king. Play high and declarer takes three tricks.
3) Play low and declarer takes two tricks. Play high and declarer can take all three tricks since his ace takes your king and partner's jack is trapped by declarer's queen.

Exercise Two
1) Play low hoping declarer will play the ace and king (eight ever, nine never) and your queen will be a winner.
2) Play low and partner's ace traps declarer's king and your queen traps dummy's jack.
3) Play low and partner gets a trick with the king and later you get a trick with your queen, since it lies behind the ace in the dummy.

Exercise Three
1) Play the 10, splitting your honors.
2) Play the 10, making sure declarer does not win a trick with dummy's 9.
3) Play the 4, hoping declarer plays the king or queen which will be his only winner in the suit.

Exercise Four
1) If you cover, declarer gets three tricks; if you don't cover declarer gets four tricks.
2) Declarer gets no tricks if you cover and one if you don't cover.
3) Declarer gets three tricks if you cover and only two tricks if you don't cover. In this example, you do not cover because you have nothing to promote.

Exercise Five
1) No	2) No	3) Yes

Exercise Six
1) 5	2) 3	3) 2
4) 9	5) Ace	6) King

Exercise Seven
1) 2♠	2) 1 NT	3) 2♥
4) 2♦	5) 3♠	6) 3♥
7) 2 NT	8) 3♣	9) 4♠

Exercise Eight
  1) One. Lead twice toward dummy, hoping either the ace or king are on the left.
  2) Two. Lead toward your hand, planning to finesse the 10 if a low card appears. If the first finesse loses, repeat the finesse, hoping either the king or queen is on the right.
  3) Three. Lead a high card from the dummy, since you can afford to have it covered, and hope the king is on your right.
  4) Three. Lead low from the dummy finessing the jack and then play the ace hoping that the defender being finessed started with a singleton or doubleton king.
  5) Two. Lead toward one of the honors and then play a low card from both hands, hoping one defender started with a doubleton ace.

Exercise Nine
The bidding
  • North has too many points to open 1 NT and so bids 1♣.
  • Yes. South responds 1♠.
  • North rebids 4♠, showing the strength of his hand and support for partner.
  • The final contract is 4♠ and South is the declarer.
The defense
  • West leads the ♥Q, top of touching honors.
  • If declarer plays trumps by leading a small spade toward dummy, West should play second hand low, the ♠5, to keep declarer's ♠Q trapped.
The play
  • Declarer can afford only three losers and has potentially four losers. Declarer has to try to avoid more than one loser in the trump suit. Declarer hopes that one opponent has a doubleton ♠A. He plans to lead toward one of the spade honors and, if this wins, play a small card from both hands and hope that a defender has to play the ♠A.

Exercise Ten
The bidding
  • East opens the bidding 1♣.
  • West responds 1♥.
  • East rebids 2♥.
  • West knows that the contract belongs in game and so rebids 4♥.
  • The final contract is 4♥ and West is the declarer.
The defense
  • North leads the ♦J, top of a sequence.
  • South will play the ♦5 if a small card is played from the dummy.
  • When West leads a spade toward the dummy, North must be prepared to play second hand low so that declarer has to guess whether to play dummy's ♠J or ♠K.

The play
- Declarer can afford three losers and has one too many. With the ♦A in the South hand, there is no way to avoid two diamond losers after the opening lead. Declarer can plan to eliminate one of the spade losers, however, by leading a small spade toward dummy's ♠K and ♠J. Declarer has to guess whether to finesse the ♠J, playing North for the ♠Q, or finesse the ♠K, playing North for the ♠A.

Exercise Eleven
The bidding
- North opens the bidding 1 NT.
- South responds 3 NT.
- The final contract is 3 NT and North is the declarer.

The defense
- East leads the ♣5, fourth highest from the longest and strongest suit.
- West should play third hand high, the ♣Q, if a small card is played from dummy.
- If declarer leads a small diamond toward dummy, East should play the ♦2, second hand low.
- If declarer leads a diamond honor, East should cover with the ♦K, covering an honor with an honor.

The play
- Declarer needs nine tricks and starts with six. The three extra tricks can come from diamonds. Declarer cannot afford to lose a diamond trick to the opponents, however, if the missing spades are divided 5–3. Declarer can hold up the ♣A only one round and must plan to take the diamond finesse, hoping to develop enough tricks in the suit before having to give the lead to the opponents.

Exercise Twelve
The bidding
- East has too many points to open 1 NT and so starts with 1♣.
- Yes. West responds 1♦.
- East shows his strong hand by rebidding 2 NT.
- West rebids 3 NT.
- The final contract is 3 NT and East is the declarer.

The defense
- South leads the ♣4, fourth highest card.
- North should play third hand high and contribute the ♣K.
- If a diamond is led from the dummy, North should not cover since there is nothing to promote for the defense.

The play
- • Declarer needs nine tricks and has six. The best chance to develop extra tricks is in the diamond suit. By leading a high diamond from dummy and taking the finesse, declarer can hope to develop extra tricks if North has the ♦K. If North had fewer than four diamonds, declarer could end up with four tricks in the diamond suit, enough to make the contract.

Lesson Five: Defensive Signals
Exercise One
1) Encourage with the 8.   2) Discourage with the 2.
3) Encourage with the 7.   4) Encourage with the 4.
5) Discourage with the 7.   6) Unblock with the ace.

Exercise Two
1) Partner dislikes diamonds.   2) Partner likes diamonds.
3) Partner dislikes spades.   4) Partner likes hearts.

Exercise Three
1) ♠2 then ♠5 (low-high)   2) ♥8 then ♥3 (high-low)
3) ♦4 then ♦6 (low-high)

Exercise Four
1) Third round   2) Second round   3) Does not matter

Exercise Five
1) ♣10, showing preference for spades.
2) ♣2, showing preference for diamonds.
3) ♣6, showing no preference for either suit.

Exercise Six
1) ♠9   2) ♣4   3)   2
4) ♦7   5) ♣9

Exercise Seven
1) Pass   2) 2♦   3) 2♠
4) 2 NT   5) 3♣   6) 3♦
7) 3 NT   8) 4♣   9) 3♥

Exercise Eight
  Declarer can afford three losers in a 4♠ contract. There are two spade losers, a diamond loser and two club losers. The diamond loser can be trumped in dummy and one of the club losers can be discarded on the extra heart winner in dummy. Drawing trumps will have to be delayed until a club loser is discarded because once the defenders get the lead they can take four quick tricks.

Exercise Nine
  The bidding
  - North would open the bidding 1♦.
  - South would respond 1♠.
  - North rebids 2♠ and South rebids 4♠.
  - All players pass. South is the declarer in 4♠.

  The defense
  - West leads the ♥10, the top of a sequence.
  - East encourages with the ♥7. The defenders have to work to get the ♥Q to go along with their three aces to defeat the contract.

  The play
  - Declarer has one loser in each suit. He will try to discard the heart loser on dummy's extra diamond winner after driving out the ♦A. Declarer will have to draw trumps first, otherwise the opponents will be able to trump the extra diamond winner once it is established.

Exercise Ten
  The bidding
  - West opens the bidding 1♣.
  - East responds 1♠.
  - West has a medium hand in support of spades and rebids 3♠.
  - East knows West has spade support and 17–18 points.
  - East bids 4♠ and the other players pass. East is declarer in 4♠.

  The defense
  - South leads the ♦A, the top of touching high cards.
  - North encourages with the ♦10.
  - South will play the ♦K and another diamond, based on partner's encouraging signal.

  The play
  - Declarer plans to trump his heart losers in dummy after driving out the ♥A.

Exercise Eleven
  The bidding
  - West opens the bidding 1 NT.
  - East raises to 2 NT.
  - West accepts the invitation and bids 3 NT.
  - West is the declarer in a final contract of 3 NT.

The defense
- North leads the ♠K, top of touching honors.
- South plays the ♠2 to tell partner he has no help in spades.
- When declarer leads diamonds, South plays the ♦9 to give count, showing an even number of diamonds.
- No. North holds up until the third round. With the ♠A already played declarer has no entry to dummy and dummy's good diamonds are stranded.

The play
- Declarer has six sure tricks and needs three more.
- Declarer needs to promote diamond winners by driving out the ♦A. The defenders, however, can make it difficult by stranding East's winners.

Exercise Twelve
The bidding
- North opens the bidding 1♠.
- South bids 2♠.
- North knows there is no game. Everyone passes and North is the declarer in 2♠.

The defense
- East leads the ♥A, top of a sequence.
- After West's encouraging ♥9, East plays the ♥K.
- West shows out and East plays the ♥10, showing a suit preference signal for diamonds, rather than clubs.
- West leads diamonds after he trumps the heart. East indicated his preference for diamonds.

The play
- Declarer plans to draw trumps by playing the ♠A and ♠K, hoping the ♠Q will drop. Declarer hopes that the hearts will be divided 3–2 and the defenders will not get a ruff.

Lesson Six: Developing Defensive Tricks

Exercise One
1) Partner would lead the queen and you would overtake with your ace or king. Then you lead your other honor followed by a low card.
2) Partner would lead the king and you would encourage with the 7.
3) Partner would lead the queen and you would overtake with the king and lead back the 4.

Exercise Two
1) Partner plays the 7 to encourage. You return the 3 so that partner can play his high card and still have a card to lead back to your winners.
2) Partner plays the king. You return one of your high cards, the jack or 10, and take the rest of the tricks in the suit.
3) Partner plays the lower of equal cards, the 10. You play a low card, the 2, when you next gain the lead.

Exercise Three

1) Duck the first trick, but play the 8 to encourage partner to lead the suit again. When you or partner next gain the lead play the high cards and take the rest of the tricks.
2) Play the 9 to encourage but, when partner leads the suit again, duck (play a low card) to preserve the entry to your long suit.
3) Play the 9 to encourage partner to lead the suit again. Duck the next trick and eventually take the ace and one other trick.

Exercise Four

1) Lead the king. Partner will discourage with the 2. When partner gets the lead, however, he should return the suit so that your queen and 10 are in a position to trap the jack.
2) Lead the queen, top of a broken sequence. Partner discourages with the 4. You want partner to return the suit in order to trap declarer's 10.
3) Lead the queen, top of a three-card sequence. Partner can encourage with the 8. You can lead the suit again and dummy's king is trapped.

Exercise Five

1) Partner has to lead the suit.
2) You have to lead the suit.
3) Partner has to lead the suit.

Exercise Six

1) East takes the first trick with the ♦A and returns the ♦2 showing a preference for clubs. After West trumps, he leads back a club and East gives West a second ruff.
2) East plays the ♦10, a suit preference signal for hearts. When West gains the lead, he plays a heart. East wins and returns a diamond for West to trump. West leads a second heart, and East gives West a second ruff.

Exercise Seven

1) Bid 1♦	2) Double	3) Bid 2♦
4) Bid 1 NT	5) Double	6) Pass
7) Pass	8) Double	9) Bid 1 NT

Exercise Eight

1) 3; 3	2) 2; 3	3) 0; 0
4) 0; 1	5) 1; 3	

Exercise Nine

The bidding

- North would open the bidding 1♦.
- East overcalls 2♣.
- West knows the partnership belongs in a game and bids 3 NT.
- All players pass. West is the declarer in 3 NT.

The defense
  - North makes the opening lead of the ♠5.
  - South plays the ♠8 to give an encouraging signal.
  - When North regains the lead, he can lead a small spade to South's ♠Q.

The play
  - Declarer needs nine tricks and has five sure winners. More than enough tricks can be developed in the club suit through promotion — if the opponents do not take too many spade tricks before declarer has a chance to develop these tricks.

Exercise Ten
  The bidding
  - West opens the bidding 1♦.
  - North overcalls 1 NT.
  - South knows there is enough for game and responds 3 NT to his partner's overcall.
  - The final contract is 3 NT and North is the declarer.

The defense
  - East makes the opening lead of the ♦9, top of a doubleton in partner's suit.
  - West knows his partner does not hold the ♦Q, ♦J or ♦10 because East leads the top card when he has a doubleton and a low card if he has three or more.
  - West plays the ♦8, ducking the trick to keep an entry to his winners if East later wins a trick. West also wants to encourage so that East will lead the suit again if he gains the lead.

The play
  - Declarer needs nine tricks and has four sure tricks. He can try to develop four winners in clubs and a trick in spades, and he can even try to promote a winner in the diamonds. All this is provided the opponents cannot take too many diamond winners when they get the lead with the ♣A.

Exercise Eleven
  The bidding
  - South opens 1♣.
  - West competes by making a takeout double.
  - North passes (although raising to 2♣ is a possibility).
  - 13. East knows the partnership belongs in game and bids 4♥.
  - All pass and East is the declarer in 4♥.

The defense
  - South leads the ♠A, top of touching high cards.
  - North plays the ♠3 to give a discouraging signal.
  - South switches to another suit, leading a diamond through the strength in dummy.

- If North wins a trick, he should lead spades since it looks as if South cannot lead the suit without giving up a trick.

The play
- Declarer can afford three losers and has six. Two club losers can be trumped in the dummy and the diamond loser could be eliminated with the help of a successful finesse.

Exercise Twelve
The bidding
- West opens 1♦.
- North competes in the auction by making a takeout double.
- East responds 1♠ to West's opening bid.
- South doesn't have to bid but does not want to let the opponents buy the contract too easily. South, therefore, bids 2♥.
- All players pass and South is the declarer in 2♥.

The defense
- West leads the ♠2, his singleton in partner's suit.
- East suspects this a singleton since the ♠2 is the lowest missing card and partner would play the top card from a doubleton.
- East wins the trick with the ♠A and returns the ♠10, showing a preference for diamonds rather than clubs.
- West trumps the next spade and plays the ♦A and another diamond based on his partner's suit preference signal. East leads another spade to set up another trump trick for West.

The play
- Declarer can afford five losers and has six, one too many. Declarer may be able to avoid a trump loser with a successful finesse if the suit divides 3–2. Declarer may choose to play the ♥A and ♥K, hoping the ♥Q is a doubleton since he suspects the finesse will lose. Two of declarer's diamond losers could be trumped in the dummy or one trumped in the dummy and one discarded on the extra spade winner after the ♠A is driven out.

Lesson Seven: Interfering with Declarer

Exercise One
1) On the first trick, partner plays the 7 to show an even number; you hold up and play a low card. On the second round of the suit, partner plays the 3 and you again hold up, playing a low card.
2) On the first round partner plays the 2, and you play the 3 to start to show an odd number of cards in the suit. On the second round of the suit, partner could play the ace knowing from your signal that declarer has only two cards in the suit.

3) On the first round partner plays the 8 to start to show two cards in the suit. You play a low card. The second time the suit is played partner plays the 6 and you play the king.

Exercise Two
1) King   2) Low   3) Jack (or 10)

Exercise Three
1) If you discard a low card, declarer gets four tricks; if you don't discard any cards, declarer gets only three tricks.
2) Declarer gets four tricks if you discard a card and only three if you do not.
3) Whether you discard or not, declarer is entitled to only three tricks in this suit.

Exercise Four
1) Five   2) Three   3) 5–1–3–4   4) Clubs

Exercise Five
1) Declarer gets three tricks without any entry problems if your partner plays the ace on the first round. Both of the defenders should play low.
2) Partner should play low on the first trick and you also should play low. Declarer may finesse again and take only one trick.
3) Partner plays the 5 and you play the king or queen.

Exercise Six
Declarer has one too many losers and may hope to trump a heart loser in the dummy. The defenders can prevent this by leading trump at the first opportunity. East has to lead the trump so that West wins a trick with the ♠K. East will have to overtake the first heart and lead a spade. When West gets the lead, he has to lead another spade. This is very delicate for the defenders because if declarer wins the second spade in the dummy and leads his remaining heart, East would have to play low and let West win the trick so that West could lead another trump.

Exercise Seven
1) 3 NT   2) 4 NT   3) 6 NT
4) 7 NT   5) 6 ♦   6) 5 ♠
7) 3 ♣ (Stayman)   8) 3 ♥   9) 3 ♣ (Stayman)

Exercise Eight
The extra tricks that declarer needs can come from the diamond suit. The danger is that you have to let the opponents in twice while promoting your diamond winners. Play the ♥3 on the first trick, letting East win with the ♥K. You are holding up your winners in the suit to try to strand West's winners.

Exercise Nine
  The bidding
- North opens the bidding 1 NT.
- The partnership belongs in game and there is no *Golden Fit*.
- South responds 3 NT, all pass and North is the declarer in a 3 NT contract.

  The defense
- East leads the ♠4, fourth highest.
- West plays the ♠Q, third hand high.
- West returns the ♠9, top of his remaining doubleton in partner's suit, to trap declarer's ♠J.
- If the first trick is won in dummy, West would encourage with the ♠9.
- The defenders want to try to prevent declarer from establishing diamonds. West holds up his ♦K until the second time diamonds are led.

  The play
- Declarer has six tricks and needs three more to make the contract. He will try to get them from the diamond suit. Declarer plans to lead the ♦Q, taking a finesse. Declarer should duck the first spade trick, holding up to try to prevent the defenders from taking too many spades. The second problem for the declarer is that the diamonds could be stranded.

Exercise Ten
  The bidding
- East opens the bidding 1 NT.
- There are at least 33 combined points. The partnership belongs in slam.
- There is no known *Golden Fit* and so West responds 6 NT.
- All pass and the final contract is 6 NT and East is the declarer.

  The defense
- South leads the ♥10.
- South guards the diamonds and North guards the spades and clubs.
- North gets clues as to which cards to discard and which to keep by watching the cards partner and declarer play.

  The play
- After the ♥A is driven out, declarer has three sure spade tricks, two heart tricks, three diamond tricks and three club tricks. The last trick can come from either the spade suit or the diamond suit, if either suit divides 3–3 or if the defense errs while discarding.

Exercise Eleven
  The bidding
- South opens the bidding 1♠.
- North has 21 points in support of spades.
- The partnership belongs in slam in spades.
- North responds 6♠.
- All pass and the final contract is 6♠ with South as the declarer.

311

The defense
- West leads the ♦J.
- East sees that West might have a heart or a club trick.
- If a heart is led to dummy, East ducks hoping that declarer might have a guess in the heart suit.
- West has to avoid discarding hearts to keep the ♥J guarded.

The play
- Declarer can afford only one loser. There are two possible losers in the heart suit. Declarer plans to lead up toward dummy's hearts, hoping that West has the ♥A.
- If East has the ♥A, declarer can hope West has the ♥J and lead the ♥10 for a finesse.

Exercise Twelve
The bidding
- West opens the bidding with 1♠.
- East can support partner's suit and bids 2♠.
- All pass and the final contract is 2♠ by West.

The defense
- North leads the ♦K, top of touching high cards.
- South would play the ♦7 on the first trick to encourage.
- North leads a trump to try to stop declarer from trumping a diamond in the dummy.
- South cooperates by winning the ♠A and leading another spade.
- If declarer leads a second diamond from dummy South has to play low, not the ♦A.
- South wants North to be able to win the trick and lead another trump.

The play
- Declarer can afford five losers and has one too many. Declarer may be able to eliminate a diamond loser by trumping one in the dummy. Declarer plans to give up two diamond tricks before drawing trumps.

Lesson Eight: Making a Plan

Exercise One
First pause to consider your objective. You need four tricks to defeat declarer's 4♥ contract. Next look at the tricks you have. You likely have a trick with the ♦A and perhaps the ♥K. You might get a trick with the ♦Q. Although you are not sure where all your tricks will come from, your best lead is probably a spade. You hope partner has a trick in that suit and will be able to lead a diamond to trap declarer's ♦K. Together with the ♥K, the prospects are not too bad. You will lead the ♠10, top of touching high cards and wait to see dummy.

Exercise Two
  This time partner leads the ♥2 and you are third hand to play. Before automatically playing third hand high, consider your plan. You need four tricks. You have two aces. You have the potential for a trump trick by getting a ruff in the diamond suit. Take the first trick with the ♥A. Now, instead of returning partner's suit, play the ♦A. Then return partner's suit by playing the ♥4. Then you wait for partner to get the lead and return a diamond.

Exercise Three
1) 2♥	2) Pass	3) 2♦
4) 3♥ or 4♥	5) Double	6) 2♠

Exercise Four
  You need 12 tricks and can afford only one loser. You start with a heart loser and a trump loser, one too many. Since you cannot do anything about the trump loser, you will have to eliminate the heart loser. You can create an extra diamond winner if the finesse in diamonds works. If it loses you will be down two instead of one, but this is a chance you have to take if you are going to make your slam.

Exercise Five
  The bidding
    • East opens 1♠.
    • West makes a limit raise and bids 3♠.
    • East rebids 4♠.
    • All pass and East is the declarer in 4♠.

  The defense
    • South leads the ♦J.
    • The defenders need four tricks. North has two tricks. The other tricks will have to come with partner's help. Neither diamonds nor clubs looks promising. The heart suit is the best possibility. North plans to lead back a heart rather than return partner's suit.

  The play
    • Declarer has one more loser than he can afford. He could try to eliminate a heart loser by discarding it on dummy's extra club winners after the ♣A has been driven out. Another possibility is to take a finesse in hearts.

Exercise Six
  The bidding
    • East opens the bidding 1♦ and West responds 1♠.
    • East rebids 1 NT to show a balanced minimum hand.
    • The partnership belongs in game in a known *Golden Fit,* so West bids 4♠.

The defense
- North leads the ♥A and plans to take as many hearts as possible.
- After the first two tricks, North knows that partner has three hearts and that declarer has only two.
- Partner might hold the ♣Q and ♣A or the ♦K and the ♣A.

The play
- Declarer has two heart losers and two potential club losers.
- He hopes to discard the club losers on dummy's extra diamond winners.

Exercise Seven
The bidding
- North, having too much to start with 1 NT, bids 1♥.
- South responds 1 NT.
- North bids 3 NT.
- All pass and South is the declarer in 3 NT.

The defense
- West leads the ♠J.
- Although East likes partner's suit, there is a better chance for the defense in the diamond suit.
- East, therefore, discourages with the ♠2.

The play
- With two sure tricks in spades and four in clubs, declarer plans to promote tricks in the heart suit to make the contract.

Exercise Eight
The bidding
- North opens the bidding 1♥.
- South responds 3♥.
- North bids 4♥.
- All pass and North is the declarer in 4♥.

The defense
- East leads the ♦10.
- Although West does not particularly like diamonds, he can see no better suit and so encourages East to continue in diamonds.

The play
- Declarer has a spade loser, a heart loser and two club losers. The main hope is that the heart finesse will work. If not, declarer may have to find an opponent with a doubleton ♣A. He will lead toward one of the club honors and then play low from both hands on the second trick.

Exercise Nine
  The bidding
- East opens 1 NT.
- The partnership belongs in game.
- West uses the Stayman convention and bids 2♣ to see if there is a *Golden Fit*.
- East shows a four-card spade suit and bids 2♠.
- West bids 4♠ and all pass. East is the declarer.

  The defense
- South leads the ♦9.
- South hopes to ruff a diamond.
- East would probably not have five diamonds and four spades and open 1 NT.
- North encourages with the ♦8.
- The next time South gets the lead he can return a diamond and North can take the ♦A and give South a ruff.

  The play
- Declarer has only three losers and will have to draw trumps as quickly as possible to make sure the defenders do not get an extra trick by ruffing one of declarer's winners.

Exercise Ten
  The bidding
- South opens 1 NT.
- North responds 3 NT.
- All pass and South is the declarer in 3 NT.

  The defense
- West leads the ♠5. East wins the ace and returns a spade.
- West ducks to keep an entry in the spade suit.
- East does not plan to hold up the ♦A.
  The play
- Declarer plans to get the extra tricks he needs by promoting diamond winners.

Exercise Eleven
  The bidding
- South opens 1 NT.
- North knows there is a *Golden Fit* and the partnership belongs in game.
- North responds 4♠.
- All pass and North is the declarer in 4♠.

  The defense
- East leads the ♥J
- After taking the ♥A, ♥Q and ♣A, West returns another heart hoping that declarer will have to ruff in the dummy to promote West's ♠J.

315

The play
- Declarer has potentially four losers and hopes either the ♥A is in the right place for his ♥K to take a trick or that there are no losers in the trump suit.

Exercise Twelve
The bidding
- West opens with 1 NT.
- East responds 3 NT.
- All pass and the final contract is 3 NT. West is the declarer.

The defense
- North leads the ♥Q.
- South hopes the defense has enough heart tricks to defeat the contract.
- South plans to lead hearts at every opportunity. If declarer leads a club, South will take the ♣A immediately and return a heart.

The play
- Declarer hopes to get the extra tricks he requires from promotion in the club suit once the ♣A and ♣K have been driven out.

INDEX
(Also see Glossary)

A

ACBL (The American Contract Bridge League) iv
ACBL Club Series, 1987 by Audrey Grant .... iii, 87
ACBL Diamond Series, 1991 by Audrey Grant iii
ACBL Spade Series, 1990 by Audrey Grant iii

B

Blocking plays 8, 85, 181, 201, 288

C

Captain 55, 87, 165, 288

Conventions in bidding 56, 87, 288
  Baron 87, 124
  Stayman 87, 124, 235, 290, 315

D

Dangerous opponents 236, 237, 288

Discarding............. 39, 57, 83, 146, 154, 156, 160, 161, 167, 189, 217, 223-226, 232, 238, 241, 248, 255, 263, 266, 268

Doubles
  Penalty 47, 48, 197, 271
  Takeout 196, 197, 212, 213, 271, 308

Ducking 17, 187-189, 199, 201, 227, 228, 288, 307

E

Echo (high-low) 151-154, 156-158, 161, 162, 168, 216, 219, 221, 226, 289, 304
  (low-high) 152, 153, 156, 157, 159, 161, 162, 168, 216, 262, 289, 304

Elwell, Joseph (1873-1920) 151

Entry-creating 109, 164, 167, 180, 186, 199, 200, 216, 221, 274, 288

Entry-killing 109, 220-222, 238, 240

Entry-preserving 17, 24, 167, 180, 183, 187, 199, 228, 255, 269, 288

F

Finesse 16, 24, 57, 88, 89, 105, 107, 116, 121, 123, 127, 128, 139, 146, 180, 184, 186, 188, 190-193, 199, 201, 205, 218, 224, 227-230, 238, 243, 254, 274, 288, 297, 299, 303, 304, 309, 313

  against dummy 77
  repeating finesse 116, 123, 127, 139, 219, 227, 229, 299, 301, 302,
  when not to (eight ever, nine never) .. 107, 301

Five-card majors 55

Forcing defense 45

G

Game contracts:
  3 notrump 4-6, 10, 11, 13, 18-20, 27, 30-35, 76, 79, 86, 100, 102, 109, 142, 143, 157, 159, 171, 177, 183, 184, 186-188, 191, 210, 211, 218, 220, 222, 246, 247, 257-259, 269,281, 284, 286, 292
  4 spades........ 41, 42, 45, 48, 49, 54, 61, 62, 65, 67, 70, 99, 117, 140, 152, 153, 163, 164, 174-176, 182, 207, 225, 226, 233, 259 264, 266, 274, 277, 279, 280, 283, 285
  4 hearts 43, 50, 53, 63, 66, 68, 82, 113, 114, 141, 148 149, 150, 171, 193, 195, 212, 232, 276, 282
  5 diamonds.....................................47, 48

Glossary of bridge terms 288-291

Grand slam contracts
  7 Notrump 160

H

Holdup play 8, 85, 156, 158, 160-162, 216-219, 222, 236, 238, 239, 247, 289, 303, 311
  when not to 85

Honors, when to cover 115-118, 130, 131, 135, 142, 230, 254,
     when not to 119-123, 131, 230, 270

J

Jump shift 125

L

Lead through strength and up to weakness .
40, 192, 194, 201, 206, 254, 256, 265, 268, 308
Lose control 45, 289

O

Opening bids
   1 notrump 22, 30, 31, 97, 101, 124,
   142, 171, 177, 234, 247, 248, 257, 283-286
   1 spade 4, 27, 31, 41, 46, 62, 69, 178,
   210, 225, 249, 250, 262, 263, 266, 279, 292
   1 heart 20, 30, 39, 43, 62, 68, 139,
   208, 259, 267, 268, 272, 278, 281, 282
   1 diamond 6, 31-33, 35, 50, 62, 67,
   173, 175, 211, 213, 271, 280, 292,
   1 club 23, 47, 48, 54, 65, 99, 100,
   140, 141, 143, 176, 212, 265
   2 notrump 23, 31, 34, 88, 124, 235,
   245, 292, 294
   2 spades 31
   2 hearts 23
   Three level or pre-emptive bids............. 23
      3 spades 23
      3 diamonds 31
      3 notrump 23, 88, 102

Opening leads against notrump contracts 2-28
   broken sequence 12-14, 16, 19, 25,
   150, 183, 185, 191, 288, 292
   fourth best 3, 19, 29, 34, 53, 58,
   101, 142, 143, 210, 247, 254, 257, 284, 289
   interior sequence 12, 14-16, 19, 20,
   25, 83, 84, 220, 289, 293
   long suit leads 5, 12-19, 24, 38, 40,
   41, 45, 52, 53, 57, 58, 70, 88, 102, 146, 177,
   180, 186, 254
   partner's suit 4, 7-11, 19, 27, 28, 32,
   40, 51, 58, 100, 157, 186, 187, 189, 190,
   211, 213, 252, 256, 260, 262, 290
   the unbid suit 6, 20, 25, 41, 42, 50,
   54, 294

Opening leads against suit contracts
   fourth best leads 99
   "MUD" leads 7, 51, 59, 289
   partner's suit 39, 67, 213
   short suit leads
     (singletons & doubletons) 42-44, 50,
     58, 70, 283
   passive leads 48, 49, 290
   top of nothing 59, 290
   top of sequence 69, 140, 141, 175,
   176, 178, 212, 248-250, 279-282, 285, 286
   trump leads 38, 46-50, 58, 62, 69,
   231, 238

Overcalls 11, 63, 67, 100, 196, 210, 211,
259, 271
Overruffing 195, 232, 233, 238, 289

Overtaking 76, 85, 289

P

Part-game contracts
   4 diamonds 273
   1 notrump 5, 27, 30, 74, 100, 154, 268
   2 spades 46, 47, 178, 194, 229,
   231, 244, 250, 265
   2 hearts 69, 192, 213, 267
   2 diamonds 62

Principle of, play the high card from the short
side first 8, 17, 85, 88, 180, 183,
199, 216
Probabilities of distribution 88, 89

Promotion 24, 57, 72, 74, 88, 115-117,
120, 130, 146, 180, 183, 185, 200, 203, 216,
221, 230, 233, 238, 254, 258, 295, 299, 300,
308, 314-316

Q

Quick losers 167, 273, 274, 290

R

Rebids:
   by opener 124-126, 138, 165
   by responder 165, 166, 173
   by take-out doubler 198

Responses:
   to one-bids 55
   to notrump bids 87, 88, 97, 124
   to 3 notrump 88
   to overcalls 196
   to takeout doubles 197, 271
   to two clubs..56
   to two-bids 56, 88
   to pre-emptive bids 56, 126

Ruffing play 38, 194, 195, 207, 231, 290

Rule of eleven 19, 26

S

Sacrifices 16, 18, 47, 48, 290

Second–hand play 2, 104-144, 254, 269, 290

Signalling 288
   attitude signals 146-155, 168, 169,
    181, 190, 191, 255, 288
   count signals 146, 156-160, 162, 164,
    168, 170, 171, 216, 219, 221, 226, 262, 288
   suit-preference signals 146, 163, 164,
    168, 171, 191, 194, 261, 290, 304, 307, 309
Sign-off bids 124, 125, 165, 290

Small slam contracts:
   6 notrump 27, 106, 170, 248
   6 spades 39, 249
   6 hearts 270
   6 clubs 278

Spot (small) cards 3, 290

Splitting honors 110-112, 290

Sure tricks 2, 24, 180-182, 202, 218, 290

T

Third-hand play 2, 72-102, 155, 157,
   180, 254, 290

Trumping losers 46, 57, 58, 163, 167,
   194, 231, 232, 238, 254, 255, 270, 274, 310

U

Unblocking plays 85, 86, 90, 95, 102,
   180, 181, 185, 201, 291

Uppercut 233, 191

W

Whist 72

Answers to exercises 291-316

♥ *NOTES* ♥

Official ACBL Playing Cards

Made exclusively for ACBL by U.S. Games Systems, famous for top quality playing cards. Extremely durable and long-lasting. These are the same cards used at all ACBL North American Bridge Championships.

Item #: **110129**   6 ACBL double decks in plastic holders.
  List Price: **$18.50** *ACBL Member Price:* **$16.65**

Item #: **110146**   Cello-wrapped single decks.
                 Tuck flap box. By the dozen only.
  List Price: **$15.50** *ACBL Member Price:* **$13.95**

Item #: **110139**   Cello-wrapped single decks.
                 By the dozen only.
  List Price: **$13.75** *ACBL Member Price:* **$12.38**

Convention Cards

ACBL CONVENTION CARDS (PRIVATE SCORE — Form SS1). The "official" convention card approved by the American Contract Bridge League. Includes "red dots" for Alerts. Sold in multiples of 100 and 1,000.

Per 100   Item #: **170316** Price: **$3.00**
Per 1,000 Item #: **170314** Price: **$14.95**

Golf Pencils

SCORE PENCILS The standard "golf pencil" - 3 ½" long - sharpened - imprinted "American Contract Bridge League." Per gross (144). Item #: **170581**
Price: **$9.95 per gross**

♥ ♦ ♣ ♠ ♥ ♦ ♣ ♠ ♥ ♦ ♣ ♠ ♥

Official ACBL Duplicate Boards and Carrying Case

Attention Club Managers and home duplicate bridge players . . . Handsome, lightweight, durable plastic boards, available in your choice of white, pink, green, yellow, orange or blue. Sold in sets of 4, 32 and 36. Vulnerability is identified in bold gold lettering. Optional vinyl carrying case is virtually indestructible. Case holds up to 36 boards with extra room for pencils, pads and table-number cards.

Item #: **BOARDS 4**	Set of 4 Boards.	List Price: **$8.95**	*ACBL Member Price:* **$8.05**
Item #: **BOARDS 32**	Set of 32 Boards.	List Price: **$49.95**	*ACBL Member Price:* **$44.95**
Item #: **BOARDS 36**	Set of 36 Boards.	List Price: **$54.95**	*ACBL Member Price:* **$49.45**
Item #: **120102**	Carrying Case.	List Price: **$29.95**	*ACBL Member Price:* **$26.95**

Red Inserts for Boards (To identify vulnerability)

Set for 4 Boards — **INSERT 4**	List Price: **$.75**	*ACBL Member Price:* **$.68**
Set for 32 Boards — **INSERT 32**	List Price: **$5.50**	*ACBL Member Price:* **$4.95**
Set for 36 Boards — **INSERT 36**	List Price: **$6.25**	*ACBL Member Price:* **$5.63**

♥ ♦ ♣ ♠ ♥ ♦ ♣ ♠ ♥ ♦ ♣ ♠ ♥ ♦ ♣ ♠ ♥

Official ACBL Student Texts

Audrey Grant has done it again. ACBL's premier teacher has developed a series (eight lessons in each volume) that takes you from an absolute beginner to confident player. Currently used by ACBL accredited teachers in all official lesson programs, the series is designed to make learning the game of bridge easy and fun.

Item	Item #	Price
Volume 1: *Club Series* (Introduction to Bridge)	210121	$ 9.95
Volume 2: *Diamond Series* (Play of the Hand)	210142	$ 9.95
Volume 3: *Heart Series* (Defense)	210156	$11.95
Volume 4: *Spade Series* (Introduction to Duplicate Bridge)	210184	$11.95

ACBL E-Z Deal Cards

Use these special decks in conjunction with ACBL's Student Text Series in a classroom setting or simply use them at home with friends. Each of the 52 cards in the deck has been coded to help you construct with ease the exercise hands in the eight lessons contained in each of the four books of the student series. The hands are noted across the top of each card and the lessons (1 to 8) are numbered down the side. Reading down from top and across from the side, you will find the position at the table for the card as each is dealt. E-Z Deal Cards really help you IMPROVE YOUR GAME!

Club	Item #: **210107**	List Price: $3.00	*ACBL Member Price:* **$2.70**
Diamond	Item #: **210110**	List Price: $3.00	*ACBL Member Price:* **$2.70**
Heart	Item #: **210114**	List Price: $3.00	*ACBL Member Price:* **$2.70**
Spade	Item #: **210118**	List Price: $3.00	*ACBL Member Price:* **$2.70**

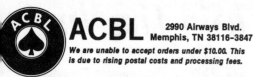

ACBL

2990 Airways Blvd.
Memphis, TN 38116-3847

We are unable to accept orders under $10.00. This is due to rising postal costs and processing fees.

CREDIT CARD HOLDERS
CALL TOLL-FREE
1-800-264-2743 (U.S. callers)
1-800-264-8786 (Canadian callers)
or 901-398-7754 (FAX)
8:00-4:45 Central Time

ORDER FORM

---

1 Ordered by: ACBL # _____

Name _____

Address _____
(No P.O. Box, please)

City _____ State _____ Zip _____

Phone _____

2 Ship to: (If different from Ordered by)

Name _____

Address _____
(No P.O. Box, please)

City _____ State _____ Zip _____

***ACBL GUARANTEES* Your Satisfaction!**

3

Item #	Quantity	Description	Size	Color	Price	Total

SAME DAY SERVICE
We are proud to offer you "same day" service.
If you phone in your order before 12:00 noon Central time,
it will be on its way to you that same afternoon.

Sorry, no discount allowed on ACBL scrip, computer-dealt hands, bid-boxes and ACBL Handbooks.

4 Subtotal .... [   ]

5 Subtract appropriate discounts .... − [   ]

6 TN residents add 8.25% sales tax .. + [   ]

7 Shipping & Handling .... + [   ]

8 TOTAL .... [   ]

7 Shipping & Handling

Order Amount	up to $10.00	$10.01 to $20.00	$20.01 to $30.00	$30.01 to $40.00	$40.01 to $50.00	$50.01 to $75.00	$75.01 to $100.00
Add	$3.00	$3.75	$4.50	$5.25	$6.00	$7.25	$8.50

All orders within the contiguous 48 states over $100.00 will be billed actual freight. Shipments outside the contiguous 48 states will be charged actual freight. Alaska, Hawaii, Canada, Mexico and Bermuda add $1.50 handling. All others outside the contiguous 48 states add $3.00 handling.

Prices subject to change without notice.

ACBL members deduct 10% off listed prices!

☐ *Check here to receive ACBL membership information.*

9 Method of Payment (U.S. Funds only)

☐ Check or Money Order (make payable to ACBL)
☐ MasterCard   ☐ VISA   ☐ Discover

Acct. # _____

MC Bank # _____ Expiration Date _____

Cardholder's Signature _____

American Contract Bridge League — *Serving the Bridge Players of North America*

Sorry, no discount allowed on ACBL scrip, computer-dealt hands, bid-boxes and ACBL Handbooks.

CREDIT CARD ORDERS:
Call our toll-free order line
1(800) 264-2743 (U.S.)
1(800) 264-8786 (CANADA)
Fax (901) 398-7754 (or use order form)

DISCOVER N))VUS   VISA   MasterCard

Join the fun!

Thank you for your interest in the game of bridge. The American Contract Bridge League (ACBL) is happy to extend you a special invitation to join our organization.

We know you will enjoy the game of bridge, and we believe you'll enjoy it even more once you become a member of the largest bridge club in North America.

ACBL membership includes

- The *BULLETIN*, our monthly magazine
- Local, regional, national and international tournaments (choose from more than 1000 each year)
- Access to 4200 clubs throughout North America
- Discounts off purchases of merchandise offered in our Products Catalog
- Opportunity to obtain a major credit card through ACBL's affinity program
- Discounts on airline fares, hotel rates and car rentals
- Group insurance
- FRIENDLY COMPETITION AND FUN!

Please join us today!

When we receive your paid membership application, you will receive your player number and a new member packet. You will be on your way to greater enjoyment of the game we all love.

For just $ 28.00* (U.S.) you can purchase a full 12 months of bridge entertainment and information — a real value!

MEMBERSHIP APPLICATION
American Contract Bridge League
2990 Airways Boulevard, Memphis TN 38116-3847

Send to: ACBL - Membership

☐ NEW MEMBER APPLICATION (YEAR)

☐ $ 28 U.S.

☐ $ 2.00 U.S. for membership in Educational Foundation

☐ MEMBERSHIP REINSTATEMENT OR RENEWAL (1 YEAR)

ACBL Player Number __ __ __ __ __ __

☐ $ 40.65 Canadian (includes $4.50 for Canadian Bridge Federation)

☐ $ 2.60 Canadian for membership in ACBL Educational Foundation

ACBL Membership\ Service fees are not tax deductible.

Name of School:

☐ $ 10.00 U.S./$ 12.90 Canadian *Student* Membership (under 26 years of age) _____

☐ Ms.   ☐ Miss   ☐ Mr.   ☐ Mrs.

_____
First Name   (Please Print)   Last Name

Address _____

City _____
Prov/ State ____   Postal Code _____

Phone(s) ( ) _____   ( ) _____
Day   Evening

☐ Male   ☐ Female

Signature _____

Date _____

$ Enclosed _____

AGE GROUP: ☐ Under 30   ☐ 31-39   ☐ 40-49   ☐ 50-59   ☐ 60 or over

Note: ACBL membership\service fees are subject to change at any time.

* Fees applicable January, 1994. Please confirm current fees by phoning 1-800-264-2743 (U.S.) or 1-800-264-8786 (Canada)